9/12/06

D0855580

DATE DUE

THE TECH WRITER'S
SURVIVAL GUIDE

THE TECH WRITER'S SURVIVAL GUIDE

A Comprehensive Handbook for Aspiring Technical Writers

JANET VAN WICKLEN

Facts On File, Inc.

THE TECH WRITER'S SURVIVAL GUIDE

Checkmark Books
An imprint of Facts On File, Inc.
11 Penn Plaza
New York, NY 10001

Library of Congress Cataloging-in-Publication Data

Van Wicklen, Janet.
    The tech writers survival guide : a comprehensive handbook for aspiring technical writers / Janet Van Wicklen.
        p. cm.
    Rev. ed. of: The tech writing game c1992.
    Includes bibliographical references and index.
    ISBN 0-8160-4038-9 (hardcover : alk. paper)—
    ISBN 0-8160-4039-7 (alk. paper)
        1. Technical writing—Vocational guidance. 2. Communication of technical information. I. Title.

T11.V368 2001
808'.066—dc21   00-062231

CONTENTS

PART THREE   A DOCUMENT IS BORN

CHAPTER 10 Planning a Writing Project, on Paper and Online

CHAPTER 11 Organizing a Technical Document

CHAPTER 12 Designing Online Documentation

CHAPTER 13 Planning for Visual Impact

PART FOUR DOING BUSINESS

CHAPTER 19 Career Excellence

Appendixes

Annotated Bibliography

Index

CHECKLISTS

ACKNOWLEDGMENTS

In writing this book, I've had to depend on so many people for help, advice, and information. I want to begin by thanking those writers, publications managers, and graphic artists who allowed me to interview them. Their real names appear herein, unless they requested otherwise. I believe their worldly advice enlivens these pages more than any other aspect of the book.

I could not have written this book without the help of those who have made superior contributions to the field of technical writing: Jonathan Price, R. John Brockmann, JoAnn Hackos, William Horton, Dr. Stephanie Rosenbaum, and the many others whose work I have learned from in the course of writing this book.

I am also grateful to Dr. William Stolgitis, executive director of the Society for Technical Communication, for providing me with unpublished data from STC surveys and for permitting me to use information from their surveys and Web pages.

Special thanks goes to Jonathan Price, who generously returned my phone calls and acted as my mentor through the inception of the first version of this book; to Dr. Donna Dowdney, who used it in her De Anza College classes and later helped me teach from its pages; to my students at De Anza and at UC Berkeley Extension, who have used its contents to move beyond my accomplishments; and to the friends who encouraged me, particularly Rod Bondurant, whose support and feedback so enriched my efforts.

And finally thanks to Anne Savarese, my editor at Facts On File, for believing in this book.

PREFACE

When I first considered becoming a technical writer, I wanted to know not only what technical writing is but also how a tech writer really spends his or her time. I requested informational interviews with writers, visiting them in their work environment and listening to their candid opinions on the profession. From these interviews, I concluded that I would try technical writing.

My efforts evolved into a challenging career, through which I truly fell in love with the writing process. And eventually, the idea came to me for a book in which I would give other aspiring technical writers the advantages I had had from knowing what I was getting into. I went on to produce this book's predecessor, *The Tech Writing Game.*

Since then, several big changes have affected the tech writing field, most notably the shift of documentation from paper to online, the growing role of the Internet in all forms of communication, and the acceleration of all business processes, including the process of technical publishing. These and other changes needed to be honored in an updated edition. Thus, the book you now hold.

The book's mission remains that of a mentor—to guide you through the process of developing a technical writing career. Consequently, the first part of this book takes you on an informational interview, with me and other writers, so you can acquire a "streetwise" view of the profession. From the impressions you gather, you can conclude whether or not it's for you.

If you decide to proceed with a tech writing career, the rest of this book guides you through the technical publication process and on through business skills you'll need to advance your career.

To read this book is to take a tour of the kinds of experiences a new technical writer can expect. Along the way, you will receive practical guidelines for developing the skills required by this dynamic profession.

These skills include active listening and logical thinking, as well as writing.

This book differs from other books about technical writing in that it is not just about writing. Although it offers detailed guidance about writing and editing, this book is as much about communication, because interview and communication skills are central to technical writing.

This book is also about doing business, especially because technical writers are most often either creative people or technical people who by nature may not relish the politics of the business world. However, as a technical writer, you sometimes must play diplomat between marketing and engineering factions that enjoy less than congenial relationships. You also must understand the larger needs of a company, in order to best serve them. And at some point you may face the question of going into business as an independent consultant. Then you need to know about marketing your services, drawing up a contract, and setting your rates. This book addresses the business questions a serious technical writer will face.

Good writing and editing habits are the heart of the technical writer's craft. In this book, writing and editing are treated as the critical skills that they are, and are complemented by an emphasis on quality: proofreading every draft, proofreading format as well as grammar and spelling, and working with artists to create a visually appealing document.

In this guide you'll find tips on how to use the latest technology available to technical writers: online authoring. This fascinating world of publishing capabilities puts added demands on the technical writer, requiring you to continually learn new technical tools, as well as to understand the elements of screen design.

Lastly, this book discusses where to go from here. What career paths are available to the technical writer? You will find that many paths lead toward professional enrichment: careers in writing, management, technology, and more open up to the successful writer.

You will find my biases as a technical writer have shaped some of the material and terminology in this book. I have worked predominantly as a computer software writer in California's Silicon Valley. This means you will find I often call technical people "engineers," "product developers," and just plain "developers," instead of "physicists," "chemists," or any of a number of titles applied to the people who will be your primary sources of technical information.

I think that the principles of communication and clear writing are universal. I have sought to aim this book at as diverse a readership as possible.

I became a technical writer out of a desire to do creative work and still make good money. My objective as a writer, and my primary joy in my work, has always been to grow in the craft of writing. It is that objective which has led to the writing of this book.

THE TECH WRITER'S
SURVIVAL GUIDE

PART 1
WHAT AM I GETTING MYSELF INTO?

1
Why Begin?

You picked up this book because you're curious about technical writing. Either you're a new tech writer or you're considering taking the plunge and becoming one. But first, you want to know what you've gotten—or are getting yourself—into. What are the rewards in this field? Will they satisfy you?

The book in your hand is a comprehensive guide to the field of technical writing. It gives you a chance to look before you plunge; then guides you through the day-to-day realities of being a tech writer. It includes tips about handling on-the-job situations not usually discussed in technical writing books, such as how to get information from a reticent engineer and how to deal with office politics in a high-tech environment.

You'll learn from working writers what they do from nine till five, what they find rewarding and frustrating, and how they broke into the field. You'll learn how to research and produce a technical document, including interviewing engineers, scheduling a writing project, and planning illustrations. You'll learn about professional associations and career development.

You can use this book both to decide about a tech writing career and to begin one. But first . . .

WHAT IS TECHNICAL WRITING?

Stated very simply, technical writing involves translating technical ideas into words a specific audience will understand. Technical ideas are initiated by scientists or engineers.

For example, a computer incorporates technical ideas that originated in an engineering laboratory. Engineers use combined knowledge of electronics, programming, and usability studies to come up with the optimal shape and internal arrangement for the computer.

Once the computer is produced, its operation must be communicated to the audiences that will market, repair, and write programs for the computer. At least three technical writers might be involved. They'll take notes on the computer's characteristics and create documents: One will write marketing brochures, another will write a hardware trouble-shooting manual, and a third will write a software reference manual.

It is up to a technical writer to weave a connection of words between the scientist and his or her audience. And most often, this connection includes images. Technical writers not only write, but frequently design the whole document. They think up visual ideas to illustrate technical ideas. They provide tables, graphs, and simple drawings and work with artists to create more elaborate drawings.

The technical writer's audience almost always knows less about the subject than the scientist or engineer initiating the ideas. This means that the technical writer has the job of (1) understanding technical ideas initiated by a scientist, (2) understanding who the reader is, and (3) expressing the ideas according to that reader's education level, ability to understand, and familiarity with the subject.

Linda Lininger, a successful Silicon Valley writing consultant, sees technical writing as a craft:

> I look at technical writing as being more of a craft than a profession; it's like being more of an artisan than an artist, because technical writers more or less make shoes. Either you make O.K. shoes or you can make really fine shoes. They both do the job, but some are better to look at, they feel better, they're pretty, and people go "Ooo Ah." The [recently finished manual]—I really put my heart and soul into it. Not only did I have a peak experience doing it, because it was a lot of work, pressure, drive, and crunch crunch, but it's nice to look at.

In the sense that Linda is talking about it, technical writing challenges the writer both to communicate effectively and to create a quality product. In her situation, a demanding schedule added further challenge. We see a picture emerging of technical writing as something of an adventure.

Technical writing is an adventure in yet another sense, in that technical writers are at the scene of many scientific breakthroughs. They enjoy the privileged knowledge of insiders. When technology allows humankind to take another giant step, a technical writer is there to learn and tell about it.

> Writers have supported and reported the nation's space programs, from its weather, communication, and navigation satellites to its Herculean effort to place man's footsteps on the moon. . . . Writers have supported and reported the nation's atomic energy program, from the excitement of the first self-sustaining chain reaction to the development of nuclear power plants. In the future, writers will document and describe the nation's battle to control pollution, its struggle to save the cities, and its search for alternative transportation systems. They will continue to

report man's fight against disease and disability. Where the action is, there the writer is.[1]

Thus wrote Clark Emerson and Vernon Roote in their 1972 career guide, *Your Future in Technical and Science Writing*. Since 1972 science has produced more wonders than Emerson and Roote could have anticipated, from organ-transplant operations to laser weapons in space. And for each wonder, writers have participated.

But, what kind of people become technical writers, what do they really do from nine till five, and where did they learn how to do it?

WHAT'S IN IT FOR ME?

It really is terrific being an insider, knowing about exciting new products that are coming, before your neighbors do. That's part of working at any high-tech company. I'm sure that people working in the design studios of automobile companies feel the same way or people in the movie or record business . . . I know about things that the whole industry is going to be talking about or the whole office is going to be talking about—later. I know about them now.

With these words, John Huber, senior technical writer at eTranslate, describes one of the satisfactions of being a technical writer. Another reward he describes is "being published, without the uncertainties of being a freelance writer." And for him, as for me, being paid well to learn is another big reward.

Every tech writer has a different list of payoffs they find in their job. Most writers include the following:

- producing a tangible result
- being published
- being paid well
- meeting interesting people
- learning new technologies and skills
- enjoying writing

Tangible Results

One technical publications manager reminisces about her writing days when, in contrast with her current job, her accomplishments were in print:

You have a finished product at the end of your efforts. You have something that is the fruits of your labor, and it's all printed and nice, and it's going out with the product. You can hold it in your hands and say, "I did this."

[When you're a manager] you solve problems, you talk to people, you write performance evaluations, so you never have a finished product that you can hold and say "I did this." Especially in retrospect, that's something that I always liked; that I never realized how much I liked until I left it.

Linda Lininger also appreciates this aspect of technical writing:

It's not like some jobs where you work and work and work and have nothing to show for it. When you work, it's in black and white. . . . There's something you can touch.

Being Published

Being published is a big tangible result. A writer whose book is published before setting pen to paper is rare. In the commercial publishing world, a writer goes through queries, proposals, and negotiations before even the prospect of a monetary advance comes into view. To be automatically published is a privilege enjoyed—nay, taken for granted—by technical writers. Although a technical writer's name usually does not appear in the book, and some writers have strong feelings about this omission, a published book is still a source of pride:

When this manual comes back from the print shop—my very first manual all by myself—when that comes back from the print shop, that'll be a hell of a wonderful day. It'll be time to buy a bottle of champagne. I'm very object oriented. I want to produce some*thing*. For this manual, I'm handling everything—the writing, vending it out to an editor, getting the art done. I'll be handling it through the print shop. So I'm the writer and the production editor, too. I think that's a hell of a production.

These comments by computer hardware writer Billie Levy point out how a technical writer often needs to be a jack-of-all-trades, and she obviously enjoys that aspect of her job.

Good Pay

Getting paid well to write, while you are writing, is another privilege of the profession. A 1999 survey, conducted by the Society for Technical Communication (STC), revealed technical writers received an average annual salary of $47,560 in the United States and $47,700 in Canada. These figures don't accurately reflect higher salaries found in high-tech areas like California's Silicon Valley, where some senior writers earned a great deal more. According to the STC survey, the highest salaries were found in Virginia, California, Massachusetts, and New York; the lowest were in New Mexico, Iowa, and Kansas.

Income is also tied to technical knowledge. The ability to write online documentation, including online help and Web pages, has rapidly become technical writers' most lucrative skill. According to a 1999 WinWriters survey, the average salary for Microsoft Windows help authors was $57,000, with a high of $150,000.[2] And of help authors, those with Web experience earned 14 percent more than those without.[3] This survey found that for hourly contractors, online help skills increased beginning technical writers' hourly rates by 40 percent; Web development skills increased rates by over 100 percent.[4] Both the WinWriters and STC surveys found salaries for men significantly higher than for women.

Tech writers' salaries grew 42 percent between 1988 and 1998. If they continue to grow at that rate, a tech writer working in 2008 can expect to make about $68,500 a year and a senior writer significantly more.

It's not unusual for a technical writer in the computer industry to double his or her salary in the first year. Most tech writers I interviewed did so. And if a book gets canceled, for whatever reason, the staff technical writer still gets a regular pay check.

Interesting People

Meeting different kinds of interesting people is another plus. How many professions put you in contact with successful engineers, artists, marketing wizards, and, of course, other writers? These contacts can provide product information, as well as friendships and possible references when it's time for a job change.

When John Huber wrote a book called *The Human Interface Guidelines*, he needed to explain the aspects of computer design that make computers easy for people to use. To do research for this book, John spent a whole year working with a group of psychologists and graphic artists. The group traveled together, used the research facilities of a number of major universities, and enjoyed an enriching synergy.

Learning New Skills

Another reward in technical writing is the opportunity to constantly learn about new technologies and better ways to communicate. Says Billie Levy:

> One quality that a technical writer ought to have is a joy in learning. I spent a lot of time going to college, and I didn't care what college class you dropped me into, as long as it had a good teacher and some good material. It could be on some subject that it never occurred to me before to be interested in. But once I'd start working on it, I'd get interested. It's part of my personality that I love to learn. And that's one of the reasons I got into this business and that's one of the reasons I love learning about this machine. I love learning about new things.

If you want to do the same old thing day after day, don't be a writer. Some people like to be on automatic pilot. They like to learn how to do a job, and learn how to do it so well that they don't really have to put a lot of energy into learning new things. They just keep cranking. That's not me and that's not technical writing.

Besides learning new technologies, tech writers get to learn the latest computer programs for word processing and for composing, or "authoring," documents online. And they're repeatedly challenged to learn better communication skills, because they need information from people and they need to harmonize as part of a team that produces a product.

Enjoying Writing

One reward in being a professional writer is the enjoyment of writing. This seems obvious, but it's a subtle truth. Most of what technical writers do is not writing, but research, organization, learning, human interaction, and book production. I feel the writing time is really the appetizer or dessert course of a meal composed of grittier dishes. It's my favorite part of the meal, which is why I'm writing this book!

Being published, receiving good pay, working with interesting people, learning new concepts and skills, and enjoying writing are probably the major benefits writers find in their jobs, but most writers find others as well. If these are things you care about, or could come to care about, you'll experience tech writing as a richly rewarding career.

However, there's a catch. Technical writing is considered by many to be one of the most stressful professions today.

WHAT PROBLEMS COME WITH THE TERRITORY?

"On the one hand, you're told to be complete, correct, concise, perfect, personal, accurate, and on the other hand, finish it by tomorrow."

Thus one tech writer sums up what he considers the stresses of the job. Every tech writer has his or her own grief list. Many will include the following:

- difficulty obtaining information
- reticent or uncooperative engineers
- canceled projects (after the work's been done)
- unreasonable or unclear deadlines
- unwieldy tools and equipment
- office politics

Difficulty Obtaining Information

Difficulty getting product information is a common experience among writers who've been at it a while. Sometimes the product is not finished yet, and its developers have not had time to write down anything about it. Sometimes a product developer is the only source of information and is difficult to communicate with.

According to one technical writing manager, who prefers anonymity:

> There is a developer here who is quite a character. He doesn't focus on the technical information but rather uses the interviews with the writer to express his political opinions about the company. So he gets up on his high horse, "At [this company], we'll put any product out there for anybody, and we never have a chance to do any of them right." The frustrating thing for the writer is trying to get technical information and keeping this guy focused on what he's supposed to be telling them, rather than expressing all this vehemence against the way the company's run.

This manager sympathizes with her writers' difficulties communicating with this engineer and understands when they need extra time to get the information they need from him.

Reticent Engineers

I remember meeting with a man I'll call Max Engineer who was my primary source of information about a computer networking product. I asked him a series of well-prepared, detailed questions about the product, and he answered all my questions with "probably" and "I'm not sure." No matter how I rephrased my questions, Max was not forthcoming. Later, my boss met Max at an office party and happened to mention to him that he was my key source of technical information. Max was shocked. He thought writers pull information from air, like magicians pulling rabbits from hats.

In that particular situation, I was too new to technical writing to know that I could have educated Max. I could have told him a bit about what technical writers do and informed him of his crucial role in that process.

According to computer hardware writer Billie Levy:

> There's no point in brow-beating the individual engineers. You have to go upstairs and say, look, if you want this manual done, it has to be looked at. It has to be passed by those people whose O.K. is important.
>
> Problems getting information are endemic to our profession. The engineers are very busy and they have a lot of demands on their time. So you have to be persistent and tactful.

The chapter "Communicating with Engineers" describes some effective ways to deal with reticent, uncooperative, and just-plain-overworked engineers.

Canceled Projects

I count canceled or postponed projects high on my list of the non-rewards of technical writing. After putting months of work into a manuscript, I anticipate its completion somewhat as a pregnant mother anticipates delivering a baby. When a project miscarries, for whatever reason, the next project seems harder to begin.

One technical writing manager I spoke with sees postponed projects as a result of shifting priorities:

> In a company like ours, you have so many projects and so many products going on at the same time, and you have a limited number of writers. So you have writers working on things based on an understanding of what the priorities are. The most important products get their attention first.

This manager believes it's counterproductive "for a writer to get ramped up on a product, become productive writing, get to know the other team members, the technical people, and all that; then be yanked off of that onto whatever is next week's fire—'Oh, well, we have to do some preliminary documentation because they want to send something out to a customer, so drop what you're doing and go . . . throw together something.'"

Because conscientious managers see their job as helping their employees succeed, they can get as frustrated as the writer when projects get "reprioritized."

We Want It Good and Now

> The worst thing about technical writing that happens again and again is this business of having to meet a deadline when you sense that the project isn't going to be ready and your book doesn't need to be ready. The deadline is unreal, the boss is holding you to it only to make himself look good, or the deadline slips and it just starts all over again. That's the worst part.

With these words, a computer-software writer describes his real feelings about unreal deadlines.

Nowhere else is the deadline so malleable one day and unforgiving the next as it is in fiercely competitive computer companies. The book must be ready *now*; then the product is delayed and, anyway, two reviewers think the book needs a rewrite.

Unfortunately, deadlines are a high-tech fact of life. The push to get out the latest computer, car, VCR, or biomedical breakthrough is the frenetic reality of our competitive marketplace. It's why we have wonder toys and miracle cures. If you're going to write about them, you sometimes have to write on your feet, as you follow the product out the door.

Tools Won't Work

Most tech writers have experienced the printer breaking down in the heat of a deadline. Office jokes abound about machines that sense panic and refuse to cooperate. Machines do tend to break down when they're used more heavily than usual, which happens around deadlines. So there's good reason for such "crashes." They are probably not the act of a rebellious machine consciousness or of demons residing within. (I say "probably.")

Other frustrations with tools occur because of poor maintenance or bad choices. The computerized workplace is like an ecosystem. It contains an intricate balance of software and hardware that must interact. This environment requires a knowledgeable system administrator to keep the machines talking to each other and listening to the people who use them. If a computer uses the wrong "protocol" (set of rules) to communicate with a new printer, the printer won't work. If the people who use machines don't choose and maintain them carefully, production suffers.

Technical writers are at the mercy of these office machines and are also vulnerable to the failings of their text editing, desktop publishing, and online authoring tools. Writers often need knowledge of the underlying software, attention to detail, and persistence to get the final document to look the way it's intended.

Technical writing requires patience with tools. If you are comfortable with the personality of computers, all the better, because you will spend some time "debugging" your tools.

The Writer Diplomat

Office politics provide another source of stress. For example, a technical writer can become caught in the middle of a miscommunication between departments. Marketing says the product is one way, engineering knows it's not, and neither is speaking to the other about it. The tech writer must play diplomat, clarifying the communication between these two departments.

Occasionally, powerful personalities can make a writer's job difficult, if not impossible. At one glamorous company known for its wonderful documentation, a writer acquaintance (who requests his name not be used) was assigned to write a book about a data communications product. He did not know when they gave him the assignment that a powerful engineer did not want the book written. The engineer had already written one about the product—a book that was almost unreadable. He liked his book and wanted to see it published with his name.

The writer tried to create a reasonable schedule and write a high-quality manuscript, but his efforts were thwarted. His manager kept encouraging him to leave the engineer's prose intact. My acquaintance eventually detected the pressure being exerted by the engineer, chose not to take the matter personally, and requested a different project.

Another way to handle this pressure would have been to leave the engineer's prose alone. If you are idealistic and care about your work, however, such compromises can lead to burnout (discussed in the chapter "The Hazards of Being a Tech Writer," later in this book).

To withstand the criticisms, pressures, and obstacles of technical writing requires emotional distance from the day-to-day crises. It also requires a sense of humor. Fortunately, most writers have a sense of humor, and their camaraderie is one of the joys of the profession.

A MENTOR CAN HELP

You will have more success dealing with stress if you have a mentor—a business acquaintance, perhaps even a boss, who has been there before. A mentor can tell you when a crisis is just typical silliness resulting from a bad combination of business pressures and human nature. "We have no control over the lunacy around us. Remember that," a favorite client once remarked.

If you are not fortunate enough to have a mentor and you haven't yet developed suitable caution, you might fall prey to some of these pressures. You might suggest a more realistic deadline to a manager too harried to listen. You might suggest an important improvement for a rushed book that no one really cares about. These suggestions can make you unpopular. Take heart! Almost every seasoned tech writer has had these experiences. As one colleague put it, "In this business, you're either a bum or a hero."

Every writing job has limits and opportunities. If polished writing isn't possible in a particular writing department, because of deadlines, politics, or uncooperative developers, you can find other ways to grow and learn. Maybe you can acquire technical knowledge by attending in-house training courses. Perhaps the company will sponsor you as a part-time student at a community college, where you can acquire technical skills that will help you understand and write about the company's products.

In one particularly frustrating job, where equipment never worked and engineers were always too busy to explain things, I took company training classes in everything from beginning data processing to "packet switching," a complex technology that prescribes how computers transmit data.

The tech writing field is far more an opportunity to expand yourself and grow than it is a series of frustrations, although sometimes it may seem the latter. If you distance yourself and learn to recognize the silliness of typical crises, you'll be the calm one others turn to for perspective.

The chapter "The Hazards of Being a Tech Writer," later in this book, goes into greater detail about ways to deal with the stresses of a technical writing career.

SUMMING IT UP

This chapter talked about some of the rewards of tech writing and some of the grief. Now you know more about what you're getting yourself into. If you're still game, read on. In the next chapter, you'll learn about the history of technical writing and its emergence as a profession.

---

[1] Clark Emerson and Vernon Roote, *Your Future in Technical and Science Writing* (New York, N.Y.: Richard Rosen Press, Inc., 1972), p. 21.

[2] WinWriters, "WinWriters Salary Survey," January 2000, at http://www.winwriters.com/salarysurvey.htm

[3] WinWriters, "The Future for Help Authors (or 'How We'll Learn to Love the Web')," January 2000, at http://www.winwriters.com/future.htm

[4] WinWriters, "On the Clock," January 2000, at http://www.winwriters.com/survey_contractor.htm

2

A Little History

"**W**e have now made clear how the axle is to be constructed;" wrote Hero of Alexandria in the first century A.D., "so now we shall describe its use."

Having explained how to make a winch, Hero added these user instructions, which are probably the first in human history: "If you want to move a great burden by a smaller power, you fasten the ropes that are tied to the burden on the grooved places of the axle on both sides of the wheel. Then you put handspakes into the holes that we have made in the wheel and press down on the handspakes, so that the wheel is turned, and then the burden will be moved by a smaller power . . ."[1]

Hero's instructions exemplify good user documentation, at least in this translation from A. G. Drachmann's *The Mechanical Technology of Greek and Roman Antiquity*. They address the user directly; they're simply phrased and clearly organized.

Through most of history, scientists have documented their work for fellow scientists. However, examples of technical writing for consumers exist from as early as 1748 in America, when the English handbook, *The Instructor*, was revised for American use. The handbook is described in Evald Rink's *Technical Americana* as "Containing spelling, reading. . . . Together with the carpenter's plain and exact rule: shewing how to measure carpenters, joyners, sawyers, bricklayers, plaisterers, plumbers, masons, glaziers and painters work. How to undertake each work, and at what price. . . . Likewise the practical gauger made easy; the art of dialling . . . instructions for dying, colouring, and making colours. . . . The whole better adapted to these American colonies. . . ."[2] This manual's reader was the original jack-of-all-trades! Were its author alive today, he wouldn't believe how far and fast technology has advanced—nor how specialized it's become.

In the 1700s technical information about industrial processes and machinery was called "useful knowledge." Such knowledge was imparted in lectures to early professional associations, like the Providence Association of Mechanics and Manufacturers, which formed in the late 1700s. But technical writing was not recognized as such until well into the 20th century.

The earliest book specifically on technical writing is probably Sir T. Clifford Allbutt's *Notes on the Composition of Scientific Papers,* which he wrote for his students at the Faculty of Medicine in Cambridge in 1904. The writing in Allbutt's profession appalled him, and he wanted to correct its defects in his students' work. "The prevailing defect of their composition" wrote Allbutt in his preface to the third edition (1923), "is not mere inelegance; were it so, it were unworthy of educated men; it is such as to perplex, and even to travesty or to hide the author's meaning."[3] The good doctor would find similar flaws in the writings of scientists today.

In flowery Victorian English, Allbutt offered advice about plain language: "Let him not search afield for long and complicated forms and elaborated words, nor for large and decorated vestures; if he can get well home on his ideas the simplest and closest words are best. Let him consider not how finely, but how plainly and directly he can express himself." He then goes on for several long sentences before concluding: "If the essayist, stripping off all encumbrance, will look nearer home for his words, and put these together concisely, the figure of his thought will move more freely in the lighter garment."[4] By modern standards, he was a long-winded fellow, but his heart was in the right place.

Almost all early books about technical writing were written for the education of engineers and scientists, according to Gerald J. Alred et al. in *Business and Technical Writing: An Annotated Bibliography of Books, 1880–1980.* "As far as we can determine," say the authors, "the first technical writing book aimed strictly at a professional audience is Thomas Arthur Rickard's *A Guide to Technical Writing* (1908). This work, aimed at metallurgical engineers and geologists, has a modern flavor throughout, especially with its emphasis on audience."[5] By professional audience, the authors mean professional scientists, not writers.

THE TOWER OF BABEL

Until the 1940s, there were no technical writers. Technical products were primarily designed for technical experts, and technical experts wrote any instructions or explanations that went with these products. So scientists and engineers wrote for each other, or more precisely, for themselves. They took pride in their use of scientific jargon and sometimes affected a high tone. Long words, sentences, and paragraphs enhanced the scholarly effect (or affectation, if you will). Often technical documentation produced by one scientist proved incomprehensible to another.

The fact that jargon and complexity fail to communicate was lost on scientists and engineers trained within a tradition of obscure verbiage. Robert Gunning, in *The Technique of Clear Writing,* tells the story of a great American scientist, Willard Gibbs, many of whose discoveries remained unknown because his colleagues couldn't understand his writing. Says Gunning, "It became a scientific joke that it was easier to 'redis-cover Gibbs than it was to read him.'" Gunning quotes Gibbs:

> For the equilibrium of any isolated system it is necessary and sufficient that in all possible variations of the state of the system which do not alter its energy, the variations of its entropy shall either vanish or be negative.[6]

What did the man say? This is a good example of poor technical writing. It contains an unclear subject, unclear referents, and passive voice. The long sentence wanders into obscurity, as did its author.

During World War II, science and technology increased in importance and so did scientists. Because of their need to work unhampered by the demand for documentation, scientists acted as unwitting midwives in the birth of a new profession. They began requiring writers to interpret their creations to others.

"When I was in the Second World War," remembers 65-year-old tech writer Mark Smith, "I was working on aircraft using military specifications as sources of information, and sometimes the information was quite clear. But sometimes it wasn't, and I didn't know what I was reading. The choice of words and the way it was put together were clumsy, and perhaps a picture would have done better. But there wasn't one." Although Mark was not a writer at the time, he remembers thinking that if he ever got the chance, he would write better "specs" than the ones he had to work from.

World War II led to a huge increase in the number of military con-tracts. After the war, the government required that these contracts be accompanied by documentation. Additionally, the peacetime uses for war-related technology fed a technological boom in consumer products, which also required documentation.

"Usually the engineer kept an engineering notebook on his work," says Mark Smith. "It was the writer's job to come along and pick up on the facts to tell what the product was for and how to use it. And that developed into what's called an operator's manual."

Operator's manuals were written by the new breed of people who were hired just to write. "During the war and shortly after the war," says Mark, "it started more or less as just a documentation effort and then developed into technical writing. I know at the time, I never heard of a technical writer. I heard of writers, but not technical writers."

THE BIRTH OF A PROFESSION

As technical writers increased in number, they sought validation for their profession by forming associations. Between 1953 and 1957, writers formed half a dozen professional societies around the country, including the Society of Technical Writers (1954) in the eastern United States, the

Association of Technical Writers and Editors (1953) in New York City, and the Technical Publishing Society on the West Coast. The Society of Technical Writers and Editors (STWE) was formed out of the two eastern societies in 1957.

In the late '50s and early '60s, the Vietnam War again placed a demand on military industries, the number of military contracts increased, and more technical writers were required.

The late '60s saw the first graduating college class of technical writing majors, which at the time was quite an oddity. Scientists were perplexed by this group of graduating engineers who had made a commitment to the writing profession. And engineers they were, heavily trained in science and technology. They entered the business world with many of the biases of earlier scientists—that technical writing should sound formal and be written in third person and passive voice.

Fortunately for everyone, technical writers today are much more aware of the requirements of clear communication than they were in the '60s and '70s. What has brought about this change? The commercialization of technology.

THE COMPUTER REVOLUTION AND BEYOND

The biggest commercialization happened when the computer became widely available for business use in the '70s. The second most revolutionary development happened when it became widely available to consumers in the '80s—industry needed to sell its genius to us, the public.

When the microcomputer (the forerunner of personal computers) first appeared, it was a very mysterious thing indeed. If your computer could not successfully process information, it displayed a number, which corresponded to an error message. You could look the message up in a book, but you'd be lucky to understand what you found. Then computer programmers started writing messages in English—messages like "SOURCE IS READER" and warnings like "BDOS ERR ON A: SELECT." These messages were understandable only to programmers.

Office automation and the commercial availability of personal computers put pressure on industry to produce larger quantities of documentation. And the audience had changed. Technical people, and those selling their creations, came to realize they needed to explain technology to the nontechnical public—the "end user"—and they needed someone other than a computer programmer to make their documents understandable.

Enter the professional technical writer—someone who knows how to use language and graphics to teach technical concepts to nontechnical people. When the computer industry began to expand, or rather explode, the demand for professional technical writers also exploded.

Today, technical writing has evolved into technical communication. Writers in all fields now have access to sight-and-sound media. Sometimes writers design computer tutorials for end users who will never pick up a document. Their computer teaches them, through graphics and sound, all they need to know about how to use it. Computer technology today allows you to record, store, and send voice messages inside documents; to compose music; to manipulate full-color, three-dimensional objects in space; and more. Technical writers both describe these products and use them to communicate technical information.

So you can see the technical communicator's role is changing as technology changes, and has already evolved well beyond the role of writer. The field continues to evolve and grow rapidly.

In 1991 over 100,000 technical communicators were employed in the United States alone. This number is estimated to increase to 166,000 by the year 2009.* With the proliferation of multimedia and data communications technologies, discoveries in biotechnology, new microprocessor-based devices, and other technological products, an unimaginable number of new opportunities will become available to technical writers in the next decade.

SUMMING IT UP

In this chapter, I delved into the history of tech writing and found that it is very old. I talked about the relatively recent birth of technical writing as a profession and its flight from the printed page into realms of color and sound. The next chapter describes people who do well in this field and the kinds of skills required.

---

* The Society for Technical Communication's *1991–1995 Strategic Plan* estimated the number of technical communicators in the United States in 1991 to be more than 100,000. In the ensuing 10 years, STC membership grew 31 percent. If this growth rate reflects the continued growth of the profession, about 166,000 technical communicators will be working in the United States by the year 2009.

---

[1] A. G. Drachmann, *The Mechanical Technology of Greek and Roman Antiquity: A Study of the Literary Sources* (Madison: University of Wisconsin Press, 1963), p. 56.

[2] Evald Rink, *Technical Americana: A Checklist of Technical Publications Printed Before 1831* (Millwood, N.Y.: Kraus International Publications, 1981), p. 18.

[3] Sir T. Clifford Allbutt, *Notes on the Composition of Scientific Papers* (London: Macmillan and Co., 1923), p. v.

[4] Allbutt, p. 140.

[5] Gerald J. Alred et al., *Business and Technical Writing: An Annotated Bibliography of Books, 1880–1980* (Metuchen, N.J.: The Scarecrow Press, Inc., 1981), p. 2.

[6] Robert Gunning, *The Technique of Clear Writing* (New York: McGraw-Hill Book Company, 1968), pp. 254–5.

3

Who Becomes
a Tech Writer?

Who are successful technical writers? What are their personal qualities and work-related skills? The reason you might ask these questions, of course, is to find out if you are such a person.

Tech writers come from as varied educational backgrounds as you can imagine, from philosophy to computer science. The only background they seem to have in common is a degree of some sort, and even here, it's tough to generalize.

A 1999 survey by the Society for Technical Communication (STC) found that 95 percent of its membership had a bachelor's degree or higher.[1] This means that 5 percent did not. A 1999 WinWriters survey of online help writers' salaries shows some members without degrees were doing very well:

> Individuals with a four-year degree coupled with heavy management responsibilities averaged $69,000 [in annual salary]. Those having a high school diploma coupled with 3–5 years of Web experience averaged $60,000.[2]

I recently spoke with two highly successful technical writing consultants who have no bachelor's degrees. While they are exceptions, they also prove that if you don't have a degree and you think this field is for you, you can still go for it. (Hiring managers I interviewed agree, but stipulate that a job applicant with no degree needs lots more experience in the field than an applicant with a degree.)

The profile of the tech writer is changing. Hiring managers are beginning to perceive technical communication degrees as more desirable now that such degrees are widely available. Nonetheless, the high demand for technical writers, coupled with their history of diversity, makes for fairly permissive hiring practices. By permissive, I mean that many different kinds of backgrounds are acceptable to hiring managers. (You can find more about that in the chapter "Breaking In.") This chapter analyzes the backgrounds, personalities, and skills of working writers today and gives you some ways to explore your own aptitudes.

TECH WRITERS HAVE VARIED BACKGROUNDS

If you're an undergraduate deciding on a major, you might find it useful to turn to the next chapter, "Get Ready," and read the section "If You're Considering a Degree," before proceeding with this chapter. That section will give you a better idea of the degrees hiring managers now look for in new grads. If you already have a degree or are a career changer, read on.

Many—probably most—working technical writers are career changers who started in some other profession. Their educational backgrounds vary widely. According to the 1999 WinWriters survey, 60 percent of 1,136 respondents had no degree or certificate directly related to technical communication. And only 15 individuals reported that they had learned core skills through their formal education.

The 1999 STC survey found most working technical writers had been humanities majors, with 42 percent coming from English curriculums, 23 percent from technical communication, and another 10 percent from journalism.*

Tech writer Jan Roechel took a theology major and a journalism minor in college, and eventually got a job in the accounting department of a computer networking firm: "When I was working in accounting as a supervisor, I worked with the programmers and I set up a computer system. . . . I had an interest in programming, and I wanted to take courses so I could write programming applications for accounting." Jan's boss wanted her to go into accounting management and wasn't open to training her as a programmer. In scouting around the company for an opportunity to learn programming, Jan stumbled upon a technical writing job, realized it combined her writing skills and her interest in computer software, and took the opportunity to begin a new career.

Some technical writers are former teachers and feel that teaching contributed to their skills as technical communicators. Says hardware writer Billie Levy:

> What the technical writer is basically doing is an educational process. A technical writer should be literate, and secondly, have a background in education, because as a technical writer, you're essentially an educator. And [a background in] education can teach you how to organize material to present it to other people so that they can absorb it.

---

* Multiple majors caused survey results to exceed 100 percent.

The 1999 STC survey found the physical sciences well represented in the tech writing profession: Ten percent of its members majored in computer science, 10 percent in other sciences, and 9 percent in engineering.

Programmers and engineers sometimes switch to technical writing after some years of industry experience. When I spoke with independent consultant Mark Smith, he had been a technical writer for 36 years and a consultant for the last 11. He started as a service engineer in the aerospace industry.

> I was a service engineer for an F-102 and F-106 and also for the Atlas missile for about nine years. In that time, I became a service specialist in the hydraulic and pneumatic fields and I had to write the tech orders for the government on those systems. At the time I was doing that, I was also writing accident reports for an air force magazine and every time I'd write one I'd get an award—about $150.00. That was kind of an incentive. The feedback was that these were good articles, and so maybe I'm some kind of a writer [laughs] after all and don't know it! So I just stayed with it, always writing engineering specifications, and I seemed to have a knack for it.

About becoming a technical writer, a former quality assurance tester and customer support engineer says:

> I didn't see it as leaving the scientific training behind. As a matter of fact, the longer I stay in this business, the more I see that scientific training is very valuable for a tech writer. There's a lot of research involved. Training in scientific method and logical presentation of data or evidence are things that people who are exclusively oriented in the humanities sometimes are neither interested nor capable of appreciating. I think a tech writer has to have a certain balance in their mental makeup and their approach to their job. Tech writing, in one sense, is a literary activity, but I see it as a sort of scientific—or semi-scientific—endeavor.

Another background worth mentioning is in foreign languages. Senior technical writer John Huber reports:

> This is the third time my foreign-language experience has been the key to a great job change. The three things that got me my first tech-writing job (Itel, 1978) were writing ability, computer experience, and knowledge of German. Etak (1994) hired me because of my German and because I'd lived and traveled extensively in German-speaking countries. And eTranslate (1999) doesn't hire anyone who isn't multilingual.

John expands on the demand for technical writers with diverse cultural and language backgrounds:

> E-commerce is global, work teams are diverse, and multilingualism and multiculturalism are highly valued. Our little engineering team includes a Hollander who speaks Frisian, Dutch, English, and German; a Bangladeshi who speaks Bengali and English; two Americans who speak English and German; an Indian whose first language is (I think) Hindi; a Canadian who speaks English and French. . . . You get the idea.

These writers' stories give you some sense of the variety and permissiveness of the technical writing field. The chapter "Breaking In" describes how managers view requirements for this field and guides you on how to break in.

WINNING QUALITIES

Despite their varied backgrounds, successful tech writers all have certain personal qualities and work-related skills. You may already possess many of these. Top of the skills list is the ability to communicate, not just on paper, but interpersonally and graphically. For this reason, many authorities, including the STC and the American Medical Writers Association, prefer the term *communicator* over writer. While I'll continue to use the terms interchangeably, I mention this to stress the interpersonal and visual communication skills required.

Now, here are those skills—successful technical writers are able to

- write
- communicate interpersonally
- communicate visually
- tenaciously track information
- learn quickly
- take criticism
- be flexible
- meet deadlines

Write

Technical writers can analyze, organize, and verbally communicate information so that it is easily understood by the intended audience. This requires both analytical skills and empathy for your reader. Says one senior writer:

> You have to be able to put yourself in somebody else's position. Especially if you're writing to end users—people who've never used a computer before—and you want to give them confidence. You have to sit in their chair and remember what it was like, and not assume too much knowledge.

Communicate Interpersonally

Technical writers need to communicate well to get information from engineers and other experts. And, as mentioned in the chapter "Why Begin," writers are often political go-betweens. They need to be both diplomatic and assertive to get their work done. According to a writer at Apple Computer:

> A project team can be full of contradictory goals, and its members don't become aware of it until the book has to be written. And the writer is the one that has to say "Look, it's either that way or it's that way. You've got to choose. It can't be both 'cause I have to write it down." And sometimes that's an unpleasant truth, and they don't like the writer for pointing that out to them. But you get to do it anyway.

Communicate Visually

Technical writers create graphs and charts to illustrate technical concepts and they provide artists with ideas for illustrations and online graphics. Writers also need to know how to use desktop publishing software (those computer programs that allow you to produce a typeset-looking document) and be skilled at manipulating the visual elements of a page. Online authors need to understand screen design as well.

As mentioned in the chapter "A Little History," some technical communicators also design presentations in other visual media, including video and multimedia.

Says biomedical writer Dan Liberthson:

> I spend a lot of my time doing slide sets to educate physicians and sometimes lay people in medical matters, and a slide has to be visually interesting. You do write an annotation—a legend—that goes with the slide, but the slide itself has to be visually gripping and interesting. You get some help from graphics people in the refinements, but you have to come up with the concept.

Tenaciously Track Information

Technical writers are thorough researchers who can recognize holes in the information they've received. They're willing to pursue questions until they have answers, through any means available. Says one publications manager:

> You have to be a little bit aggressive, because there are going to be people who don't want to talk with you, who don't want to spend time with you, and they don't want to review your manuals, either. So you can't be afraid to go and pound people on the head and say "I need this [information] or the manual is not going to be ready on time" or to ask your boss to do the same thing.

Learn Quickly

Technical writers need to understand complex technologies enough to describe a high-tech product. Says Dan Liberthson:

> To be successful, I think you have to be very intensely project-focused. Learn like a sponge. You soak up like a blotter as quickly as possible, like cramming for an exam, everything that you need to know for a particular project. Then you do the project and then you let it go.

Take Criticism

Technical writers have their work reviewed to ensure its technical accuracy. Reviewers will say anything—even obscene things—about a writer's work. The chapter "The Review Process" goes into how to handle this in detail.

Be Flexible

Technical writers are faced with undefined product development schedules, canceled projects, and myriad other situations in which they are forced to switch gears rapidly. Says publications manager Carre Mirzadeh:

> Often at the beginning of a project, the project isn't well specified, the schedule isn't well known, the players on the project aren't well known, and you have to have a great deal of flexibility to be able to adjust to the requirements and constraints during the time of the project. And more than one writer I've known have been driven from technical writing because they weren't able to function in that type of an environment.

Meet Deadlines

Technical writers need to manage an entire writing project. The final deadline, while affected by many forces outside the writer's control, must ultimately be in the writer's control. If a writer's schedule is jeopardized, he or she communicates that fact and renegotiates. Meeting deadlines requires every skill a writer has. Usually junior writers get help with this part of their job, and companies differ a great deal over how seriously they take deadlines. If you want to excel as a technical writer, meet your deadlines.

WHO ARE YOU?

Assessing your particular combination of personal qualities and work-related skills lies in the domain of vocational counselors. Some try to quantify "aptitude"—your talent in a subject area. Others believe it's your enjoyment and desire that best determine your success at something. In the latter camp, the classic is Richard Bolles's buoyant, extremely helpful *What Color Is Your Parachute?*[3] If you still have doubts about where you are going in life (who doesn't?), read Bolles's book.

A number of career guidebooks present skills-assessment methods based on what you enjoy. They suggest listing significant achievements from your past that have afforded you the most personal satisfaction, then listing the actual work you did, the skills you used (such as organizing, advising, selling, etc.), and the rewards you experienced. You can refer to the bibliography at the back of this book for suggested career guides.

Once you have a pretty good idea of your interests and abilities, use the "Winning Qualities" described in this chapter and the questions in the following checklist to decide if you are—or if you want to become—the right person for a technical writing career.

CHECKLIST 3–1. SELF-EXPLORATION

The "correct" answers to these questions are pretty obvious. They're just here to help you think it over.

- Do you like to write?
- Do you like learning new things?
- Can you converse with "difficult" people and avoid getting into an argument with them?
- Have you ever negotiated a compromise between people who disagree?
- Have you ever drawn pictures, graphs, or diagrams to express concepts?
- When you can't get the answer to a question after several tries, do you think creatively about other avenues to explore?
- Do you try to either appease or argue with someone who criticizes you? Or can you step back and weigh the criticism objectively?
- If plans change unexpectedly, do you get upset? Or can you take a deep breath and steer accordingly?
- Do you keep your time commitments?

IT'S UP TO YOU

You can see that successful technical writers are self-directed, highly motivated learners, unintimidated by new concepts and terminology. You should have some of these qualities, if only in their embryonic form, before you consider tech writing. Many tech writers don't have these qualities, but they're not good tech writers.

This book assumes that you can develop any quality you want, if you really believe it's in your best interest. And none of these generalizations about tech writers is meant to intimidate. You can always find people to tell you how hard something is. This book is about how to go out and do it.

Says Richard Bolles in an early edition of *What Color Is Your Parachute?*, "Your interests, wishes, and happiness determine what you actually do well more than your intelligence, aptitudes, or skills do."[4]

If you don't have a skill you need, you can learn it, provided you're interested in doing so.

A former coworker, shy and conciliatory by nature, got a job at the most political, aggressive company in Silicon Valley. At the time, she told me, "The one thing I'm going to learn on this job is to be assertive." Some years later, she'd obviously succeeded, and I asked her how she did it. She replied:

> By dealing with people who were very assertive, I had to become assertive myself. I learned that I had to say no to people and not worry about what they felt, because otherwise they were going to tell me what to do and it's going to have an effect on me. . . . If you look at how other people do things—how the engineers do things—they might be working 80 hours a week, and they'll have those kinds of expectations of you. I have to be assertive enough to set my own limits and say no, this is what I need.

SUMMING IT UP

This chapter described the kind of person who becomes a tech writer and the kinds of backgrounds today's tech writers have. The next chapter explores different kinds of technical writing and educational opportunities that can prepare you for your chosen field.

---

[1] *STC 1999 Technical Communicator Salary Survey* (Arlington, Virginia: Society for Technical Communication, 1999).

[2] WinWriters, "School's Never Out," January 2000, at www.winwriters.com/survey_education.htm

[3] Richard Bolles, *What Color Is Your Parachute?* (Berkeley, Calif.: Ten Speed Press: Updated annually).

[4] Bolles, *Parachute* (1978 edition), p. 90.

4

Get Ready

When you first bought your VCR—or microwave oven or other technological toy—and took it out of the box, did you read the unpacking instructions? Did you wonder who the writer was? Did you curse or praise him? Technical writing is so much a part of our lives that we take it for granted. Technical writers write everything from scripts for sales videos to the directions and warnings that come with an over-the-counter drug. This diversity presents a confusing array of choices to those considering a tech writing career.

What technology will you specialize in? This chapter will give you an idea of where to begin to look. Once you decide on a technical field, you're faced with the perplexing variety of media that technical communicators use to express concepts and describe products. Will you write articles, proposals, or Web pages? Or will you design presentations requiring few words and many visuals? This chapter describes five major categories of technical writing and the communication media they use. It goes on to describe educational programs and other ways to acquire the knowledge you might still need to enter your chosen field.

CHOOSING A FIELD

You can choose a field or let it choose you. I fell into writing about data communications software—my primary subject area—because the start-up company that first hired me happened to produce data communications software products. My primary career objective was to make a decent living as a writer, and writing was my main skill. The fact that I was a sophisticated computer user helped get my foot in the door.

If you are primarily a strong writer, you will choose a technical field based on either the available job market or a technical interest you already have—say computers or conservation. If you have some technical expertise, it will guide you toward a field where your current skills will help you begin. You may already be working in a technical field where you can make a lateral move into a writing position. More about that in the chapter "Breaking In."

Many writers switch between fields. They feel that tech writing skills, once acquired, are applicable to a variety of technologies. You can leave several options open by learning the vocabulary and procedures of more than one technology and by becoming proficient in the communication media they use.

While technologies are varied and proliferating, most of the hiring is done by just a few industries:

- Computers
- Electronics
- Biotechnology
- Scientific research and development
- Aerospace
- Automotive
- Engineering and construction
- Networking and telecommunications

Within these broad categories are numerous subfields. For example, computer software alone includes such disparate subjects as accounting, medical imaging, and engineering design.

In addition to deciding on a particular field, think about whether you want to work for private industry or for government. Each provides a very different work environment and places different demands on writers. For example, in private industry you'll participate in decisions about the writing style and design of documents, and you're more likely to enjoy flexible work hours. In contrast, a job in government, or on a government contract, is circumscribed by restrictions. One writer describes his first tech writing job in an aerospace company as "quasi military. Everything had to be kept in a safe because you're dealing with security documents. If you forgot to put it in the safe you got a penalty. If you forgot three times, you got additional penalties. There was either too much work or no work. You spent a lot of time doing mindless things. The milspec [military specification] format was very restrictive." This writer has a Ph.D. in English and was initially unfamiliar with both government requirements and the company's technology. If you have a military background and interest in aerospace technology, you might find this kind of job rewarding.

The military budgets huge sums of money for documentation—over $1 billion to document the space station alone, according to William K. Horton in *Designing & Writing Online Documentation.* And the volume of military documentation is staggering. Says Horton, "World War II fighter aircraft got by with 1,000 pages of manuals and drawings. . . . Today, the B1 bomber has about 1 million pages of documentation."[1]

MARKETING OR JOURNALISM? THE MEDIUM IS THE MESSAGE

Writing is the heart of your craft. But the kind of writing you do is shaped by your medium. If you design a video, you cannot do the kind of writing you would for an environmental impact report or your audience will soon be snoring. Similarly, the purpose of the writing—whether it's to sell, instruct, inform, or entertain—will shape your style. If you're a technical journalist for a consumer publication, you'll use an informal, direct "voice" and cram your page with facts. If you're writing military specifications, you'll follow rigid guidelines to organize and express information. Each kind of technical writing places unique demands on a writer and requires different skills. The following sections describe a few purposes technical writing fulfills and the forms it takes. They're not meant to be comprehensive; an adequate description of any one of these categories could fill a book!

Marketing Communication and Support

Marketing communication is geared to sell. Its form varies with its audience. For example, in the electronics industry, marketing produces data sheets— glossy, one-page handouts with a photograph or drawing of the product and a terse description of its functions. While the writing is often dry, the graphic impact must be "sexy"—very sophisticated and appealing.

In the pharmaceutical industry, marketing support materials appeal to doctors, who are less likely to respond to glitz. One of the largest pharmaceutical firms in California's Silicon Valley takes a low-key approach by giving doctors complimentary slide sets they can use to educate their colleagues and patients about medical and pharmaceutical matters. "It supports your marketing effort," says one of their pharmaceutical writers. "It spreads your name. Somebody receives this nice slide set and they're likely to remember who gave it to them."

If you write for marketing, you must know who the customer is and what the competition is doing. You will describe your product's strengths to convince customers to buy it. You will probably work in a wide variety of media, including overhead transparencies, slides, video, press releases, and magazine ads. You will work closely with artists and the production people who photograph or lay out the finished piece.

Technical Manuals and Specifications

Technical manuals and specifications contain the most complete technical information about a product, including its limitations. These publications range from simple operating instructions to extremely technical engineering specifications. Sometimes the audience consists of customers who are new to the kind of product you are describing. Often the audience consists of engineers or scientists.

While these documents are sometimes long, dry, and complicated, they are often where the high-tech action is and where the jobs are. By writing technical manuals and specifications, you'll receive a free education in the latest technical developments in your field and you'll gain most of the skills you need to write less arduous publications.

Military specifications, which meticulously describe equipment produced for military use, fall into this category. Aerospace proposals do, too. "These are lengthy, detailed, complicated documents," says Dirk van Nouhuys, who started technical writing 40 years ago and now consults:

> The proposal for the C5A transport was shipped in a truck—one copy was shipped in a truck! [It filled boxes and boxes.] These proposals are written by a special team put together for that purpose, which includes writers and editors and technical people. It's a terrible crash-deadline situation. Some of these things—quite complicated ones—are written in six weeks. It's a bizarre Dionysian thing—people sleeping on the floor days on end and all that kind of stuff. It's still going on. Hundreds of thousands of people are employed doing it as we sit here.

So you can see that your choice of medium can have a serious impact on the quality of your life!

Tech writing has its horror stories. However, most technical manuals and specifications are produced in a standard 40-hour week, plus an occasional weekend before the deadline.

If you write technical manuals or specifications, you'll constantly learn more about your chosen technology. You'll work closely with technical experts. You will read inscrutable documents written by said experts, ask lots of questions, and organize lots of complex information. You will usually write to a fairly formal style, dictated by the publications department. For military specifications, you will follow government "mil-spec" style guidelines.

If you write manuals, you'll often use desktop publishing software to produce a finished document. If your product is a computer program, you might write help information the customer will read online. "Computer literacy"—the ability to use computer software and operating systems, and some understanding of how they work—is a must.

Training Materials

A training writer is an educator even more than other technical writers. In training, you'll produce course materials, including study guides, instructors' manuals, overhead visuals, test questions, and score sheets. You might also design interactive, online training courses employees can take without leaving their desks. Your materials will help train both company personnel who service customers and the customers themselves. For example, once a data communications company sells computer networks to several large companies, it provides training for the customers' network managers to teach them how to operate the network.

If you write training material, you'll need skill at lesson planning and experience with the communication medium you'll use. You might work closely with trainers, computer programmers, graphic artists, or animators. If you have a teaching background, it will help you break into this kind of technical writing.

Technical Journalism

Technical journalists write for several different audiences. For example, they can specialize in ghostwriting books, lectures, and journal articles bearing the bylines of well-known scientists or in writing product reviews for consumer magazines. The one thing these kinds of writing have in common is that their primary purpose is to inform, rather than train, guide, or sell. While ghostwriters might write for an audience of scientists, most technical journalists need to translate highly technical concepts for a more lay public. The reader is usually there by choice, not because she bought the product and needs to find out how it works. If your article is boring, she'll flip to another page.

Ghostwriting for scientists is much like manual writing: You will translate technical concepts into readable English for a specific audience and publication style.

Consumer journalism allows a more flexible, conversational style. Because consumer journalism is a glamour field, you will compete harder for a job and make less money than your counterparts in the tech-manual trenches. If you like playing with technical toys, this field could be for you. For example, as a staff journalist for *PC World,* you might spend your time in a lab, testing competing software applications and writing about your findings.

A degree or experience in journalism will help you succeed in this kind of technical writing.

Online Documentation

Technical writers produce online documentation to support technical products and processes, such as computer software. Their audiences are similar to those of the manual writer or training writer and can vary from new computer users to the technically sophisticated. You will probably specialize in one or more kinds of online documentation—for example, creating online help systems and converting paper manuals to online.

Online documentation specialist Freda Salatino calls converting manuals for online viewing "schlepping the book online." If you are fortunate, you will be given the time to optimize text for online use by *chunking* information and inserting helpful *links*. (For information about these terms and about online help authoring, see the chapter "Designing Online Documentation.")

Another area you might specialize in, online tutorials, overlaps the training writer's domain. Computer software tutorials, packaged with consumer software products, are one of the oldest forms of online documentation. Tutorials provide an interactive form of learning, in which the user can perform product-related tasks, respond to questions on the screen, or click for more information. Tutorials usually use lots of graphic images, and some incorporate animation and sound.

As an online documentation specialist, you also might produce online documentation products, such as a medical reference system or a multimedia encyclopedia.

You don't need a particular degree to break into this field—just experience. Experience working on a multimedia project in school or creating any kind of hypertext document will help you break into this field.

Web Sites

Web pages communicate technical information to customers through the World Wide Web, as well as to employees through corporate intranets. As a Web designer, you will focus as much on screen design as on writing. You will use online Web-authoring tools and will need to know a markup language, like HTML (Hypertext Markup Language), to format your written words for online viewing. You will also need to understand computer graphics formats (with names like GIF and JPEG) and to know how different kinds of graphics and fonts display on different kinds of computers.

Experience building your own Web site will help you break into this field.

ACQUIRING THE KNOWLEDGE YOU NEED

If you're a career changer with a degree, you'll learn the necessary skills for technical writing in different ways from someone still planning a college education. If you are an undergraduate deciding on a major, the following sections will help you with this decision. If you already have a degree or work experience, skip to the section "If You Already Have a Degree" for information on ways to gain additional knowledge. The next chapter, "Breaking In," will help you make the most of your current skills in a job interview.

If You're Considering a Degree

If you don't yet have a degree, a technical communication major is one option to consider. One advantage of many technical communication programs is an internship opportunity—a low-paid, temporary junior position, which can lead into your first real technical writing job. Appendix A lists academic programs in technical communication, many of which offer internship programs.

A 1990 survey of 72 organizations in diverse technical fields showed hiring managers prefer new writers to have technical communication degrees above other majors.[2] Since then, the numbers of technical communication programs and their graduates have increased dramatically.

Managers I interviewed did not have a preference for technical communication degrees. Says Dirk van Nouhuys, who has been a technical publications manager for several companies, including Sun Microsystems and Apple Computer:

> I don't think managers weight tech writing degrees very heavily. When you're trying to get a job, there's a difference between dealing with a publications manager and somebody who's not a publications manager but who happens to manage a group that needs a technical writer. And I think that latter group—because specialized degrees are very important to them—is more likely to give weight to a degree in technical writing. But I don't. I know a bunch of publications managers and I don't know any publications manager who is explicitly looking for people with degrees in technical writing. I've seen some people who can't write who have degrees in technical writing and I'm so far not impressed with them. But it's not a handicap to have one.

Dirk's comments make sense when you realize that many hiring managers with technical writing backgrounds did not come from a technical communication curriculum. And managers, by their own admission, tend to hire people like themselves. However, many writing jobs are offered by people with engineering and business backgrounds, who feel less at ease hiring writers and are reassured by a technical communication degree. Also, the growing academic community in this field is promoting the desirability of technical communication degrees.

In deciding the kind of degree to aim for, consider not only what employers think but, more important, what will prepare you to do well as a technical writer. The skills you need can be gleaned from many different combinations of course work and practical experience. You can use the recommendations under "Academic Programs in Technical Communication" later in this section to guide you.

Also, there is life after technical writing, and you may want to move on to a career in business or some other field where a different mix of course work or a less-specialized degree will have prepared you better than would a technical communication major. A narrowly focused major can open some doors but close many others.

Finally, let your unique set of interests lead you toward the curriculum you're most enthusiastic about. Your interests will guide you to the areas in which you perform best.

OPINIONS FROM THE FIELD

When I asked what background they look for in technical writers, managers differed.

Publications manager Carre Mirzadeh reports:

> Our job descriptions say "degree in computer science, English, journalism, technical writing, or equivalent." My experience has led me to believe that a person from the humanities side or from the scientific or technical side can be a successful technical writer. However, I don't believe that a person with a technical background who's interested in writing will necessarily be able to become a successful technical writer. You need something more than an interest in becoming a writer.

When I asked her what that was, Carre talked about interpersonal skills and flexibility.

Says Dirk van Nouhuys:

> My favorite educational background is journalism and that is because people in journalism know how to ask questions, they know how to deal with getting information from people, they know how to write, and they have a clear image of an audience.

Biomedical writer Dan Liberthson reports:

> People in the medical and scientific disciplines have a bias toward hiring people with science backgrounds and science degrees. There are some industries, like bioengineering, in which I'd say you almost have to have a master's or a Ph.D. in science in a very specific area, like molecular biology. Extremely technical fields. I can't say whether a person with a general humanities background could understand them or not. I suspect they could, but the bias is to say that you need a scientific background.

Dan has a Ph.D. in English and is a successful biomedical writer.

ACADEMIC PROGRAMS IN TECHNICAL COMMUNICATION

In the mid-1980s, educational institutions offered over a hundred academic programs in technical communication, according to the 1985 edition of the STC publication, *Academic Programs in Technical Communication*. The number of programs has at least doubled since then—an indication of the rapid growth in this field.

A closer look at these programs reveals a wide range of focuses, some of them less than practical. One program titled "Technical and Professional Writing" provided journalism and English courses, with no technical requirement or practical experience. Another program not only provided writing courses directly related to technical industries, but also required a technical or science minor, some graphics and design training, and an internship in the field. This would seem to prepare you much more thoroughly for the realities of the tech writing field.

In a 1990 survey by the Association of Teachers of Technical Writing, 124 members were asked which of 48 undergraduate courses in 37 tech writing programs they considered most important. They ranked technical writing highest, followed by technical editing, graphics and design, an internship or research project, business and industrial report writing, and lastly, interviewing. (I would rate interviewing and interpersonal skills a lot higher than this.)[3]

If you are considering an academic program in technical writing, try to talk to graduates from the program who are working in the field. Ask them how well their education prepared them for their careers.

CHECKLIST 4–1. TECHNICAL COMMUNICATION CURRICULA

Below are characteristics you should look for in an academic program in technical writing:

- Several writing-intensive courses, equivalent to at least a minor in English or journalism, with a minimum of one course in your chosen field (for example, science journalism or medical documentation).
- Several courses in your chosen science or technology.
- Courses and labs in desktop publishing and online-authoring tools, including HTML, XML, or a similar markup language.
- An opportunity to learn interpersonal communication skills in a real setting, such as through a journalism course that requires you to perform interviews.
- An internship in the technical writing field, with opportunities to attend meetings and experience the dynamics of a technical publications department in your chosen environment.

The five characteristics listed in the preceding checklist are probably essential elements of a tech writing program. You would also benefit from a course in logic or rhetoric, a course in graphics or design, and courses teaching the production techniques involved in your chosen medium, be it paper documents, online documents, or multimedia. An education course that teaches lesson planning would also be helpful.

If I had it to do over again, I would seek the educational opportunities I've just described. When I entered the tech writing profession, I already had my degree—a major in fine art, a minor in English, and a teaching credential. So I'm in the group I'll talk about next.

If You Already Have a Degree

If you already have a degree or some years of related work experience, you may be able to get your foot in the door without further study. The chapter "Breaking In" discusses how to do this in some detail.

With most degrees, you probably still need more technical knowledge to become a tech writer in a given slot. If you have a liberal arts background, or a science background from an unrelated field, you still need to learn product-specific information. You can learn this kind of information by taking a class or through a company training program once you're hired.

If you have a primarily technical background, you can develop writing abilities that will bridge the gap between your understanding and that of your more technically naive reader. (Later chapters tell you how.) If you learn better from people than from books, consider taking writing and editing classes to fill out your knowledge.

TAKING CLASSES

Before signing up for a class, watch for one pitfall—many people think they need to go to school or take one more class before they go for their real goal. Most real goals are scary, and school is a handy way to put off pursuing them. If you already have strong writing or technical skills, you may have everything you need to get hired. And often companies will train writers.

On the other hand, classes can help you in several ways. One important reason to take a class is to master some of the current technical writing tools. In the early days of word processing, if you knew one tool, you could come up to speed quickly on similar ones. However, as software products have become ever more "powerful" and feature laden, they have also become more difficult to master. Classes in desktop publishing programs like FrameMaker and online authoring tools like RoboHelp can give you the skills you will need.

Another reason to take a class is to show prospective employers that you're up on the latest technological advances. Hiring managers admit they look for buzz words on résumés. Buzz words are product names and technical terms that indicate very specific experience.

Thus, if you want a job in a particular field, take a night course in its latest developments. For example, if you were applying for a job as a computer software writer in the late 1990s, a course in the Java programming language or UNIX operating system looked very good on your résumé. Such trends change fast, and tomorrow a different buzz word will attract the hiring manager's eye.

Classes in either writing or technology can give you knowledge and confidence while you're pursuing your goal. Colleges and universities offer writing and technical classes you can attend in the evening or in summer school. If you don't live in a college town, phone your state university for information on summer school opportunities or extension classes you can take by mail.

In high-tech regions, you'll find a dizzying variety of course offerings. For example, De Anza College in California's Silicon Valley lists

- Business Communication
- Business English
- Word Processing Production
- Desktop Publishing Software
- Computer Applications and Office Systems
- Introduction to the Internet and World Wide Web
- Introduction to Data Communication and Networking

and 20 microcomputer classes, ranging from using a microcomputer to understanding its hardware. This college also offers more than two dozen computer programming classes, as well as classes in physics, ophthalmics, chemistry, and engineering.

If you need writing skills, take a class in expository writing, business writing, technical writing, or copyediting. I took a night course in copyediting at the University of California, Berkeley Extension, taught by a master editor, Max Knight. Not only did he cover the mechanics of editing, but he also spent most of the course illuminating the principles of good writing. This he did with great clarity and enthusiasm. Take an editing course. You might get lucky, as I did.

LEARNING ON THE JOB

Once you land your first job, you can acquire technical knowledge both on the job and through outside classes. I did both. My first technical writing job at a start-up company allowed me to come up to speed informally, by talking to the programmers in the cubicles next to mine and by attending weekly lunch meetings in which a staff programmer would present some technical topic. I also took the company's training course designed to teach customers about the product, a software package that allowed different kinds of personal computers to communicate over a local network (revolutionary stuff at that time!). This course allowed me to see how the training department presented the same material I would write about to the same audience I would address.

I next worked for a larger networking company, which offered weeklong courses in data processing, data communications, and the company's networking products. I took as many of these as I could. Later, I attended a computer programming course at night at a community college. Last, I continue to build my own reference library of technical material about my strongest technical area, data communications. And, of course, the educational process continues every time I research a new product and interview a technical expert.

Other writers report that they do a lot of self-directed study. Says Dan Liberthson:

> I went out, picked up a physiology book, and studied it as though I were taking a physiology course. I picked up an anatomy book. I studied it as though I were taking an anatomy course. . . . I outlined the books and

learned them—basically, memorized them. So I gave myself a course. And I found that physiology, as far as the pharmaceutical industry was concerned, was the most important course because it gave me a basic grasp of the anatomy and processes of the human body.

The other thing you have to do is read the journals. That's very important because doctors often talk in code, as engineers talk in code. There are certain terms that they use that are abbreviations, that are current terms, and if you don't read the journals and the medical magazines, you're not up on things.

Whatever your background, if you are an enthusiastic learner, know how to communicate with people, and enjoy writing, you can develop the skills needed to be a tech writer.

SUMMING IT UP

This chapter described major areas of technical writing and talked about some ways you can acquire knowledge you may need to enter the area of your choice. In the next chapter, you'll learn ways to break into your first, or next, technical writing job.

---

[1] William K. Horton, *Designing & Writing Online Documentation, Second Edition* (New York: John Wiley & Sons, 1994), pp. 1–2.

[2] Dorothy Corner Amsden and Ann Parker, "Up the Ladder or Off the Track: Career Paths for Technical Communicators," 37th ITCC Proceedings, May 20–23, 1990, Santa Clara, Calif., p. CC-27.

[3] Earl E. McDowell, "Survey of Undergraduate Technical Communication Programs and Courses in the United States," 37th ITCC Proceedings, May 20–23, 1990, Santa Clara, Calif., p. ET-112.

5
Breaking In

"What do I look for in a résumé?" says Dirk van Nouhuys. "One thing I look for—and I'm somewhat embarrassed to admit this—is closely related experience to the job. Now the reason I'm embarrassed is that I know perfectly well that any smart person can learn very quickly quite a wide range of things that are not in their experience. But when you read résumés, you have to pick out one from another somehow, and that's one way to pick out one from another."

Everybody knows the job seeker's paradox: You've got to have experience to get a job and you've got to have a job to get experience. What's a person to do?

THE CHILL OF THE HUNT

A woman phoned me this morning seeking advice on how to break into technical writing. She's had 15 years experience as a journalist, including a position as editor of a corporate newsletter, and she knows how to use several word-processing programs and microcomputers. She's extremely well qualified for a technical editing or junior technical writing position. Yet her first few conversations with potential employers left her with a cold, unwanted feeling.

This conversation reminded me how hard it is to be a job hunter, particularly breaking into a new field. It reminded me to remind you up front that self-confidence, perseverance, and luck are essential in any job search. Bolster your self-confidence and courage by any means necessary. The career and job-hunting guides listed in the bibliography can help you with this. For example, Bolles's *What Color Is Your Parachute?*, mentioned earlier, provides excellent guidance through the harrowing process of looking for work.

The rest of this chapter focuses on the particular requirements of the technical writing field and gives you some ways to improve your luck there. You'll find suggestions from managers on how to break in, and guidance on résumés and portfolio preparation. You'll learn how to figure out where the jobs are and how to arrange and survive an interview.

SOME SUGGESTIONS FROM MANAGERS

Hiring managers I asked recommended three ways to break into technical writing:

- a lateral transfer within your present company, where you have already shown some writing ability
- an internship placement through an academic program in technical communication
- a junior writer position in a company too small to afford an experienced writer, or in a company large enough to mentor an inexperienced one

For career changers—particularly those with technical jobs, such as lab technician or product tester—a lateral move is probably the best way to break into technical writing. Says writing manager Carre Mirzadeh about how she broke into technical writing:

> I worked for a company that needed some writing done and there wasn't anyone else to do it, so I began to do it. And once I started, I realized that I enjoyed it. When I first started writing, I didn't do it full time. I did it in conjunction with some QA [quality assurance] testing and tech support. Writing was initially maybe 10 or 20 percent of my job. And as the company changed, we hired people to take over some of the functions I was doing, and I spent more and more time writing. After the first year-and-a-half to two years, I was writing full time.

If you are already working for a company that needs a technical writer—whether or not they know they need one—you can volunteer. Think about what kinds of documents could enhance your current job; then write them. For example, if you deal with customers who repeatedly telephone with the same questions, write a question-and-answer sheet and send it to them. This sheet could save you telephone time and later help prove your writing abilities. Even if your writing efforts don't work into a full-time position, as they did for Carre, your question-and-answer sheet and other product-related pieces will provide writing samples to start your portfolio.

Another way to break in, mentioned by managers, is through an internship within an academic program in technical communication. If you are an undergraduate, this is one good reason to choose a technical communication major—your school will get you your first job.

Consultant Daunna Minnich hired new writers through a college internship program when she needed help. "I had some extra training to do but I figured I'd rather train somebody up the way I wanted than try to untrain somebody. Who wants to write unpacking instructions and things that are one to four pages? A junior tech writer." Thus the importance of an internship as part of a tech writing program! If you are interested in technical writing but have an unrelated degree and no related experience, consider getting a technical writing certificate in a program that offers an internship. Start by looking through Appendix A, which lists academic programs in technical communication; then contact the ones in your area for more information.

A third way to break in is to sell yourself "cheap" as a junior writer or editor. Companies that might hire junior writers include small companies that cannot afford to hire experienced writers and large companies with a layered publications department set up to mentor less-experienced writers.

To break into a junior writer position, you need either academic or job experience in some writing field or in the technical field you will document. You also need to be aggressive about getting your foot in the door, and you may have to make some "cold calls." More about cold calls later in this chapter.

All working technical writers I've asked have told unique stories about how they broke in. While no map emerged of a straight path to a tech writing career, their stories indicate that you, too, can find your own way. Who do you know who might help you? What unique skill do you have to offer?

RÉSUMÉ PREPARATION FOR WRITERS

A résumé is a selling tool. That's all it is. This section focuses on résumés for writers, but no section on résumés can ignore these basic principles:

- A résumé should contain only those details about your education and work experience that will spark the reader's interest enough to get you the interview.
- A résumé should be as short as possible. Over 1,000 unsolicited résumés arrive weekly at most Fortune 500 companies.[1] And each hiring manager scans hundreds to select the few he actually reads. Your short résumé assures him you value his time.
- A résumé should contain no information that will elicit negative associations. Nothing about unusual hobbies, political or religious affiliations, age, divorce, or nonconformity in any form. You can always reveal your personal quirks in the interview, should the interviewer seem the sort of person who'd be positively swayed by such revelations.
- A résumé should stand out. If you positively highlight your skills and experience through thoughtful wording and then format the information as elegantly as your tools will allow, your résumé will stand out.

If you're writing your first résumé, consult the résumé-writing guides listed in the bibliography for details about the building blocks and principles of résumé writing.

A résumé has two aspects: content and form. Think of them separately and polish each to a fine sheen. Today's résumé can take many forms, from paper to multimedia CD. But the rules of content remain unchanged.

Content

Skills and experience provide the content of a résumé. And, as Dirk mentioned at the beginning of this chapter, managers look for buzzwords. That means they prefer to hire people who've had hands-on experience with their company's specific technology and publishing system. This does not necessarily mean lots of experience.

As you learned in the chapter "Get Ready," taking a class in the current "hot" tools can suffice. FrameMaker is the current favorite and has been for years, but that could change quickly. Check the technical writers want ads, usually listed under "Writers" and "Technical Writers," and see for yourself what's hot now. It also helps if you're familiar with more that one kind of computer (for example, an IBM PC and an Apple Macintosh).

If you're basically computer conversant, a short course in a word-processing program or a computer system should give you license to add it to your résumé. Even somebody who has spent months using a system forgets how after not having used it for a while and needs to brush up upon returning to it.

"I look for a listing of both the software they've used and the equipment they've used," says Sun Microsystems writing manager Sheila Borders. "If perchance in my job description, the operating system is important, I want to see those listed separately from all the word-processing packages they've used."

In a separate section on your résumé, include every technical skill you can think of that might spark the hiring manager's interest or meet a requirement in the company's official job description. Use several sections if you need to—one for the publishing tools you've used, another for equipment you're familiar with, a third for products you've documented. Brevity is paramount. Just list the buzzwords.

The Paper Résumé

For writers, a résumé is not just a résumé. It's a writing sample. Therefore, more than for any other career goal, a writer's résumé must be well organized, clearly written, and meticulously edited and proofread. "The first thing I look for is typos," says Sheila Borders. "If they've got a typo or a bad grammatical construction or just a poor way of expressing their job assignments, then I figure they're not what I'd call a skilled writer."

Use active verbs and cut all words that don't contribute to your goal. A traditional résumé is basically a list and should follow good list form—items are of parallel structure; verb tense and form are consistent; items are of similar length, although recent jobs can take more space than past jobs. If you are unclear about any of these principles. consult the chapter "Writing Is the Heart of Your Craft."

In addition to being well written, your résumé has to look good. "I look for something that's got a fair amount of white space," says Sheila, "with type at least ten points, or bigger, because my eyes are getting old. I like it to be very dark type on white or buff paper."

When consultant Daunna Minnich was a manager at Apple Computer, she received around 50 résumés a week, even when she had no job openings. Says Daunna:

> If somebody couldn't give me an attractive résumé, I figured they weren't going to be able to figure out how to make a page look decent when they were actually writing. It was very easy to go through 30 or 40 résumés and pick out five to look at. They weren't crowded. They probably were only one page but might have gone on to a second. I didn't care if [a résumé] was chronological or functional. I really didn't care. If the thing looked attractive, then I'd decide to read it.

If you are uncertain about your design skills, have a friend with design experience look over your résumé and suggest ways to improve its appearance. A second pair of eyes can really help you create an attractive résumé.

The Electronic Résumé

An *electronic résumé* is a résumé that can be read by a computer. You can send an electronic résumé via email to prospective employers and you can post it to sites on the World Wide Web.*

The number of employers looking for employees on the Web is growing about as fast as the Web itself. According to Pat Criscito, in *Résumés in Cyberspace*, about 12 percent of employers sought applicants via the Internet in 1997, which equates to over 1 million hits per month on career-related sites, and "the number is growing exponentially every day."[2]

Do you want to take advantage of this trend in your job search? I hope you do.

Rules for paper résumés apply as well to the electronic one: Your page (or screen) layout needs to be short, clear, and easy to read. Your content is exactly the same—it presents your most salable skills in active verbs and offers no flaws or quirks that might trigger rejection.

So what's different about the electronic résumé? It's a matter of format. The most common electronic résumés are formatted for three main purposes: to be scanned into a database, to be emailed via the Internet to a prospective employer, and to be posted to Internet job sites.

---

* The term *Internet* is sometimes used to refer to the hardware and *World Wide Web*, or *Web*, to the software that runs on the Internet. I use the terms interchangeably here.

THE SCANNABLE RÉSUMÉ

A *scannable résumé* is "machine readable." Create one if you intend to apply to large companies with large human resources departments, because they can use a software program instead of a human being to read, analyze, and file your résumé. The program picks out keywords, such as "team player" and "UNIX," representing desirable attributes and skills. Later, should a position open, hiring managers can use such terms to search the database for applicants.

I never have liked the idea of résumé scanning, because I've felt this process strips every molecule of individuality from the applicant during the hiring process. But it's the way of things.

A scannable résumé needs a simple format. The easiest way to create a scannable résumé is to convert your regular résumé to a *plain text* file, a file that does not incorporate any desktop publishing fonts or frills. First eliminate any fancy formatting, such as block indents or two-column lists; then use your word processor to save your résumé as a *text* file. For example, in Microsoft Word, you would use the *save as* command and select *text only* as the *Save as type*. Some other word-processing programs use the term *ASCII* (which stands for American Standard Code for Information Interchange) to describe this file format. Alternatively, you can design a regular-print résumé to be scannable by choosing a simple format. If you choose to create a plain text file, you are already one step ahead in creating a résumé to send through cyberspace.

Your scannable résumé should also include an introductory section dense with keywords. To learn more about how to create a scannable résumé, refer to Criscito's helpful text, *Résumés in Cyberspace,* or the Adams *Electronic Job Search Almanac,* both of which are listed in the bibliography.

THE INTERNET RÉSUMÉ

In addition to being scannable, a plain text résumé can be read by nearly every computer on the planet. This feature allows you to use the résumé to perform an Internet job search in a number of ways.

You can paste the contents of your plain text résumé into an email message and mail it to hiring managers at their request. Before you do this, though, mail a copy to yourself to see how it looks on the receiving end. You may need to change the line lengths, add or delete space, and adjust the format in other ways to make the résumé look as attractive as possible.

You can also post your plain text résumé on the Web. Employer and recruiter Web sites vary in the kinds of résumés they accept. Some will take your plain text résumé as is. For others, you will need to copy sections and paste them into blanks provided on the sites.

Online writers sometimes employ additional "résumé" forms, which present their skills and employment history in their chosen medium, be it a Web page, a hypertext help file with links, or a multimedia presentation. You will learn more about these media in the chapter "Designing Online Documentation."

The Web provides an endless array of opportunities for job seekers. A thorough discussion on performing an electronic job search is beyond the scope of this book. However, you'll find titles listed in the "Careers and Job Hunting" section of the bibliography that can help you explore the job market in cyberspace.

CHECKLIST 5–1. RÉSUMÉS

Use the checklist below to make sure you've created the best résumé you can:

- Have you listed all your technical skills?
- Is the layout attractive?
- Have you used active verbs and cut unnecessary words?
- Are job descriptions consistent in verb tense and form?
- Are items parallel?
- Is the résumé free of grammatical and punctuation errors?
- Is it free of spelling errors and typos?

WHAT'S IN A PORTFOLIO?

When you apply for that first tech writing job, you need to demonstrate that you can do the work. The best way to convince a hiring manager that you can write technical documents is to show her some you've done. A portfolio should contain at least three or four pieces of writing. Familiarize yourself first with examples of good documents from your chosen field and try to emulate their style. Listen to their tone by reading them out loud and observe the layout of their pages.

Show flexibility by including samples written in different styles, even if you must write additional pieces just for your portfolio. Include a sample written in third person and one in second person; include a piece directed at consumers and one at a more technically sophisticated audience.

For example, if you want a job documenting computer software, you might include a procedure, written in second person, on how to use a consumer software product; a reference piece, written in third person, describing the actions of a set of commands; and perhaps a more complex procedure or an overview of a product or process aimed at a more technically sophisticated reader.

If you already have produced documents in your current job or through writing classes, all the better. If not, and the prospect of creating portfolio pieces from scratch seems overwhelming, try rewriting documents that already exist. Find examples that are poorly organized and unclearly written and strive to improve them. Include the before and after versions in your portfolio. These will demonstrate your skills and your initiative to hiring managers.

If you want to author online documents, include disks containing a sample help file, a multimedia presentation, or other online documents that demonstrate your skill at designing for those media and at using appropriate software tools.

PREPARING AND PRESENTING WRITING SAMPLES

I have a gorgeous writing sample that came out of a team-written book with a big budget. We had artists, production people, typesetters, and enough money for two-color illustrations throughout. The customers ended up absolutely hating this book. It did not have the information they wanted, and the information that was there was not organized for easy reference. It was a tough lesson for me. It taught me both about the importance of knowing my audience's needs and about the pitfalls of a team-written project. Nonetheless, this book remained one of my best samples for a number of years. Why? Because it's pretty. (Also, the short sample of my writing does not reveal the overall organizational problems of the book.)

Most interviewers flip through your sample and judge it by how it looks. They rarely look deeply at the usefulness of your information and organization, perhaps because they are just too busy.

What's the lesson? Certainly not that you should write badly. But do make your samples look as crisp and attractive as you can, given your available tools. Format your text with wide margins and plenty of white space, so the page is not gray. Break your text up with headings, lists, graphs, and tables. For more details about formatting, refer to the chapter "Planning for Visual Impact," later in this book.

Proofread your writing samples rigorously. Small errors have a way of leaping from the page at a casual glance.

Make sure to point out in your cover letter and in the interview that you can write in a variety of styles, so that the hiring manager does not just glance at one piece and decide you write only that way. Be aware that almost every company has its own house style and let the hiring manager know you're willing to go with it (if you are). It's part of the business.

Some writers find they can't go along with house style. For example, military specification ("milspec") writing is not everybody's cup of tea. You can determine this in the interview and later diplomatically remove yourself from the hiring process for that company. Of course, the luxury of such a choice depends on an abundant job market, where you stand a good chance of finding a more compatible house style at another company.

WHERE ARE THE JOBS?

You're fortunate if you live in a pocket of technology, like California's Silicon Valley or North Carolina's Research Triangle, where high-tech jobs are abundant. But even if your geographic area is not a high-tech area, it might support a prospering industry that hires technical writers. You can find out by looking through the Yellow Pages of your phone directory under the technical industries that interest you, by looking through the classified ads in your local paper, and by talking with career counselors. Even billboards along local highways can give you some clues about neighboring industries. For example, billboards along Highway 101 between San Francisco and San Jose advertise computer networking products and e-commerce Web sites (or "dot coms").

Look through the classified ads on a regular basis, even if you do not use them for your job search. Classified ads show the industries that hire and indicate common job requirements, such as years of experience and "hot" publishing software you should know. The classifieds occasionally show salary trends, and the number of ads goes up and down to reflect the general job market. Lots of ads mean lots of jobs.

GETTING YOUR FOOT IN THE DOOR

It's all well and good to talk about who's hiring, but how do you get that first interview? How, when most advertised job descriptions require more or different experience than you have, are you going to get your foot in the door?

As job search books attest, the best way to find a job is not through the paper—it's through someone you know or through more creative search methods. Creative job search techniques for tech writers include a lateral transfer and an internship placement, described earlier in this chapter. Another big one is called networking.

Networking

Networking means establishing friendly contacts with fellow professionals to share helpful work-related information. One 1999 study revealed tech writing contractors found 60 percent of their clients through networking.[3]

Networking through a professional organization is one of the best ways to find a technical writing job. For example, at the monthly meeting of the Silicon Valley chapter of the Society for Technical Communication (STC), hiring managers announce job openings, job seekers display their résumés at a table for that purpose and use the microphone to describe their availability and background, and a listing of current job openings is available.

Another professional organization, the National Writers Union (NWU), provides a job hotline for writers who are members of the union, and its San Francisco Bay area local holds monthly technical writers' meetings in which job leads are shared. Such organizations give you an opportunity to meet experienced writers and learn from them. In addition to job leads, you can find out what it's really like inside hiring organizations and what salaries they pay writers.

Cold Calls

You are fortunate if your contacts provide you with plentiful interviews and eventually a job. But usually you will have to face the impersonal specter of the want ads or even the phone book Yellow Pages for possible openings. If you must resort to a "cold call"—phoning an employer when no one has referred you and you don't know the manager's name— here are some things to remember:

Find out as much as you can about the company before you call. Even small companies with technical products have Web sites, so your first step is to find the company's site. Use your favorite search engine (or try http://www.yahoo.com) and type in the name of the company you want to research. From their Web site, you can usually print out their annual report, product descriptions, and recent press releases. Also ask people in your professional network for information they might have about the company. All this is so you'll appear knowledgeable when you make that cold call.

Later, if you get an interview, you can use the information you've gathered to learn even more—from acquaintances, the library, or the Web—about the kinds of products the company produces. Who else produces them? Who buys them? What are they used for?

Even if you don't fit advertised job requirements, make that call. In today's high-tech market, employers ask for the stars, knowing that they'll have to settle for the moon. If you can get through to the hiring manager with your sunny personality, obvious brilliance, or whatever other outstanding quality you offer, that manager will probably consider at least looking at your résumé and perhaps a writing sample, even if you don't perfectly fit the company's job description. A follow-up call—from you—might lead to an interview.

Never go through the human resources department, if you can help it. Human resources staff know nothing about hiring writers and will screen you out immediately on the basis of an official job description. When you call the company's main number, ask for the publications department (or training department or whatever department you intend to work for); then ask the person who answers the department phone for the name of the manager and ask if you can speak to him or her. If you need to explain your business, do so honestly. People in publications departments have stood where you stand and will usually be sympathetic and helpful.

THE INTERVIEW PROCESS

Most hiring managers do not have good interview skills. They do not know how to ask the right questions to bring out a job applicant's relevant skills and personal strengths. Therefore, it's up to you to control the interview, by anticipating the hiring manager's needs and meeting them.

Unfortunately, the interview process is uncomfortable and complex for even seasoned applicants. The bottom line of interviews seems to be that you should create a good impression, which you may be able to do in spite of your lack of experience and skills. The interviewer's subjective feeling about you can sway the result of the interview more than any other single factor.

Says H. Anthony Medley in *Sweaty Palms: The Neglected Art of Being Interviewed*: "The questions and answers of an interview are merely the tools used to make an evaluation, the trees in the forest of impression. The manner in which you answer the questions and whether or not you appear self-confident are far more important than the words you use in your answers."[4]

If you are new to the job search process, or even if you aren't, look at the job-hunting books mentioned here (and listed in the bibliography) for tips on how to handle interview questions designed to throw you off guard, how to avoid making negative statements, how to deal with interview stress, and so on. The information in these books can help turn this often painful process into a challenging, successful experience.

What Hiring Managers Want to Know About You

Once you have some idea of what to expect from any employment interview, you can present your skills as a technical writer in their best light. Job-hunting books suggest one key to a successful interview is to ascertain the hiring manager's needs and convince him or her that you can meet them. In this area you are fortunate. Technical publications managers all have a few simple needs in common. They want you to be able to ask questions assertively without making enemies, to understand the answers, to be "flexible" (a vague word but that's what they say), and to write. Let's see how these requirements affect an employment interview.

YOU KNOW HOW TO ASK QUESTIONS

Asking questions is so critical to your performance as a tech writer that it's the first thing some managers look for in an interview. Says Sheila Borders:

> I interviewed someone recently—an employee from another area in the company—and that person did not ask me one question about the job or the subject matter or anything. They told me a lot about what they had done, but asked no questions at all about this particular position. And my immediate inclination was to think, is this the way they would interview a technical subject expert?

So ask questions. The checklist "Questions to Ask a Prospective Employer," later in this chapter, suggests some you probably should ask.

YOU CAN UNDERSTAND THE ANSWERS

Managers want assurance from you that you're able to absorb and interpret technical information. They may use interview questions to find this out, or if they are not good interviewers, you'll have to volunteer evidence.

Some writing managers will ask an engineer to interview you and later ask that person how you responded to technical questions. Some managers will ask you technical questions themselves. Don't panic. You should know the buzzwords and general concepts of your technical area. But these interviewers don't expect you to know how many bits reside in the address segment of a particular data communication packet or to recite the exact structure of a particular DNA molecule. They're looking for signs of intelligence—for assurance that you'll understand these things with a minimum of tutelage. When you're asked a question you don't understand, ask one back. Continue asking until you understand the question and the answer. That's the exact process you'll use to get technical information on the job. If you do it well and learn quickly within the interview process, you'll impress all but a few literal-minded stick-in-the-muds who want only a correct response.

Even if the interviewer doesn't ask technical questions, he or she still wants to know that you can handle technical subject matter. This is particularly true if you have a liberal arts background. Find an opportunity to describe how you researched a technical topic in school or on a previous job, or ask about the company's technical products and probe for details. Indicate that you're interested in technical wizardry, which you should be by now or you wouldn't still be considering this field!

YOU'RE FLEXIBLE

Flexibility, in this sense, does not mean that you practice Hatha Yoga daily, although that might help. Managers want you to be flexible in terms of their needs:

- You will not complain to your boss when your project gets canceled halfway through.
- You will not quit when you're assigned to work with the engineer writers call Attila the Hun.
- You will not get frazzled if the product schedule changes, forcing you to produce the manual by yesterday.

In short, you will not make problems for them. Technical writing managers tend to have very tight schedules and sometimes see a writer's need for problem-solving help as a demand for hand-holding—a pastime managers generally detest. Assure them in the interview that you enjoy working independently, that you like to take the initiative in solving problems, and so on. If you can do this without using such obvious clichés, you'll make an even better impression!

YOU CAN WRITE

Be prepared to discuss your writing samples intelligently. Sheila Borders knows how to interview writers, so you can use her advice to reassure managers who don't know how:

> I usually want writing samples brought to the interview, so I can get the person explaining about the book the samples came from. I want to know who the audience is. I want to know something about the project that it was developed under. . . . What restrictions surrounded the production of the book?
>
> The physical presentation isn't necessarily the writer's choice. You see this grungy manuscript—8 $1/2$ by 11—it looks like it was done on a typewriter. It doesn't look great in our environment where we're dealing with fairly fancy-looking books. So your first impression is, is this all you can do? After I find out what the circumstances are—this was a start-up company [with dated word-processing tools]—then I get past that physical, judging-the-book-by-its-cover idea and move into the content. I see how many questions I can come up with that don't seem to be covered. In a real snap judgment sort of way, I ask those questions—see how the writer responds to that quick critique.

One reason she does this is to make sure the applicant is truly the author of the sample. "I figure if they lived it," says Sheila, "there's no hesitation in their response."

In the interview, describe the restrictions under which your samples were written and point out each document's strengths, whatever they may be. Of course, mention any positive responses or comments the document drew from customers. And mention ways it might have helped the company; for example, "This installation guide reduced service calls by 30 percent."

What You Need to Know

Finding the right job, particularly if you are starting a new career, is one of the biggest decisions you'll make in your life. You'll make this decision largely on the basis of interviews.

As you walk through the corridors to the interview, look around for cultural cues—the office humor on the bulletin board, the American flag or inflatable dinosaur or artsy mobile hanging over someone's cubicle, the overall tidiness or clutter of the place—to see if you feel comfortable in that setting. Notice the physical environment. Are there windows? Do writers have offices, cubicles, shared or private space?

While the employer is choosing a new writer, you are choosing where you'll spend most of your waking hours and energy. In the interview, you'll need to find out as much as you can to make this critical decision. Isn't it natural to ask questions?

Take this opportunity to ask about the company's writing style guidelines, as these will shape the character of the documents you produce. Find out who the audience of your documents will be—whether you'll write for technical experts, first-time product users, or some other customer. Often you'll enjoy more creative leeway writing for a new user than for a technically sophisticated user.

Find out more about the company's products. The interview also provides an opportunity to meet your supervisor and the people you'll be working with. If you get a chance to meet with writers individually, you can ask them what the manager is like to work for. You can also get a sense of their stress level. Are they frantic to get back to work? Were they in the office last weekend and the one before?

Find out who has final say over document content. Technically naive editors can sometimes introduce inaccuracies into your document, while engineers can introduce technical information that is irrelevant or too complex for your reader. Your job will be easier if you work for a publications department where writers control content.

In the interview, you can also find out how much of the manual's production will be your responsibility. If you are responsible for camera-ready copy, you'll spend a large part of your time perfectly formatting your documents for publication. If you are responsible for integrated online documentation, you'll spend a lot of time getting your authoring tools to work properly or compensating for ones that don't. You'll be a lot more hirable if you're able and willing to perform these nonwriting tasks.

You can also ask the interviewer about the company's organization chart. Who does the technical publication manager report to? The vice president of marketing or the manager of a less prestigious group? The higher the publication manager's boss is in the corporate hierarchy, the more respected he or she will be. You'll probably find a highly placed manager has the clout to help you set realistic deadlines and get information from reticent engineers. Additionally, if the publications department is high on the chart, it probably has the financial resources and equipment it needs to do a good job.

If the publications department is low on the chart or classified as clerical, the opposite is true. Writers in such an organization might lack resources and have difficulty getting cooperation from other departments.

CHECKLIST 5–2. QUESTIONS TO ASK A PROSPECTIVE EMPLOYER

Below are specific questions you might ask in an interview for a technical writing position. Don't try to ask them all. Choose those questions that will serve your unique concerns and create questions of your own.

- Are your documents written in second or third person? Active or passive voice? May I see an example of the kind of writing you do in this department?

- Is your reader technically naive or sophisticated?
- Do you have a lab where writers can use the product? Can I see the product?
- How is the department structured? Would I report directly to you or would someone else monitor and evaluate my performance?
- Is it possible to meet the writers I'd be working with?
- Is there an editorial staff? Who has the final say on edits—the editor or writer?
- Who reviews my documents? Who will be responsible for their final content?
- Are the engineers accustomed to working with writers? How cooperative are they?
- What tools will I use to produce the final document?
- Where is the publications department in the organization chart?

Obviously some of the interviewer's answers to the questions in the preceding checklist might not please you. Try not to react in the interview. Weigh your impressions later to decide if the job's good qualities outweigh aspects you don't like.

Before the interview ends, ask when the interviewer will reach a hiring decision.

The Question of Money

Most technical writers I interviewed told me their first tech writing job paid them twice what they'd been making at their previous job. Technical writing pays well. How well? The chapter "Why Begin?" named some figures from the late 1990s and described some skills and geographic areas that pay more than others. However, salary surveys, published by organizations like the STC, are usually way out of date by the time they reach you. So you will need to do some research for yourself.

On salary matters, networking is of great value. I determine my rates by periodically asking other writers how much they make. If they don't want to tell me, that's fine. But most do, and they ask the same in return. At meetings of your chosen professional organization, you can ask the question of several writers and get a sense of what writers with different experience levels make and what different companies pay. For staff positions, salaries vary quite widely between companies.

If this is your first technical writing job, you may have to accept a salary low on the company's scale. Accept it gracefully, unless it's ridiculously low. And congratulate yourself for landing the job!

If you already have an entry-level position and are going for your next job, you have more leverage and can set a higher goal. For help negotiating pay within the interview, refer to the job-hunting guides listed in the bibliography.

FOLLOW-UP

A hiring manager told me she'd recently interviewed two applicants with equally impressive credentials and was at a loss over how to choose one. Which applicant did she finally hire? The one who sent her a thank-you note after the interview. Can you afford to skip this step? Obviously not.

After the interview, send a brief letter or handwritten card thanking the hiring manager for his or her time. You'll create an even better impression if you mention a point he or she made.

During the interview, the interviewer told you when he or she would reach a hiring decision and probably reassured you that you'd be notified. Don't wait for this call. When the stated time has elapsed, phone and ask how the decision-making process is unfolding. If you receive a rejection at this point, have the courage to ask how the decision was reached. Don't take the answer too seriously—it's difficult for employers to give you a complete, honest answer as to why they rejected you. But if you ask non-defensively, you might get some feedback that you can use to improve your performance in future interviews.

Most important, don't get discouraged. Rejections are a necessary part of breaking in. And if that phone call yields an acceptance, it's time to celebrate!

SUMMING IT UP

This chapter suggested ways to break into technical writing and provided tips on résumés, writing samples, and the job interview. The next chapter lets you glimpse inside the office window. What will you find yourself doing in a typical day as a technical writer?

---

[1] Pat Criscito, *Résumés in Cyberspace* (Hauppauge, N.Y.: Barron's Educational Series, Inc.), 1997, p. 2.

[2] Criscito, p. 99.

[3] 1999 Salary Survey of the Rocky Mountain Chapter of the Society for Technical Communication (www.stcrmc.org/Salary99/survey99.htm)

[4] H. Anthony Medley, *Sweaty Palms: The Neglected Art of Being Interviewed* (Berkeley, Calif.: Ten Speed Press), 1993, p. 59.

A Day in the Life

6

The workstation lab is a large, warehouselike space. Fluorescent ceiling lights glow high above long tables, where programmers and hardware engineers sit absorbed with display screens or tangles of wire.

Ken sits on a high stool, frowning at a computer display. He's unaware of me as I move to within a few feet of him. I always feel hesitant to interrupt an engineer in the throes of a deadline. But his deadline is also mine.

"Ken . . ."

He jumps at the sound of his name. "Oh, hi. I bet you want to know what I did to the interface."

"Yes," I tell him. "It needs to be in the manual."

"Well, if the software would stop flying off into the ozone, I might be able to show it to you!"

I sit on a stool, looking over his shoulder for the next hour, while he "debugs the code" (figures out what parts of his computer program are causing the trouble) and intermittently tries to show me how it's supposed to work. I take notes and sketch a few screens, all the while doing my best not to disrupt his debugging process.

This scene from a day in my life illustrates one way technical writers spend their time. Ask a technical writer what he or she does in a typical day and you'll hear an extraordinarily varied list. Said one writer, "I don't have a typical day."

TECH WRITERS WRITE, RIGHT?

How much time does a tech writer actually spend writing? Estimates vary between 25 and 35 percent.

Says consultant Dirk van Nouhuys, "We did a survey at Apple Computer at one point about how much of a technical writer's time is actually spent sitting in front of his or her terminal writing, as opposed to being in meetings or interviewing people or greasing the skids in other ways." They found that writing time amounted to about 25 percent. "But that was Apple at a certain stage," Dirk explains. "I think probably for the average technical writer it's somewhat higher—say 35 percent."

Other writers concur with Dirk. Says consultant Linda Lininger, "In-house writers tend to be bludgeoned with meetings. As a freelancer, I avoid them. I'd say most in-house writers are lucky if they write a third of the time, because there are numerous interruptions and all those crazy meetings they go to."

Says another writer, "It's probably one third meetings, one third other stuff—dealing with politics and personalities and office supplies and overhead of some sort."

One thing is clear—tech writers spend most of their time at activities other than writing. One purpose of this book is to prepare you for some of the nonwriting tasks you'll perform, like researching a technical product in a corporate environment, where information is usually not neatly catalogued and communication is your primary research tool.

WHAT DO YOU DO BESIDES WRITE?

What you do in a day depends on the kind of technical writer you are and on the stage of your project. A training-film writer's day will be different from that of a technical journalist. Says a computer software writer:

> As a writer of books, in a typical day I might interview a couple of programmers, maybe with a tape recorder, to ask them what they meant by their obscure scribbles in a review copy of something I'd written; go to a staff meeting, where a manager tells us what work is on its way and how deadlines are shifting and so on; maybe go to a meeting of a project team; spend a couple of hours revising my current draft in the light of what I'd learned from the earlier interviews. Gee, there really is no one typical day. I've used up over 8 hours already.

Says hardware writer Billie Levy about her day:

> It'll be a combination of mashing away on the terminal, maybe getting up and looking at drawings, maybe making a drawing that I want to be in the book. I don't like sitting at a desk. I get restless and my neck hurts. So I go in and see what the technicians are doing, and the engineers, and I watch what they're doing, and I ask questions.

ADDITIONAL RESPONSIBILITIES

Besides undertaking the varied activities inherent in producing a technical document, writers enjoy additional responsibilities within a high-tech corporation. These can include:

- contributing to team project planning and scheduling
- participating in product design decisions

- testing the product
- editing the *user interface*—the part of a computer program that the customer sees

As a technical writer, you will often participate in product team meetings, which include those representatives from the scientific, marketing, and testing departments that are directly involved with the product. At these meetings, team members decide scheduling, product design, packaging, and other issues that are constantly reexamined during the product development cycle. When should you join the product team? The earlier the better.

At the beginning of a project, you can act as the user's advocate, suggesting design modifications that make the product easier to use. Sun Microsystems lead writer Shaunna Pickett-Gordon describes how some of Sun's writers work with their human interface engineers (HIE)—the people who have the job of making products user friendly—to help correct problems. Says Shaunna: "The writer's role is as a junior HIE. The writer can say [to the HIE], 'Look at that icon, it doesn't match the company standard. Look at this color that doesn't look right. . . .' They can be attacking the smaller, front-line issues."

Shaunna describes an unusually high level of writer involvement. This would certainly eliminate many of the problems writers tend to uncover later in the development process, when writer and product usually meet.

Some companies involve the writer only at the end of the product cycle, after design decisions have been implemented and the schedule is too rigid to permit unforeseen problems. Writers always uncover unforeseen problems! One of your most valuable nonwriterly roles is product tester.

You'll perform this role because you need to use the product to see how it works and to check it against the document in progress. In doing so, you will uncover and report functional failures as well as features that are difficult to use. For example, most large computer companies have established a procedure for reporting product flaws (bugs) and provide a "bug report" form you can fill out and submit. For the sake of your document and the customer, try to gain access to the first working version of the product.

If you are documenting a computer program, this is the stage at which you'll suggest rewording error messages, system messages, and other text that are part of the user interface. You should inform developers of any grammatical and punctuation errors, inconsistencies in use of terminology, terms and acronyms that need definition, and just plain incomprehensible stuff. Many developers speak English as a second language and design some rather surprising sentence structures into the user interface. Developers welcome a writer's input on these errors. But watch how you say it. Diplomacy is paramount.

DIFFERENT STAGES, DIFFERENT DAYS

Different stages of a writing project demand different skills of a writer. The planning stage involves a different set of activities from the production stage. The following subsections list activities you might perform at different stages. Projects interweave, however, and you'll find yourself in the planning phase of one, while another needs last-minute changes.

Says John Huber, "While you're working on project B, you might be interrupted seventeen times with questions about project A, which you thought you finished three weeks ago, but the artist wants clarification on your request for a graphic, the editor wants to talk to you about a word you used, or whatever. While you're working on B, A keeps biting you on the ankle, and maybe the one before A, as well!"

So be aware that some of the following activities lists are more tidily arranged than in the real world.

A Research Day

- You read the internal reference specification ("spec") for a computer program and determine which part of the information will affect the user.
- You write a list of questions to ask the spec's author.
- You set up interviews with the product designer and implementer.
- You talk with the editor about "house style"—how is this type of manual organized? Can you see others that have been produced in the past?

A Planning Day

- You ask your boss about the "product freeze," the date beyond which the product will not change. The boss sends you to find that out.
- You ask the engineering manager about the proposed freeze date, then write a memo to the manager and your boss that summarizes the conversation.
- You attend a product team meeting, in which everyone reports on their schedule in relation to the product.
- You sit down at your computer and outline what you know about the product.
- You print your outline, then scribble notes all over it.

A "Writing" Day

- You talk with the artist about ideas for illustrations. She asks you to sketch your ideas.
- You sketch a group of workstations and draw arrows showing their relationships.
- You go to the engineering lab to look at a processor board. You make note of the number of cable attachments it has.

- Back at your desk, you sketch four more art ideas, number them as figures, and create a numbered list of proposed figures for your manual.
- You photocopy the list for the artist.
- You continue writing instructions on how to install the processor board.

A Production Day

- You insert index entries in your word-processed document file; then run a computerized index generator to create an alphabetized list of entries with page numbers.
- You send the list to the laser printer. When you go to the printer to retrieve it, you find your index list full of unintelligible characters.
- You phone tech support and ask to have someone look at the printer. The technician on the phone tells you how to "reload the printer fonts."
- You follow the instructions, which do not work, and then get a cup of coffee.
- You phone tech support again, and the technician comes over to fix the printer.
- You are late for a staff meeting.
- You stay overtime and finish your index.

TABLE 6–1
SKILLS USED IN A "TYPICAL" DAY

Activity	Skills
Reading specs and listing questions; writing an outline	Clear thinking; organizing ideas
Sharing a team project	Clear communication; active listening; negotiation
Determining the project schedule	Time management; diplomacy; assertiveness
Writing a memo	Organizing ideas; clear writing; diplomacy
Planning figures	Visual thinking
Creating an index	Organizing ideas; computer literacy
Getting the printer fixed	Clear communication; computer literacy; persistence; diplomacy

Obviously, a tech writer uses many skills besides writing, as we already know from previous chapters. How many do you use on a typical day? Table 6-1 lists some of the activities described in the preceding lists, together with the skills they require.

SUMMING IT UP

This chapter gave you a detailed picture of a day in the life of a technical writer and continued to describe the kinds of skills you need. The next section of this book tells you how to begin the documentation process, starting with concrete ways to research a technical product.

PART 2
GATHERING INFORMATION

7

Know Your Subject

"Technical writing is probably about 70 percent research," says Billie Levy. "You just don't go in and sit down and start spitting out words. You can feel sort of guilty about this at first, but the research—looking at drawings or at the system and tracing down the air lines or the water lines—is legitimate. You can't do a good job of writing without it."

Billie's comments remind me of an ancient story about three blind men trying to understand an elephant. The first felt the trunk and said, "An elephant is like a long cylinder." The second patted its side and said, "The elephant is like a large wall." The third, stroking its tail, said, "No, it's much more like a snake." If you don't take the time to understand the product, your document might lack some vital details.

BECOMING A SUBJECT EXPERT

Some people think tech writers don't need to know much about their subject. They see the writer as a mechanical editor, cleaning up the grammar and punctuation and "prettying up" the format. Experienced writers think otherwise.

"The thing that I learned the most from my initial experiences is, whenever I come to a new project—before I even set finger to keyboard— I read *everything*," says consultant Linda Lininger. "And I didn't do that at first. I mean, I didn't know to do that. But now, if I am confronted with a new product, I read the manual, cover to cover."

Knowing as much as possible about your subject helps you in several ways. First, the more you know, the more technically accurate your document will be. Unlike other kinds of writing where verbal agility is paramount, technical writing demands accuracy first. You may be a superb stylist, but if your material isn't accurate, your readers will experience confusion and anger when they read your work.

Self-confidence is the second payoff for subject knowledge. You can press developers for information, because you're confident about the terminology and nature of the product. You can express your questions clearly and organize them effectively.

Also, engineers are more likely to cooperate if you speak their language and are familiar with their subject. If engineers need to teach you a lot before you are able to talk about the subject, they're likely to lose patience. (In the next chapter, I'll give you tips on how to be assertive when you know nothing—a skill you may need when no information is available.)

KNOWING YOUR PURPOSES

The first question to ask yourself, in researching a technical topic, is what is the purpose of the product? The second—what is the purpose of my document?

When you first receive your writing assignment, you'll probably get a brief description of what the product does. Think about this information. Try to imagine how customers will use the product and what they'll expect from it. What primary and secondary purposes does it fulfill? Approach the product from the customer's point of view. (Later, the chapter "Know Your Audience" will help you refine your understanding of the user, so your writing will address the user's needs.)

Next, ask yourself, what is the purpose of the information I'm seeking? For example, if you're writing a marketing brochure about a computer program, your purpose is to convince the customer to buy the product. So, in your research, you'll ask questions about the program's features and how those features fill a customer's specific needs. Those questions will elicit information that serves your marketing purpose—convincing the customer.

On the other hand, if you're writing an online tutorial about that same program, you'll need a different kind of information. Your purpose, in this case, is to teach the user how to use the program. You can step into your reader's place by learning how to use it yourself. You'll also need to know about the user's experience with computers and about the nature of the tasks the program helps the user perform. You'll look for information that serves your purpose—telling the user, step-by-step, how to use the product.

You can see that the kind of document you're creating shapes the kind of information you need.

LEARNING ABOUT A TECHNICAL PRODUCT

You will learn about a technical product by

- reading technical documents
- questioning technical experts
- attending in-house training classes
- using the product
- thinking clearly about the data you've gathered

Your most important sources of current product information are the technical people working on the product—its designers, implementers, testers, and quality assurance specialists. Because your communication with them is so important, the next chapter, "Communicating with Engineers," is devoted to that process. It also describes ways to create and order questions in preparation for the interview. The rest of this chapter explains how to research your subject before you approach these specialists.

Gathering Information Sources

To learn about a technical product, first find out what sources of information are available. The Information Source List in this section can help you. Your manager will know some of the answers to these questions and can direct you to people who will answer the rest.

At this point, also ask your manager for a preliminary list of people who will review your document and the names of their departments. Later, if you need information from marketing or product testing, you'll know whom to contact.

When you fill out the Information Source List, you'll probably leave some questions blank. For example, questions 1 through 3 ask for the names of the primary resource person for your document, the product designer, and the product implementer. If your company is small, these may all be the same person. In a large company, these roles might be filled by three different people, and you'll need to go through one to find out about the others.

INFORMATION SOURCE LIST

1. Who will be my primary resource (or first contact)?
   Name _____   Phone number _____
2. Who is the product designer (or second contact)?
   Name _____   Phone number _____
3. Who is the product implementer or developer (or third contact)?
   Name _____   Phone number _____
4. Does my company offer training classes I can attend on the use of this product?
   Name of Class _____
   Date offered _____ Register with whom?_____
   Phone number _____
5. What documentation is already available on this product? _____

   _____

6. What engineering documents (e.g., functional specifications and change notices) are available? _____

   _____

7. Is an operating version of the product available for me to use? Who can show me how?
   Name _____   Phone number _____

It helps to have more than one person to contact with questions. Sometimes your primary technical resource won't be available or won't know the answers to all your questions. You can use your other contacts to get your answers.

Once you've filled out the Information Source List, you'll know where to find copies of product specifications and whom to ask for information.

Reading Technical Documents

To ask intelligent questions, you first must read available documents and identify where information is missing or incorrect. The checklist in this section can guide you. The subsections after the checklist provide details about the different kinds of documents you might read to research your topic, as well as tips on how to read them.

CHECKLIST 7–1. IDENTIFYING MISSING INFORMATION

Use the following questions to make sure your information is complete and accurate:

- Do procedures seem complete or are there steps missing?
- Does the sequence of steps seem logical?
- Is the information specific? "Developers occasionally write *is recommended* or *is suggested* when they mean *is required*," says Daniel Nolan in an article in *Technical Communication,* "and they write *should* or *may* when they mean *must.* . . . When you see *is recommended, is suggested, should* or *may,* . . . you *should* probably ask questions."[1]
- What is the active agent? Often technical documents are written in passive voice, so the cause of action is unclear. For example, "a secondary station response must be initiated." Who or what is doing the initiating?
- Is the information current? Question numerical values to be certain they haven't changed since the spec or previous manual was written. Check version numbers, dimensions, ranges, limits, and default values.
- Are all technical terms defined? List all terms, along with their definitions, and question the ones you can't define.
- Are all acronyms spelled out? List all acronyms and question the ones you don't understand.

KEEPING TRACK OF QUESTIONS

Keep track of your questions in one or more of the following ways:

- Write them in a notebook that you reserve for information about the product.
- Write them on your copy of the spec or previous manual or on a hard copy of an online document.
- Write them on sticky notes that you can use to flag the pages in question.

I like the sticky notes, because I move them to the middle of the page when a question is answered, or I stick them to my computer display screen when I have trouble finding an answer.

READING PRODUCT SPECIFICATIONS

The first step in researching a product is to read all available product specs. Specs differ between product types and between companies. For example, if you're writing a product monograph for a drug company, you won't find anything called a spec, but other documents serve the same function.

Says one pharmaceutical writer, "The first thing you usually do is a library search through Medline. Medline is a database. You design a literature search to pull out everything having to do with the drug. You look through your company's literature, the final reports on clinical trials, on toxicologic trials, and so forth."

If you write about computer software, you'll encounter

- Functional specifications
- Internal reference specifications
- External reference specifications
- User interface change notices
- Software change notices

and a host of other technical-sounding documents. You'll probably refer to them by acronyms—the ERS or the UICN—but for the purpose of this discussion, they're all "specs."

Specs have two uses to you as a writer: They are (1) a source of information about the product, and (2) a source of questions for the product developer (who may also be the author of the spec).

Some specs are extremely well written and clear, but many are not. Spec writers usually don't define jargon or acronyms. They tend to use terminology inconsistently, calling something an "index unit" in one place and an "index object" in another. Therefore, some skill in reading specs will help you extract the information you need, without succumbing to confusion or boredom. The following tips should help.

TIPS ON READING A SPEC

1. Make a photocopy of the spec so you can mark it up.
2. Write your purpose at the top of the spec. What kind of information do you need from the spec? For example, "Installing the software."
3. Skim the whole spec and highlight everything you might need— draw a line along the side of relevant sections.

4. Go back and read the sections you've highlighted. As you read, do the following:
   - Mark or circle paragraphs that you can use verbatim in the first draft of your manual. (Plagiarism in tech writing is totally legit, as long as you "lift" material from within your company.)
   - List terms and acronyms, as recommended earlier in this chapter.
   - List questions that seem relevant to your purpose. For example, if the spec says, "The default of 300 applies for most configurations," you might ask, "Under what circumstances would the user need to use a different value?"

READING PREVIOUS DOCUMENTS

In addition to specs, other written materials can be sources of information and questions. Most commonly, you'll be able to read previous documentation written by technical writers about earlier versions of the product. These documents can be both on paper and online. They are valuable not only for technical information but also as examples of the manual formats, online organization and screen layouts, and the "house style" used by your company.

Reading previous documentation is similar to reading specs, only easier. The following tips will help you read a manual for information and questions.

TIPS ON READING PREVIOUS DOCUMENTATION

1. Whether the document is a paper manual or online, get a paper copy you can write on. Now you can mark it up as you did the product specification.
2. Highlight useful information.
3. Cross out information that you know is outdated.
4. In a notebook, list terms and acronyms next to their definitions, as described earlier. The acronyms and terms in previous documentation should already be defined.
5. List questions that you think need to be clarified before you can begin writing.
6. Talk to the previous document's author, if available, to find out what problems and questions came up while documenting the last version of the product.
7. If you think you can use a lot of the previous document, ask for the most current online version or "source file"—one that you can manipulate on your computer. Later, you can build your new document using large chunks of existing material.

Sometimes no spec, previous documentation, or written material is available about a product. If the product is a groundbreaking, one-of-a-kind new gizmo, you may have to go straight to its designer for information. However, most products are like something else that already exists, perhaps from a different company. To increase your knowledge of your subject, read manuals about competing products, which you can sometimes get from your marketing or engineering department. At least you'll understand some of the concepts that went into your product. This knowledge will help you when you talk to your product's developer.

Attending In-House Training Classes

Many companies have training classes for customers and for field support personnel—the folks who go to the customer site to fix things. You will probably be permitted, if not encouraged, to attend. As I mentioned in the chapter "Get Ready," I recommend taking as many as possible.

During the research phase of your writing project, training classes can teach you generally about a technology and specifically about your company's products. They also help you make your terminology consistent with the terminology used by the training department.

Additionally, you can make valuable contacts within the training department—people who can answer your questions or review your work at a later date. The following tips will help you get all you can out of in-house training classes.

TIPS ON USING IN-HOUSE TRAINING

- Ask the trainer if he or she is willing to be contacted later to answer questions about the product.
- Ask if the trainer is willing to be on your list of reviewers. If so, add the trainer to your reviewers list, along with his or her *mail stop* (address within your company), email address, and phone number.
- During the class, ask lots of questions, particularly about the product characteristics you'll be documenting. Everyone in the class will benefit from your questions.
- List terminology and one or two short sentences defining each term.
- Ask the trainer to clarify any definitions you don't understand.
- Ask the trainer to define acronyms, if he or she hasn't already.
- Hoard all class handouts.
- Later, go through class handouts and highlight any information that would help your reader understand the product. Remember, you can plagiarize from in-house documentation. Lift whatever is helpful.
- File class handouts for later reference. For example, you can refer to them to see how the training department uses certain terms.

Using the Product

Some people learn best by doing. If you are such a person, do everything you can to get your hands on a working model of the product. If you are not such a person, you should still use the product in its final phases, to make sure the developers have accurately communicated all its features and have not incorporated new features that they haven't told you about. This is critical. Most of the time you'll document a product that is not finalized or "frozen." Developers, creative folks that they are, will try to squeeze as many features as possible into the product between its inception and the rush out the door. The only way you can check the final accuracy of your documentation is to read it while you use the product.

If the product is too specialized or easily damaged for you to use, ask to observe it in use at a test site, in the quality assurance lab, or wherever your company puts the finishing touches on the product.

If you cannot possibly view the product's final operation, make at least one close contact among the product's testers (who may be called, among other titles, "field engineers," "test engineers," "quality assurance testers," or the product developer). Ask your contact to use your documentation with the product and mark on a hard copy anything that works differently or appears different from its description.

If you can't check your document against the final product, you might be writing fiction without even realizing it.

CLEAR THINKING

"Learning without thought is labor lost," said Confucius.

Clear thinking is an important part of research. You don't need a course in logic to become aware of your assumptions: Learn to distinguish between when you know something and when you are just guessing. You will do a lot of guessing in technical writing and will sometimes have to write information that you are not sure about. Be aware that you are guessing and *check your facts* later.

Sometimes writers don't distinguish between guesses and facts. They think, "It's obvious that the product must work the way I describe it here," without questioning the parts they've assumed. Such fuzzy thinking is usually the result of deadline pressure, shyness, or technophobia—three frequent enemies of clear thinking.

When you're under deadline pressure, you do experience reluctance to follow up on technical questions. How does the product really look? Does this old drawing still describe it, or should I go into the lab and see how it looks now? If I find out it looks different, I'll have to ask the artist to do a new drawing right away, and I might not make my deadline. Well, maybe this drawing is close enough.

Dealing with uncooperative developers can bring out latent shyness you never knew you had. How does the product work? Does it *replace* another device or *attach to* the other device? I'll ask Pat. Hmmm. Last time I interviewed Pat, she fumed, "Let's get this over with. My schedule is full." Maybe I'll just say the product attaches to the other device. That can't be too far off.

Technophobia goes something like this—my God, this thing is complex. I'll never figure out how it works. I can't even understand the spec enough to ask intelligent questions. I'll make a fool of myself with the developer. I know. I'll take his spec, add a few commas, break up the long paragraphs, and format it to be the manual.

So, pressure, shyness, and technophobia are enemies of clear thinking. How do you know when you're making false assumptions? Ask yourself *how do I know* what I know?:

- From studying similar products
- Reading the product specification
- Talking with the product developer
- Using the product recently
- Guessing

If you need to guess to finish writing something, turn your guess into a question to ask the developer. For example:

"To include a user logo on the header page of a print job, the following eight lines must be placed [WHERE?] . . ."

Embedding questions in your draft is one way to avoid making assumptions. Just remember to flag questions so you can delete them from your final draft.

SUMMING IT UP

In this chapter, I described the importance of knowing your subject and I summarized the ways to research a technical product. I then provided tips on how to get the most out of your sources of information. Getting information from your most important source is described in the next chapter, "Communicating with Engineers."

---

[1] "Analyzing Technical Input," *Technical Communication,* Journal of the Society for Technical Communication, Third Quarter 1990, p. 260.

8

Communicating with Engineers

The richest source of current, accurate technical information about a product is the technical person working directly with it. In this chapter, that person is called an engineer, though he or she may be a chemist, computer programmer, or chief scientist. A critical part of your job is to communicate effectively with the engineer.

Technical writers and journalists have a lot in common. Both have to find things out quickly, by asking focused, well-organized questions; both have to write concisely; and both have to meet deadlines. The interview skills that good journalists use work equally well for technical writers. These skills involve:

- choosing the authority most likely to have the desired information
- carefully preparing questions to ask
- effectively communicating during the interview
- taking accurate notes
- fleshing out notes after the interview

PREPARING FOR THE INTERVIEW

The more prepared you are for an interview, the better it will go. If you know ahead of time what you will ask, who you are asking, and how you will use the information, you can relax and concentrate on making contact with this person, the engineer.

A story goes that a press conference was held to celebrate the rerelease of the movie *Gone With the Wind*, starring Vivien Leigh. And Vivien Leigh was to be there. At the last minute a cub reporter found himself assigned to the event. He rushed to the scene, notebook in hand, and singled out the striking actress at the center of the crowd. Under his breath, he asked an onlooker who the actress was. He was told, "Vivien Leigh," whereupon he thrust himself through the crowd and questioned her loudly, "Tell me, Miss

Leigh, what part did you play in the film?" The story has it that Miss Leigh turned and walked out of the press conference.

As the Boy Scouts of America advise, be prepared.

The first preparation for an interview is to learn as much about your subject as you possibly can. The preceding chapter, "Know Your Subject," told you how to research a technical product. Now that you have background knowledge, it's time to prepare the questions you will ask.

Preparing Interview Questions

Preparing a list of interview questions can help you in a number of ways. It lets the engineer know that you have given thought to the interview and that you value his or her time. The engineer is more willing to answer questions carefully knowing that the questions were carefully preplanned.

A written list also helps you keep control of the interview. Often, the interviewee will answer only the first few questions in order before unwittingly jumping ahead to a later topic, or going on a tangent that brings other questions to mind. Your written list gives you a structure you can refer to when you need to bring the engineer back to the questions you want answered.

A questions list can make the job of writing easier. You can arrange your questions in the topical order you plan to use for your document. It only follows that you'll ask the questions, and write the answers to them, in that order. Later, when you write your document, you can do so without having to jump back and forth through your notes. The information is already in the order you intended to use.

Write down your interview questions. Write more questions than you can ask in the time allotted. That way, you can be sure you'll take full advantage of the engineer's time. You won't have to cut the interview short because you ran out of questions (as I did in my first-ever interview).

CHOOSE QUESTIONS THAT WORK

> I keep six honest serving men
> (They taught me all I knew);
> Their names are What and Why and When
> And How and Where and Who.

Just about every English-speaking journalist has been taught this Rudyard Kipling verse. It summarizes the basic questions journalists must ask in almost every interview. These questions apply for technical writers, too.

To call these questions "serving men" is apt, because they serve you in any interview situation, even when you don't know much about a subject. If you've been unable to find out much background information, or if a product is totally new, you can still ask the engineer:

- *What* is the purpose of the product?
- *Why* would the customer want it?
- *When* will it be put on the market?
- *How* does it work?
- *Where* can I see a working prototype?
- *Who* is the customer?

ORDER QUESTIONS LOGICALLY

Arrange your questions in some logical order. As suggested earlier, you can arrange your questions to match the order of information in the document you're writing. Another arrangement you might choose is the order of information in an existing document, such as the product specification. Often the engineer you interview is the author of the product specification. In this case, use sticky notes to keep track of questions on the specification. During the interview you can turn to the pages with the notes on them and ask your questions, perhaps quoting the passages you're not sure about.

A third way to arrange questions is to move from general questions to more specific ones. Journalists call this a "funnel" sequence: moving from more "open" (general) to more "closed" (specific) questions. When you move from general to specific questions, the engineer has a better chance of following your train of thought and perhaps providing additional information that you hadn't thought to ask for. You begin with your "What is the product's purpose?"; then proceed through more and more tightly defined questions. Finally ask those questions that can have only one specific answer. For example, "What baud rates does the modem support?"

Group specific questions by subject. In other words, don't ask a question about a particular hose, then one about the release date for the product, and then another question about a hose. Move methodically from subject to subject.

Move methodically within each subject as well. For example, move from general to more specific questions, or ask questions chronologically. This doesn't mean the interview will tightly follow your chosen order, nor should it. But by grouping your questions logically, you will keep track of them easily and think more clearly about the information you need.

You will most likely have to skip around during part of the interview, asking questions out of order. So number your written questions in advance. Then place a check mark next to each one as it's answered. That way, you can glance at your list and know which questions remain.

PHRASE QUESTIONS CLEARLY

Make sure you phrase your questions clearly and in detail. That way, the engineer will understand each question and not have to ask you to repeat or explain it. This means including background information.

Let's take a real example. To research an index generator—a computer program that makes an index for a document—you need to find out how the user includes terms in the index. You might ask the engineer, "Does the user need to type a list of terms?"

The engineer, with much on his or her mind, might not know exactly what you're talking about. Perhaps the user needs to type several lists of terms—some to include in the index, some to exclude, etc. Perhaps the user will not type any list at all, but will highlight terms directly in the computer version of the document. If the engineer knows the latter to be the case, he or she won't understand your question immediately. The engineer will have to pause to figure out what it is you really want to know.

Besides being vague, this question is also an example of a yes/no question: "Does the user need to type a list of terms?" The engineer might well say no.

The ideal interview question gets the engineer talking—in detail. It cannot be dismissed with a simple yes or no, which gives you very little information.

A clearer, more specific question about the index generator might include some introductory comments: "This software generates an index for a document. But I don't quite understand how the user tells the software which terms to index. Would you explain how the user does this?" The introductory remark places the engineer right where you are. Your ensuing question lets the engineer know exactly the kind of information you want.

Besides phrasing questions clearly, make sure to write them clearly. This may seem a trivial point now, but it won't seem that way during the interview. There's nothing more annoying than squinting at your list of questions during a hard-to-arrange interview and wondering what on earth you meant by a particular scribble. Write your questions in your best handwriting or type them.

Basically, you are going to ask the engineer all the questions about the product that you haven't been able to answer elsewhere. Sometimes, you won't have answers for some of the simplest, most mundane questions and you'll be stuck asking the engineer. This brings up a critical point. Whether fresh out of school or very experienced, a technical writer always has to be willing to *risk looking stupid*. As a Chinese proverb says, "He who asks is a fool for five minutes. He who does not is a fool forever."

Sometimes the only way to find something out is to ask the expert. And no matter how long you're at it, there'll always be some term or concept you don't know, particularly in complex, rapidly evolving technologies. You will have to hear the incredulous "You mean you don't know what a supergizmokaffoble is?" and just hang tough. Take it on the chin, as the saying goes. If you fail to ask about the obvious, you might end up omitting it from your document.

The following checklist summarizes the tips discussed in this section. You can use it as a checklist when you prepare questions for an interview.

- Choose an order for your questions.
- Move from general to more specific questions.
- Group questions by subject.
- Phrase questions clearly.
- Ask specific questions, aimed at getting the kind of answer you need.
- Avoid yes/no questions.
- Number your questions.
- Use clear handwriting or type your questions.
- Don't be afraid to ask the obvious or to appear stupid.

Who Is the Interviewee?

Before interviewing the engineer, find out as much as you can about him or her. Does the engineer have a reputation for cooperating with technical writers? Or is that person supposed to be an ogre? Ask your manager or other writers what their experience with the engineer has been like. But don't let a bad reputation prejudice you. You might be the first writer to favorably impress that engineer with your courtesy and intelligence.

You may have moral difficulty asking for gossip about a person, but it can prove invaluable. You can use what you learn to make a good impression or at least break the ice at interview time. For example, you might find out not only what the engineer is like, but that she's got two sons, is recently divorced, and collects Gary Larson cartoons. Then you know she's very busy with her personal life, not just work, and she's under extra stress, but she's got a sense of humor. When you interview her, you might choose to start with a humorous comment as an icebreaker, then move briskly into your questions, to assure her that you value her time.

Setting Up the Interview

Phone the engineer to arrange an interview *after* you've organized your questions. That way, you're ready if the engineer says "Can you come over right now? I'm leaving for Argentina in an hour and won't be back for two months."

When you phone the engineer, introduce yourself and give your credentials for taking his or her time. You can do this by mentioning the names of your department and manager, or by giving your job title and the name of the project you've been assigned:

"This is Gary Meade. I'm a technical writer in the Software Documentation Group. My boss, Sheila Channing, suggested you might be the person to answer some of my questions about the Software Troubleshooting Guide I'm working on."

Next, tell the engineer the kind of information you need. Make sure to tell the engineer why you need him or her specifically, unless it's obvious. For example, if you need clarification about a product specification that the engineer wrote, it should be obvious why you're calling.

If you need general product information, a busy engineer might try to refer you to someone else. If you've been told that he or she is the best authority on how the product works, mention it now. Make sure the engineer knows that he or she is a valuable resource for you.

Usually you will work with an engineer whom I'll call your "primary technical resource." This particular engineer will be responsible for the technical accuracy of your document. You will turn to this person for answers to your questions, as well as for leads to other authorities who can help you. If your primary technical resource cares about documentation, he or she may also pave the way by telling other engineers to expect your calls. He or she will be your key reviewer when you send your written drafts out for feedback. You can find details about the key reviewers' roles in the chapter, "The Review Process."

Sometimes your primary technical resource is a relatively inexperienced technical person who is willing to track down information for you. He or she may be more graciously received than an inexperienced writer by the upper engineering echelons of some companies.

If your manager has told you that the engineer will be your primary technical resource, the manager should have informed the engineer first. Check that your manager has clarified your relationship with this engineer, who should then be expecting your call.

Scheduling More Interviews

You will meet with your primary technical resource on an ongoing basis and sometimes work very closely with that person. You need to tell the person about how often you anticipate needing to meet, and how long each meeting should take. Engineers who've had experience working with writers will usually ask for this information. They need to know, so they can include the interview time in their schedule and let their manager know how their time is being spent.

Estimating how much of an engineer's time you will need is tricky. Every writer seems to need different amounts, and the amount of time will vary between projects. I strongly recommend never asking for more than an hour at a time because you need to be very sharp during the interview. You need to listen intently and digest vast quantities of new, complex information. More than an hour of this can lead to burnout for you and the engineer. Also, an engineer's schedule is tight. He or she may postpone meeting with you if you ask for more than an hour. Sometimes you may be able to get only 15 minutes.

You should press hard to find one dependable technical resource who is willing to meet with you for an hour at least twice a week, even if you don't feel you need that much time. Otherwise, gathering enough information later may become grueling or impossible.

Start by meeting with your primary technical resource twice the first week. Then estimate how much time you'll regularly need, based on how many questions were answered in those two meetings and how much more information you'll need. You'll meet more frequently during the research part of a project than during the final editing stage. But make sure to establish a continuing relationship with the engineer, in which he or she expects your requests for time.

TO TAPE OR NOT TO TAPE

To capture the responses to your interview questions, you'll either use a tape recorder or write detailed notes. Again, the similarities between technical writers and journalists come to mind. Both must decide whether to tape or take notes; both have personal preferences. There are many good reasons to use a tape recorder:

- When a topic is very technically complex, you can record concepts and statistics accurately.
- You can maintain eye contact with the interviewee.
- You can listen more fully. You know all the details are being captured by your tape recorder, so you can concentrate on understanding the bigger picture.
- You're free to think about tying in your next question, because you're not frantically taking notes.
- You're freer to reorganize your questions creatively, should the interview take an unexpected twist.
- You'll never have to ask the interviewee to stop talking while you finish writing something.

If You Tape

If you tape, remember to turn the tape recorder off during interruptions. For example, if the engineer answers the phone or someone drops by with a message, don't record the event. You'll only have to listen to it again later. For the same reason, if you and the engineer get involved in a prolonged discussion about raising puppies, you probably don't want to record it—unless you're writing for Purina.

If you turn the recorder off after an interruption or social digression, remember to turn it back on.

There are two main drawbacks to taping: One is the occasional reluctance of an interviewee to be taped, and the other is mechanical failure.

I have never had anyone refuse to be taped when politely asked. Some people feel self-conscious while being taped, however, because they don't like the sound of their voice or they have poor language skills. Others feel their privacy somewhat threatened. Therefore, it's very important that you ask permission before you begin to tape someone.

Mechanical failure is another drawback to consider. One precaution you can take is to bring both a cord and batteries with you to the interview; then plug the tape recorder into an outlet whenever possible. This eliminates one cause of mechanical failure—dead batteries.

Another precaution is to test the tape recorder twice—once before and once during the interview. Request the engineer's patience, stop the tape, rewind it a bit, and play the last few seconds of the interview.

During a recent interview, the interviewee asked me why I was taking notes at the same time as I was taping. I told him I don't trust machines (an attitude gained from working with computers!). Taking notes is another precaution against mechanical failure. You can take sketchier notes than you would without a tape, but at least write down terminology, definitions of acronyms, and statistical data. That way, if the tape recorder fails, you can recapture much of the interview from memory and fill in the definitions and facts from your notes. You're saved the embarrassment of requesting a repeat interview.

One very good reason *not* to use a tape is the amount of time it takes to transcribe it. Taping is a two-step process: First you record; then you transcribe, or take notes from, your tape. Transcribing a tape almost always takes longer than the time the interview took, unless you are lucky enough to have a secretary to transcribe the tape for you. Taking notes is a one-step process: If you can take good, detailed notes quickly, you can work directly from them.

If you use tape, transcribe it within a day or two. Within that time, you can usually remember thoughts you had during the interview that you might want to write down.

If You Take Notes

You can choose to take notes rather than use a tape recorder. You might not feel comfortable relying on a tape recorder, or you might be a whiz at shorthand. Perhaps your topic is simple and you can get most of what you need by taking notes and making a few sketches.

If you take notes, rather than tape, go over them immediately after the interview. You probably heard more details and nuances than you were able to write quickly. You can write them now, without the time pressure of the interview. Human memory is a fragile recording device. Most impressions and extra information will evaporate in a day or two, whereas they're still fresh after the interview. Also, if your rushed handwriting is hard to read, you'll be better able to decipher it immediately. You'll remember what you tried to write.

THE INTERVIEW PROCESS

Bob, a tech writer friend of mine, always begins an interview by scanning the engineer's office, then asking about the photo or trophy on his desk. If no photo or other knickknack is in sight, this writer focuses on the engineer's tie, coffee cup, whatever, and offers a compliment. When Bob first recommended this tactic, I thought he was a cad. But after a while, I came to see the wisdom in it. I don't recommend insincerity, but an opening remark that's somewhat personal can relax the atmosphere.

For most interviews, keep your opening remarks fairly brief. Your time, and the engineer's, is valuable. You can make your ice-breaking overture while you're setting up your tape recorder or readying your pens and notebook. Then launch briskly into your first question.

Asking for an Interview

Asking for a product overview is a good way to start a first interview with an engineer. Getting a product overview from a technical person's point of view is particularly valuable if you are a new writer or the product is new. It also helps even if you are an experienced writer working on a known product, because it gets the interview off to a good start. The engineer talks for a while. You sit back, listen, and take notes or nod encouragingly. You learn not only about the product, but also how the engineer thinks about the product. And more important, you learn how the engineer *thinks*. Does he or she go on tangents and jump around a lot in explaining things? If so, you can be ready to take firmer control of the interview.

Does the engineer use a lot of jargon and unfamiliar terms? List them as you listen to the product overview. When it's ended, ask the engineer to define those terms for you. He or she will probably use less jargon in answering your subsequent questions.

The nature of your interview will vary a great deal depending on the willingness of the engineer and on your level of experience. Many engineers take great interest in documentation and understand the process of producing a manual. They can be extremely patient with a new writer. I knew one writer who, when she first started out, had the good fortune to work with such an engineer. He met with her every day, providing technical information and reviewing her writing as she wrote. This is an uncommon situation and may not always be desirable. Writers usually need to maintain some professional distance to keep engineers from taking control of a writing project.

Winning the Engineer's Respect

You are always more fortunate to have an interested, supportive engineer working with you than a reticent, critical one. However, the outcome of the interview is largely up to you. It's up to you to come prepared; up to you to make a good impression; and up to you to win the engineer's respect. Winning respect is easier the more experience you have. After being a tech writer for a while, you will know how to organize questions, time your interview, and use the information well, even in a new subject area. Also, the more technical expertise you have in a subject area, the easier it is to win an engineer's respect. No question about that. However, you can enhance your working relationship with an engineer even if you know next to nothing about things technical.

First, treat the engineer with respect, but don't be deferential. Being deferential puts you at a disadvantage. It's important not to let the engineer think he or she is doing you a favor.

Says Shaunna Pickett-Gordon, lead writer and former manager at Sun Microsystems:

> You have to be as aggressive or assertive or demanding with the engineer as that engineer is with you. You have to reflect their manner. If a deferential manner is ingrained in you, you're going to have a hard time pushing back enough and asking questions enough and being inquisitive enough and saying, "This doesn't work."

Intelligence is an important quality that wins engineers' respect. Unfortunately, engineers will tend to judge your intelligence in terms of your technical expertise, even though the two are unrelated. If you seem to know something about the product and if you assimilate new information quickly, you will gain more respect. But be ready to admit you don't know something. By admitting ignorance, you show that you're willing to learn. You're willing to correct your ignorance. That is a sign of intelligence that should win respect from all but the dourest engineers.

When I first started as a tech writer, I had to admit ignorance a lot, and my admission didn't always go over too well. At the time, I wasn't making much money and I knew the engineer was making lots, so I'd quip, "Hey, if I already knew what you know, I'd be making your salary!" That usually got a chuckle and made the information flow more easily. This, I suppose, illustrates that humor can sometimes win respect. At least it's worth a try.

Other weaponry that win respect are communication skills, especially active listening. These skills are the subject of the next section.

CHECKLIST 8–2. WINNING RESPECT

You can use the following checklist to review the guidelines presented in this section:

- Approach the engineer with respect, but don't be deferential.
- Organize your questions well.
- Research your subject as thoroughly as possible.
- Listen carefully to the engineer's answers.
- Admit when you don't know something.
- If all else fails, try humor.

Communicating Effectively

Just as the engineer must receive a good impression of you, you will do well if you can regard him or her in the best possible light.

If you feel immediate antipathy toward the engineer whose coopera-tion you must have, put that antipathy aside. If you can't find anything to like, regard the person as a valuable source of information. Focus on the information you need, rather than the source. Direct your attention toward gathering that information as inoffensively as possible.

LISTENING

Listening is the primary communication skill for all occasions. You can't get along with your friend, spouse, parent, child, or boss if you can't lis-ten effectively. Listening is just as important to the interview process.

You and the engineer probably differ in the ways you think and express yourselves. You may have to rephrase your questions so that par-ticular engineer can hear what you mean. And you will certainly employ "active listening" when he or she answers you. To actively listen, you repeat back what's been said to you in a slightly different way—the way you heard it. Here's an example of such a dialogue:

Engineer: For a point-to-point configuration, the asynchronous modes
    work better than the normal response mode.
Writer: You're saying that asynchronous communication is more effi-
    cient for point-to-point connections?
Engineer: Yes.
Writer: Why?
Engineer: Because there's no polling overhead required.
Writer: Then, polling takes time and makes the normal response mode
    less efficient?
Engineer: That is correct.

You get the idea. You bounce concepts back and forth, like a ball, to check your perceptions. But here's an important point: You're not just checking the accuracy of your understanding. You're also letting the engi-neer know that you are really listening—that you're a real human being sitting there taking in all this wisdom and knowledge. Communication is happening.

EXPRESSING

The way you express yourself affects the interview. It might not be the way the engineer best hears things. By "hears" things I really mean "thinks" about them; people conceptualize in different ways. The field of neurolinguistic psychology defines three sensory categories for how peo-ple conceptualize: visual, auditory, and kinesthetic. For example, I started this paragraph by talking about how engineers "hear" things. Neurolin-guistic psychologists would say my thinking was auditory. I could just as easily have talked about how engineers "see" things.

The point is, if the interviewee seems confused, try stating your ques-tions and your understandings differently. You might try analogies and metaphors. For example, you can describe a machine as an animal, consuming and defecating, or as a symphony, with different parts playing solo or accompanied by other parts. You might need to speak very literally with a particular person. Another person might understand a sketch better than your words. Try drawing a picture of how you think something works. Then ask the engineer to correct it or to draw a better one. Think creatively and express yourself flexibly in the interview.

NONVERBAL CUES

Psychologists, journalists, and other professional interviewers use nonverbal, as well as verbal, communication techniques. These techniques can also help tech writers. An accepting tone of voice and facial expression go a long way in establishing rapport. If you make eye contact, nod encouragingly, and smile appropriately, you'll get more careful, complete responses than if you ask the same questions in a clipped monotone and bury yourself in note taking.

CONTROLLING THE INTERVIEW

Interviews can easily get out of hand. You and an engineer have very different views of a product—and for good reasons. The engineer has spent many loving hours in the bowels of a program or device or molecular model. This person sees it as a clever solution to a design problem, and you see it as an end product someone needs to know how to use. The engineer may be willing to talk for hours about the product's technical details. But that's not what you need.

Here's how one technical publications manager describes the problem of engineers who are too close to their job to understand what the writer wants:

> They know the information in their heads and they just can't tell you about it. Try to get them to explain an overall concept of what this product does or give a twenty-five-words-or-less description about this project that you're working on, and they immediately zoom from that down into the seven-layer protocol and what the twenty-fifth bit in the second register does. This doesn't help the writer develop any sort of framework for the information.

What you need in an interview is the information that will help your reader, plus enough extra product knowledge to give depth to your writing. You do not need to know the algorithm for a computer program in order to write a tutorial for a naive user. You do not need to know how many bits reside in each portion of a data communications packet, unless you're writing for programmers.

You will have to interrupt the engineer who launches into lengthy, detailed technical discourse. Courteously, but firmly, focus the discussion:

"Can I interrupt? I'm enjoying what you're saying, but I have many more questions that I need answers for. Could we get to some of them now?"

One technique I use with engineers who are too close to their work is to remind them who my audience is. I sometimes have to do this several times during the interview:

"The manual I'm writing is for the person using this security lock. They won't be aware of the process you're describing, but they need to know how to use the lock. What does that person see when the lock denies them access?"

On the other hand, some engineers have so much history with a product or technology that your interview with them turns unexpectedly into a private seminar. I have found myself listening to an expert who is so knowledgeable and gripping that I've shelved my questions for a future time, settled down, and listened.

DEALING WITH RETICENT ENGINEERS

The best thing you can do with a reticent input person is to ask for information in small chunks. Like being audited by the government. When they ask you for a tax audit, they tell you *exactly* what they want to know about. When you're going to a developer that you're having trouble getting information from, the day before your interview, give them a list of questions and say, "This is the information I'm digging for." And then go in there the next day and sit down and talk to them about it. The more prepared you are for what you really want, the more likely you are to be successful.

Thus, freelance writer Linda Lininger offers a way to deal with reticent engineers. An engineer can be reticent in an interview for a number of reasons. He or she can be reticent for all the reasons that any human being might be: She might not be a particularly gregarious person, she might be having a rotten day, or she might have problems at home. I call this communication difficulty the human factor. In the chapter "Why Begin?" the engineer who got on a political soapbox was an example of this human factor. He preferred expressing political views about the company to answering technical questions. Such a person needs to be politely but firmly brought back to the topic at hand, as this chapter has described.

Two other communication difficulties are more endemic to the writer-engineer relationship: (1) The engineer has a superior attitude toward the writer, and (2) the engineer has a poor command of English. Unfortunately, every writer has to learn how to deal with these two communication problems.

An engineer with a seemingly superior attitude may in fact be having difficulty answering your questions. Frequently, such a person will say "You don't need to tell the reader about that" when he or she is stumped about how to explain the answer to you or is concerned that the answer will prove complex and time-consuming. Tell the reticent engineer that you need to understand the product well enough to write about it, without always calling for help. Explain that the more you understand now, the less help you will need later. The prospect of your future independence should motivate the engineer to tell you everything you need! After you have explained why you want the information, rephrase your question.

I have good luck with a trick that seems as though it shouldn't work. When an engineer tells me "You don't need to know about that," I answer, "But I'm just curious. Could you explain it to me?" And he or she always does. This approach works to open the flow of conversation because the engineer hears that I'm genuinely interested in what he or she is doing, that I'm not just doing a job. You will find tricks that work for you.

BREAKING THROUGH THE LANGUAGE BARRIER

Sometimes your primary technical resource speaks English as a second language and has not mastered conversational English. He or she has a strong technical background but rudimentary English skills. This problem is not serious if the engineer is willing to spend time and energy communicating with you. The language barrier becomes a problem only when the person is defensive about his or her lack of English skills or is not willing to overcome the difficulty of communicating complex technical information to you.

You need to be patient in this situation. Be willing to rephrase questions several times, draw pictures, try to use the product while the engineer watches, or whatever it takes. Assume that you are responsible for making the communication work.

A writer I know made the language barrier into a problem. He complained that a Chinese engineer couldn't speak English well enough to explain certain concepts. I worked with the same engineer and found him to be very articulate, patient, and helpful. It was the writer who was defensive about his own lack of technical knowledge and sought to blame the engineer's language skills!

Sometimes you'll do everything possible to communicate with an engineer whose English skills are minimal and you'll fail to get the information you need. In this case, you must find others who know the product and can communicate with you. Get them to answer your questions.

I recently reached a dead end with a non-English-speaking programmer and couldn't find another engineer who knew the product. I ended up talking to a writer in a different part of the company, who'd already documented the product for a different audience. He was very technically knowledgeable. He agreed to be my primary technical resource and the main reviewer for my document.

CHECKLIST 8–3.   INTERVIEWING A NON-ENGLISH SPEAKER

In summary, here are some guidelines for working with an engineer whose English skills are minimal:

- Phrase your questions in simple, clear English.
- Be patient—first assume the problem is with your communication skills and be prepared to rephrase a question several ways.
- Draw pictures, when possible and appropriate.
- Ask the engineer for the names of other technical people (including writers) who've worked with the product. Then go over your questions with them.
- Ask to use the product or watch the engineer use the product.
- Seek a translator who speaks the engineer's language and whose English skills are better.

Double-check technical information you get from a non-English-speaking engineer. I wrote a document based on an interview with such a person and later found many of my understandings to be inaccurate. The language barrier can introduce more inaccuracies than you realize.

Wrapping Up the Interview

When all your questions are answered or the amount of time you've asked for has come to an end, you will close the interview. If all your questions have not been answered, you'll arrange for another interview. Don't let the interview go more than 10 minutes beyond the time you've requested, unless the engineer volunteers to go on. Even then, check your own fatigue level.

Bring the interview to a close while you and the engineer are still thinking clearly. Thank the engineer for his or her time. Mention—unless it's blatantly not true—that you got a lot of valuable information:

"This was an excellent interview. You gave me all the information I need for the first three chapters. Do you mind if I call you if another question or two comes to mind?"

Letting the interviewee know that you got a lot of information helps him or her feel that the time was well spent. That person will be more willing to meet with you again and will surely say yes to your request to make follow-up calls.

You will most likely have to make follow-up calls, particularly if the engineer couldn't answer some of your questions. In almost every interview, an engineer (who is being helpful) offers "to get back to you" about something. *Don't wait* for the engineer to get back to you with the information. Make a note—"Rich will get back to me about the Help messages"—and phone him, after suitable time has passed. You'll probably have to phone more than once, because unless he's unusually diligent, he'll have forgotten his offer to look something up.

Pave the way for follow-up calls; then be patient and courteous when you call.

SUMMING IT UP

This chapter described the art of communicating with an engineer. It provided guidelines on preparing interview questions and making a good impression. It also explored the question of whether or not to tape record an interview. This chapter then described communication skills and other tips to help you maximize the value of your time with the engineer. Finally, this chapter gave tips on how to end the interview, so that the engineer graciously receives your next phone call or request for another interview.

The next chapter talks about communicating with the most important person of all—your reader.

Know Your Audience

9

One day in May 1983, three of the four engines on an Eastern Airlines jumbo jet died in mid-flight. The passenger-filled plane abruptly dropped three miles before the pilot recovered and managed to land the plane. An investigation revealed the accident was not caused by faulty equipment; it was caused by the maintenance crew's failure to read the manual.

In this incident, reported by Jonathan Kozol in *Illiterate America*,[1] the crew had neglected to insert oil seals in the fuel line during a preflight check. In the investigation report, Eastern Airlines did not specify whether the maintenance crew never opened the manual, or opened it but failed to find or understand the instructions. Document usability experts might suggest this is a moot question—users stop opening a manual soon after they have difficulty finding or understanding information in it.

An electronics engineer I know, Rod Bondurant, who is also a recreational pilot, says it's unfair to single out airplane mechanics:

> The consequences of their actions are very dramatic. How many computer technicians have failed to set some dip switch on a computer card and spent the rest of the day trying to make it work? Lots. I talk to them all day. But a similar error by an airplane mechanic might have more dramatic consequences.
>
> Nobody reads manuals. Why the hell should an airplane mechanic read it? He's out in the rain, covered with grease. How can he read the manual?

A document is effective only if it reaches its intended audience. For your document to reach its readers, you first need to learn about them. This chapter describes the problem of reaching readers who can't read, and some real-world problems finding out about your audience. It goes on to describe ways to learn about your audience and to apply what you've learned.

THE PROBLEM OF ILLITERACY

Would knowing the manual's user have helped the writer prevent the Eastern Airlines accident described earlier? Studies have produced a profile of military airplane mechanics, who might differ somewhat from the mechanics working on passenger jets. According to one report:

> The typical [aviation] mechanic is 24 years old, has a high school diploma, never enjoyed reading, and had a ninth-grade reading ability upon graduation from high school. Through nonuse, reading ability has deteriorated to almost the seventh-grade level. The typical individual does not use the traditional technical manuals . . . for much of his work; he prefers to use proceduralized, task-specific maintenance repair cards. He gives no indication that he understands how or why the system works.[2]

A reasonable response to this discovery would be to produce extremely simple manuals with many illustrations, and that's what the military did. They created "New Look" Skill Performance Aids that depended heavily on pictures. Perhaps they even went too far. According to Kozol, some military documentation became so cartoonlike and simplistic that one manual allowed five pages to explain how to open the hood on an army vehicle.

In the end, no amount of technical writing genius can compensate for a reader's illiteracy. Illustrations didn't help the navy recruit who damaged $250,000 worth of delicate equipment, according to a report described by Kozol, because the recruit could not read.[3] He had attempted a repair by following only the illustrations. While the navy recruit is an extreme example, your average reader might not be that far ahead of him in ability or willingness to read.

You cannot teach your audience to read or force them to open your manual if they're unwilling. But by knowing your audience's reading level, preferences, previous experience with similar products, and how they'll use your manual, you can direct your manual to their needs.

THE REAL WORLD

Despite a long-standing awareness of the importance of knowing a document's audience, technical writing departments do not often look beneath the surface of what they already know or assume. They place readers in two very broad categories: technically naive and technically sophisticated. Common "wisdom" dictates that you define all terms for the technically naive, while for the sophisticated, you assume knowledge of terms and concepts that are "commonly used in the field."

Writers are left to make broad judgment calls on these issues. They are frequently urged on by harried technical experts who are quick to reassure writers "you don't need to tell the user that. He already knows," when that expert might not (1) know the answer, (2) be able to explain it easily, or (3) want to take the time to explain it.

The more you really know about the reader, the more you can know when to stand up to such pressure. At a meeting of the Silicon Valley Chapter of the Society for Technical Communication (STC), Stephanie Rosenbaum, president of Tec-Ed, told a story about a writer producing a document for an engineering audience. Whenever the writer sought help defining a term or explaining a concept, the engineering resource for the project explained, "Engineers already know about that. You don't need to put it in the manual." The writer decided to comply with all the engineer's advice about what fellow engineers needed in the document. Then, to test the document's fitness to its target audience, she sent a review draft across the country to an engineer in the same field as her resource person. The engineer sent back copious comments about the inadequacy of the document, its lack of definitions, explanations, and so on. The writer then showed these comments to her recalcitrant resource person. She never had difficulty getting information from him again.

This writer's ingenuity paid off. Most of the time, you'll be told rather tersely who the document audience is, and that's all you'll get. The section "Getting Acquainted with Your Audience," later in this chapter, tells you some ways to get to know your readers better. But first, what specific characteristics of your readers do you need to know?

CHARACTERISTICS OF YOUR AUDIENCE

The characteristics of your audience will guide you to the appropriate form and content for your document. For example, how would you provide an airplane mechanic who is "out in the rain, covered with grease" with appropriate documentation? How would your knowledge of his circumstances dictate form and content? One solution might be to give him a task card, laminated in heavy plastic, with short, clear instructions describing only those steps needed to get the job done. If you do not know the characteristics of the reader—in this case, how he uses the product—you might choose an inappropriate form of communication.

Some characteristics to consider include:

- the reader's education level or reading ability
- the reader's knowledge of the product technology
- how the reader uses the product to perform a task
- what the reader wants from a document
- how many distinct audiences will use the document

Does your document have two, or even three, distinctly different sets of readers—for example, a programmer, a system administrator, and a new user? Are the customer (the product buyer) and the product user different people? Are the product user and document user different? These questions are not obvious, and writers don't often think to ask them.

WRITING FOR A SINGLE AUDIENCE

If you have a say in planning the documentation effort for your department, strive to define a single audience for each manual in a product's documentation set. This set might include online help and video, and these too should have a single defined audience.

I was not so fortunate on one contract, where I was asked to write a user's guide for a data communication product. While the audience had not been clearly defined, the deadline loomed. Assuming I was writing for the program user, I began with a simple overview of what the product did, defined all terms in a glossary, and went on with step-by-step instructions telling the user how to use the program.

In the middle of doing this, my client requested that I tell the network administrator (audience number 2) how to configure the software. I suggested a network administrator's guide would be the place for such information, but time and funds were not set aside for such a manual. I added a chapter for the network administrator.

Then the client wanted information included about how to configure a host computer at the other end of the communication line. The host system administrator became audience number 3.

Next, an out-of-breath programmer whisked a software specification under my nose at the 11th hour. His specification would tell a programmer (audience number 4) how to design a communication program that would work with the product. The spec was almost unreadable, containing undefined terms, passive voice sentences, and poorly formatted examples of code. According to the programmer, I only needed to "clean it up a little. The audience already knows about most of this stuff."

No, that was not the final blow to this manual. Someone in technical support insisted that I document his diagnostic program, which would help customer support engineers (audience number 5) trace problems with data transmission.

The "user's guide" ended up with five distinct audiences, each with vastly differing needs, expectations, and levels of technical knowledge. My client was happy with the end result, which I considered a disaster. The reason such a document is a disaster is that each audience will find it lacking: The technically knowledgeable will feel patronized by the simpler text intended for the product user, and the poor user will feel intimidated by the inscrutable technical detail.

Make every effort you can to define a single audience for your documentation project. If you're stuck with multiple audiences, at least give each its own chapter and clarify the audience up front. For example:

"This chapter addresses the system administrator. It tells you how to install and configure the software. If you want information on how to transfer files, refer to the chapter 'Using the File Transfer Facility.'"

Once you've defined the general audience, you can get down to specifics about it. The rest of this chapter assumes you will have the time, money, and supportive management you need to learn about your readers and to implement documentation improvements based on your discoveries. In other words, it's based on an ideal—not necessarily the real world—and you might have to settle for less.

GETTING ACQUAINTED WITH YOUR AUDIENCE

You can get to know your audience by talking with people, like customer support engineers, who know something about it or by talking to members of the audience. If you have the wherewithal, you can also test the usability of your preliminary documentation with members of your target audience.

If your situation doesn't allow for formal means, use any means you can to learn more about your readers. When consultant Daunna Minnich needed to write a workstation user guide, she was able to find representative users within her company:

> I was writing about what they now would call a workstation, and they had at Memorex everybody from engineers to data-entry clerks, which was exactly who the audience was. It was everyone from people who knew nothing to people who could design the system.

Daunna astutely realized that she too was a member of her target audience and drew some valuable inferences from her own experience:

> Partly I used myself as a resource. This is the job—in the Memorex Communications Division—where I walked in for my interview thinking, "Oh, this is the communications division, so they must do all the publicity stuff here." I had no idea we were talking about *tele*communications or *data* communications. I was totally stupid!
>
> I must have figured it out somewhere between going in for the initial interview and being hired, but I didn't know what that basic term [communications] meant.

By being honest about herself and having the self-confidence to share her observations with her boss, she was able to convince him to change the nature of their manuals.

> One of the things that I did in that book was to spend four pages defining some basic terms. "Here's a monitor, here's a keyboard," and back in 1980, not everybody knew what a monitor was if they were a data-entry clerk, whereas my boss said, "Everybody knows what a monitor is." Not if you were a data-entry clerk fresh out of high school you didn't.

Talking with Customer Contacts

While employees in your company might not accurately represent members of your target audience, you might still be able to gather information within your company. As part of their jobs, some employees in your company have direct contact with your audience. The most valuable of these are in customer support, training, and sometimes marketing.

The customer support engineer ("technician," "analyst," or "representative"), who provides either telephone or field support to customers with problems, is an invaluable source of information. He or she knows where users get stuck using the product, the kinds of technical errors that can cause the product to malfunction, and the product quirks the user has to learn about. By asking customer support people about the calls they receive, you can unearth inadequacies in the product's design and documentation. The support engineer usually knows the current manual and can make valuable suggestions about the kinds of additions that would save support effort. This person should also be on your list of reviewers.

Technical trainers are another good source of information about your reader. Trainers usually use the current manual, or pieces of it, in their hands-on classes for customers. Frequently trainers rewrite portions of the manual in response to problems that show up. For example, if the manual inaccurately describes a procedure used in a hands-on training class, instructors will rewrite that section. However, somehow they don't think to tell the manual's author about errors! My eyes were opened when I took a training class for customers and discovered the manual had been heavily edited and in places, completely rewritten, mostly to correct technical inaccuracies.

In that class, I hoarded class materials and added the trainer to my list of reviewers. In addition, I talked with customers in the class to get a sense of their level of technical expertise and their problems using the product. I also watched how they used the manual with the product. Training classes are an excellent way to get to know your audience.

Marketing representatives often provide your initial information about your audience. With skilled questioning, you can glean a lot more from them than they first provide. As Stephanie Rosenbaum reports in a paper on document usability testing:

> Often, marketing groups develop a short audience description, full of buzzwords such as "novice computer users" or "power users," which they employ over and over in presentations and discussions.
>
> For each buzzword, you need to interview for more information. . . . "How much experience can someone have and still be a 'novice'? What must someone know to be a 'power user'?"
>
> By asking open-ended questions, you encourage the product manager or other respondent to think before answering. More important, you obtain specific operational information which will help you prepare rigorous user-group definitions.[4]

In some large companies, marketing groups actually perform their own audience research. Glenda Leatherman, program manager of Networked

Publishing, a marketing-oriented department at Cisco Systems, emphasizes the need to survey users' preferences in creating end-user documents: "Why are we doing this [writing] if it's not for the end-user? I mean, we're not writing this so we can look at it and say it's a beautiful piece of work!"

Talking with Your Audience

If you can, obtain information directly from your readers about their education and skills, how they use the product, and what documentation they feel they need. Two ways to do this include a visit to a customer site and a reader survey.

SITE VISIT

A site visit lets you evaluate existing documentation, based on user feedback, so you can improve your future efforts. If you can arrange a site visit, through your marketing or customer support departments, try to set up interviews beforehand with those customer employees who use the manual or online documentation. Be prepared to elicit the kinds of information that will help you improve your documentation. For example, ask users to perform a simple operation by following the previous documentation, and watch them. Do they thumb through the manual randomly? Do they look in the index or table of contents first? Are they so familiar with the guide that they turn immediately to the right place?

If they know exactly where to look in a document, chances are they've regularly found it useful.

If they've had a manual for a while and are still unfamiliar with it, you might conclude the product is so easy to use that the manual is unnecessary, or the manual is so unattractive or difficult to use that the customer is happier fumbling blindly with the product, or some combination of product user-friendliness and document user-hostility. After all, if there's user-friendliness, there must also be user-hostility!

QUESTIONS TO ASK USERS

Augment your observations with questions. The following list provides questions you can ask the user to evaluate a document. It assumes the user has access to either the previous version of the document or a preliminary draft of one you are writing.

About Organization

- Can you find the information you need easily?
- If not, what kinds of information are hard to find?
- Is there a better way to organize the document so that you can get to what you need?
- Is the index adequate?

About Completeness

- Did you need to ask someone for help to use the product?

- What information could the documentation provide such that you would not have to ask for help?
- Is the documentation too technical for you to understand the information you need?
- If so, what parts require clarification?
- Is the documentation technical enough?
- What more technical information would you like to see in it?

About Visual Presentation

- Would more illustrations help you?
- What kinds of illustrations would you like to see?
- Do you think the manual or online document looks attractive?
- How can we improve its appearance?

About Appropriateness

- Do you have additional suggestions for improving the documentation you use with this product?
- Is there an additional kind of documentation—for example, an interactive tutorial—that would help you use the product?

AN AUDIENCE SURVEY

You can use an audience survey to learn about your audience either after they've used a version of a document or before they've even seen the product. If you're conducting a survey of current documentation users, use the same questions (listed in the preceding section) that you'd ask at a customer site to discover the reader's needs.

A reader survey can also reveal the characteristics of an audience you are about to address with new documentation. One such survey, described by Heather Keeler in an article in *Technical Communication,* sought to discover three user characteristics: "how my readers process information, their preference for style and content, and their familiarity with printed material. I wanted reader responses to help me determine whether I should explain details with pictures more than text, use formal or informal language, provide overview information or just details, and use marginal notes and headings to help readers skim text."[5]

Keeler designed a survey containing affective questions a social scientist might ask. For example, she asks the reader to respond to statements like "When I read fiction, I hear characters speaking in my head," with a range of reactions from "strongly agree" through "strongly disagree." She included questions about job classification, age, and education.

Keeler found, among other things, that her readers "more effectively process information through pictures rather than words. . . . They prefer simplicity over formality. . . . Readers also want documentation to provide the whole picture, not just the details, and to include why something happens, not just how."[6]

Because Keeler surveyed an entire company, her respondents included audiences for a variety of documentation. By differentiating them, she was able to see how, say, manufacturing documentation needs more visual elements than are needed in documentation for a more print-oriented audience.

One of Keeler's final recommendations is "if in doubt, ask" the user.

Usability Testing

"Usability testing is very simple," say Carol Bergfeld Mills and Kenneth L. Dye in an article in *Technical Communication:*

> You just find users who know nothing about a product and have them use it with the manual. By watching where they have problems using the product or where they need help, you can identify problems in the manual (and sometimes in the product).[7]

In my technical writing seminars, I ask students to write simple procedures, such as how to load a staple gun or how to tape-record a message, and then to test each other's instructions. "Testers" are usually able to identify numerous omissions and distortions. Students are amazed by the assumptions they make in documenting these everyday actions.

Some would argue with the simplicity of "just" finding users who know nothing about the product. Selecting users for such a test can be a very detailed process. Some testers first formulate a measurable definition of the manual's prospective user, which can include a complex catalog of traits, similar to the characteristics Keeler investigated in her survey, described in the previous section. They then match this definition with a group of people who will take the test.

Why a usability test? Why go to all this trouble when you can simply ask users about their education and experience, adjust your document reading level and vocabulary accordingly, have the document reviewed, and be done with it? Because, say cognitive psychologists, we bring to any task a complex agenda of past experiences and associations. While not simple to measure, these associations affect how we think and act. By observing a sampling of typical users, we can allow for the eccentric differences people bring to tasks and observe some of their less predictable responses.

THE TEST LAB

Usability testing of both products and documentation is now done by a number of in-house and consulting laboratories, as well as universities. The labs usually consist of two rooms connected by a one-way mirror, through which testers can observe and record users' attempts to use the product and its accompanying documentation. The process is also videotaped, and other measurements, such as rate of keystrokes, might be taken.

I've seen two such tapes, produced by Digital Equipment Corporation and Apple Computer. In both cases, users were either thoroughly confused or enraged with the product's manuals. Besides leading to product improvements, the taped sessions made excruciatingly clear the need for improved documentation.

A quality assurance engineer at Cisco Systems recently told me about a usability test he observed in which a workstation user flipped through the accompanying documentation. When the user got to an illustration, he would stop and read for a while, then skip forward until he reached the next illustration. When asked for his opinion of the document, he described it as "fragmented"! Had this user not been observed in the act of using the document, document designers might have wrongly concluded that the document itself lacked continuity. In fact, this user had not read the document. He processed information visually, and only the images held his attention.

THE RESULTS

What are the elements usability testers measure? According to Mills and Dye, "Three main classes of information are collected in usability tests: logs, objective measures, and subjective measures." Logs record testers' observations, users' keystrokes, and "verbal protocols (thinking aloud)." Objective measures include things like the number of errors made and the amount of time it takes to perform a task. Subjective measures include the users' feelings and opinions about the product, which testers will collect through interviews and questionnaires.[8]

Conclusions drawn from these data depend on the kind of documentation and the nature of the tasks the user performs. You wouldn't need to be a trained social scientist, though, to understand the grosser problems expressed by test subjects in the sessions I observed.

FOLLOW-UP

No amount of research will help you if you don't use what you've discovered to improve your documentation. You may think this goes without saying, but I've found it's not as obvious as it seems. At one company where users were disgruntled about documentation, I was sent to find out why. "Design a survey," my boss suggested. I designed one, with questions similar to those you'll find earlier in this chapter in the section titled "Site Visit." I submitted it to user groups both in the United States and in Europe. Customers were obviously pleased to have their opinions solicited, because a large percentage returned my questionnaire. The results were easy to analyze, because the majority of users requested the same improvements: more illustrations, a better index, and more technical information on a more sophisticated level. They didn't care about the attractiveness of the manual's cover. They just wanted the facts.

I presented the results at a department meeting and made concrete suggestions about how to give the users what they'd requested. Everyone was in agreement. But it never happened. The survey, it turned out, had been a gesture of diplomacy. Management did not intend to implement changes. Seven years later, that company's customers still complained about documentation, and the company had lost revenue. Then, when the company was acquired by a larger corporation, the publications department was disbanded, followed shortly by the company itself. The moral of the story? Pay attention to your audience!

Enlist the support you'll need from management and fellow workers before you begin to investigate your audience. Prepare a concrete plan to give your readers what they need.

What are some of the elements you'll modify based on your findings about your audience? Some obvious ones already mentioned include level of technical complexity, amount of detail, number of illustrations, and formality of language.

When Keeler found a significant minority of her test subjects were "nonreaders"—that is, they read fewer than five newspapers, books, or magazines per month—she recommended using "lots of headings, marginal notes, illustrations, and bulleted lists."[9] These recommended elements are standard tools tech writers use to break up the printed page. More about them in the chapter "Planning for Visual Impact."

Other document features based on audience might be unique to your user and might require you to find a more creative solution. The example of the airplane mechanic in the mud is a good one, and the plastic-laminated task card is, I think, a good solution. Others might include providing the following:

- labeled, colored tabs in a binder that is used often as a reference
- a quick-reference card that folds to stand up by itself, for users who need both hands to perform a task
- extra blank pages for taking notes, should your readers have a specific need to do so in a document
- an online document, a portable computer, and a modem, for traveling workers who need instant access to most-current data

These are just a few examples of ways to creatively apply what you know about your audience to your documentation choices

SUMMING IT UP

This chapter described ways to find out who your audience is and what they need from your manual to do their jobs. It recommended some ways you can use this information to improve document usability. The next chapter begins a new section, which describes the birth of a document and its passage through writing, editing, review, and production. It provides guidance for planning both paper and online documentation.

---

[1] Jonathan Kozol, *Illiterate America* (New York: Anchor Press/Doubleday, 1985), p. 20.

[2] Thomas M. Duffy et al., "An Analysis of the Process of Developing Military Technical Manuals," *Technical Communication,* Journal of the Society for Technical Communication, Second Quarter, 1987, p. 70.

[3] Kozol, p. 18.

[4] Stephanie Rosenbaum, "Selecting Appropriate Subjects for Documentation Usability Testing," *Work with Computers: Organizational, Management, Stress and Health Aspects,* Proceedings of the Third International Conference on Human-Computer Interaction, Boston, Mass. September 18–22, 1989 (Amsterdam, Netherlands: Elsevier Science Publishers B. V., 1989), p. 621.

[5] Heather Keeler, "A Writer's Readers: Who Are They and What Do They Want?" *Technical Communication,* Journal of the Society for Technical Communication, First Quarter, 1989, p. 9.

[6] Keeler, pp. 10–11.

[7] Carol Bergfeld Mills and Kenneth L. Dye, "Usability Testing: User Reviews," *Technical Communication,* Journal of the Society for Technical Communication, Fourth Quarter, 1985, p. 40.

[8] Mills and Dye, pp. 42–43.

[9] Keeler, p. 11.

PART 3

A DOCUMENT IS BORN

10

Planning a Writing Project, on Paper and Online

This chapter begins the odyssey of producing a document. Along the way, you'll travel through the mental realm of organizing thoughts on paper; the visual world of graphs, illustrations, page and screen design, and animation; the businesslike trail of schedule milestones; the creative adventure of writing; the editorial forest of rules and semicolons; the diplomatic forays of the review process; and the final road to your destination—producing a print-ready book or fully integrated online document.

This chapter describes planning and organizing a writing project and presents the differences between paper and online documentation.

Until the mid-1990s, paper documentation was the dominant medium in technical communication. With the explosion of computer networking as a popular medium, online communication caught up with and pulled ahead of paper. Fortunately, the guidelines to good writing remain essentially unchanged. In fact, some guidelines, like terseness and correctness, are even more critical online. And technical writers, whether working on paper or in cyberspace, still must answer to ever-tightening deadlines. The best way to meet a deadline is to follow a plan.

THE DOCUMENT PLAN

The document plan (or "doc plan") contains the guidelines you'll follow to produce a document. Sometimes it's called a document design, a blueprint, or some other name, and its characteristics vary among organizations. A doc plan usually contains the following elements:

- the document title
- a statement of purpose
- a statement of audience

- a brief product description, including version number or other identifying product-release information
- a list of reviewers and their departments
- a list of other documents that support the same product
- a detailed document outline
- for online documents, a visual representation of the document structure
- a schedule showing milestones (described in detail later in this chapter)

For paper documents, your outline can include positions of figures, graphs, and tables. You might also be asked to include a description of the physical characteristics of the final document (for example, three-hole bound, 8 $1/2'' \times 11''$, with colored tabs showing chapter titles), an example of the document's format, and a plan for updates. Appendix C, at the end of this book, contains an example of a detailed document plan for a software user's guide.

For online documents, your outline provides a detailed list of topics, but the document structure will be presented in an additional document, sometimes called a *map*. This map might be anything from a rough sketch, in the beginning of your project, to a printed document showing screen captures with arrows between them. The arrows represent *links*, those connections users can follow to get from one part of the document to another.

Says online documentation consultant Linda Urban:

> The outline doesn't represent the hierarchical order in the same way an outline for a paper document does, but it includes all material to be covered. The navigation plan, or map, is a visual representation showing how the different types of topics will connect to each other, but it may not include every single topic, as the outline does. The outline is still important because it lets the writer and others on the team see what information is being included.

As a beginning writer, you will probably follow someone else's structure to create your online document. When you become more sophisticated with online authoring tools, you will not only design the structure, but you also might create a working prototype demonstrating to reviewers how the finished online document will look.

SCHEDULING

How long should the planning process take? "The drafting of specifications normally takes from 25 to 30 percent of the entire writing time," says R. John Brockmann in *Writing Better Computer User Documentation:*

> This may sound like a lot of time, but probably a great deal of what you now consider writing time is really planning time. And, even if this is a lot of time, the time spent developing writing specifications is much more cost-effective than unplanned time spent rewriting pages or screens

during the testing, editing, or reviewing stages that try to make up for planning mistakes or organization problems. The hidden cost of unexpected problems can be greatly diminished by planning.[1]

Brockmann's specifications are very like the document plan described in the previous section. Brockmann's time estimate for planning is a generous one, but you can certainly use his arguments, and other reasons listed here, to justify more time in your schedule for this vital activity.

Scheduling Constraints

Document scheduling is strongly affected by the schedule for producing the product. More and more, product deadlines inflexibly dictate document deadlines, as technological advances move new products out at ever faster rates. Documents that once took three months to produce now must be produced in three weeks. Artificial scheduling constraints can force you to write a final draft about an unfinished product, so the documentation will be ready by the product release date. You can imagine how such constraints produce inaccuracies—and angry customers.

Rules for scheduling a document are difficult to formulate, because writers require vastly different amounts of time during different documentation stages. One writer might research painstakingly and write at the speed of a comet. Another might be a very slow writer, but will polish style and check facts in the process, producing a much more finished draft than the comet writer.

Scheduling Milestones

When you write a schedule, you'll probably include dates for the following document "milestones":

- research phase complete
- document plan distributed to reviewers
- document plan review comments due
- first review draft distributed
  (For online documents, this can be a software version, accompanied by either a printout of actual screens or for online help, a revised list of help topics.)
- first review comments due
- second review draft distributed
- second review comments due (sometimes a third review is required)
- final editing, formatting, table of contents, and index complete
- for paper documents, graphics inserted by artist
- for paper documents, print-ready copy, in electronic or camera-ready format, sent to printer
- for online documents, final version sent to product developer to be integrated into the product
- printed, bound manual or online document available to customers

These stages will vary, depending on your production tools and responsibilities. For example, usually the "research phase" is an ongoing process, stretching beyond the distribution of the document plan.

Some writing departments also schedule review meetings, where reviewers and writer get together to reconcile differing views about changes to the document.

As you gain experience, you'll learn your own rhythms and be able to assess how much time each phase takes you. You'll also gain the confidence you need to assert your scheduling needs as part of the entire product scheduling process. (An example of a document schedule is included in the software-manual document plan in Appendix C.)

THE IMPORTANCE OF DOCUMENT ORGANIZATION

The document plan allows you to pace your work by giving you milestones to meet. As such, it gives structure to your work. However, the plan's most important components are the outline and for online documents, the map representing how the content will be structured. These written plans dictate the organization of your document. Why is this so important?

Organization is the key to comprehension and document usability. It directs the reader to your intended communication goal.

The benefits of an outline and visual map more than compensate for the struggles some of us (and I include myself) go through to create them:

- A solid structure, expressed on paper, greatly speeds the writing process. You are no longer confronted with a blank page. Your structure is in place, waiting to be filled in.
- An outline, or map, can be reviewed and revised. Reviewers can suggest changes to the document's organization early, eliminating the need for drastic changes after the complete document is reviewed.
- You can prevent redundancy within a document by ordering information logically in the beginning.
- You can eliminate redundancy among documents written by different writers within the group, because each is aware of what the others' documents will cover.

You will find details about writing an outline in the chapter "Organizing a Technical Document." The chapter "Designing Online Documentation" describes the elements to include in a map.

THE REAL WORLD

Before looking at the ideal, let's look at how you can expect to organize a document on your first technical writing job. For now, let's assume a "document" can be either on paper or online.

At least at the start, your document's style and organization probably will be dictated by your writing department. Even more likely, you'll be given a book (or a Web site) to update and won't have the opportunity to consider whether it's organized for maximum usefulness.

As you participate more in department decisions, you'll have a chance to suggest changes that will improve the organization of documents as well as changes to an entire documentation set. These may be your biggest contributions to documentation quality.

Time is an obstacle you'll confront in planning a document. The up-front effort of organizing your material into a purposive whole is not always valued or understood by nonwriting managers and other members of a product team. After all, writers just sit down and write, don't they? If you ask for a significant amount of time in the planning stage, you might be met with suspicion, unless you've already proved yourself to be a "fast" writer. (A fast writer is one who meets deadlines without obvious signs of panic.)

Despite real-world obstacles, careful preparation is worth fighting for. Even more than the ability to write tidy prose, your ability to organize technical information will endear you to your readers.

PRINCIPLES OF DOCUMENT ORGANIZATION, ON PAPER AND ONLINE

The way you structure information directs your audience's thought process or actions toward a specific goal, be it to understand the results of a study, to install a device, or to manipulate a computer program. If you place information on the page as if you were writing a grocery list, with no regard to the relationships among ideas, the reader has no sign-posts to guide thought or actions and must organize—mentally rewrite—the information before using it.

Organization sets up relationships among the kinds of information you'll communicate and provides clear paths from one to the next.

Effective documentation, whether on paper or online, follows two organizational principles:

*   Recognizable structure
*   User orientation (versus product orientation)

The first principle—to give the reader a clearly recognizable path through the material—is accomplished differently for paper and online documentation. For paper, you reveal the document's structure both through logical writing, which includes transitional words and phrases, and through rhetorical signposts, like headings, introductions, and summaries.

Online, you provide navigational aids, like graphic symbols labeled **Next, Back,** and **Top,** which allow the user to move about, and you maintain consistency in the ways you link information. For both paper and online, reference aids, like a table of contents, further help readers find their way.

The second principle has to do with the fact that people have unique characteristics and needs that dictate how they use documents. In the chapter "Know Your Audience," you read about the importance of addressing your audience. Now you can use what you know about them to organize your documentation. For both paper and online documents, that means considering the way the user does his work and giving him the information he really needs where he is most likely to find it. By contrast, product-oriented documents often provide tons of product information the user doesn't need or care to know.

For online documents, user orientation is particularly important. If the user doesn't find what he most needs up front, he'll click out of the document in a millisecond!

DIFFERENCES BETWEEN PAPER AND ONLINE DOCUMENTATION

While the need for recognizable structure and user orientation guides both written and online projects, these media differ in some important ways. Once you know their characteristics, you can choose the one most appropriate to your communication goal.

Characteristics of a Book

"Books take their place according to their specific gravity as surely as potatoes in a tub."
—Ralph Waldo Emerson *(Journals, 1832)*

A book is a substantial object. You can touch it, heft it, and even throw it, should the need arise.

If you need to find information in a book, you remove it from a shelf, turn to a table of contents, flip the pages until you come to the right spot, read, then close the book, and reshelve it. Many physical steps are involved.

If a book is very thick, you might feel reluctant to open it. Once you do, you'll passively absorb what you find, proceeding in a fixed, linear direction. While you can move back and forth through its pages, the book's character is essentially static and linear. You always know where you are in relation to its beginning and its end.

Because larger amounts of text are easier to read on paper than online, a book allows for long discussions and complex, detailed information.

A book usually requires an outside vendor to manufacture it. And books still take longer to produce. However, the arrival of "just-in-time" printing has closed the time gap between what was once a three- or four-week book-printing process and the faster technology of burning online documentation onto CDs. Just-in-time printing incorporates smaller print runs and faster operations to enable manuals to ship in as few as three or four days.

Today, books are often placed online, where readers can choose to view or print them. Thus, the boundary between paper and online documentation is not as clearly defined as it once was.

Characteristics of Online Documentation

Online documentation is intangible and dynamic. By merely typing a key or clicking a mouse, you can select a topic and get a virtually instantaneous response.

Your relationship with online documentation can be interactive, like a conversation. For example, you ask a question; the software provides a general answer, then displays the message:

Click here for related topics

Good online documentation lets you select layers of detail and move among different kinds of information quickly and easily. Bad online documentation leads you into corners from which you can't escape. Unlike a book, which has a beginning, middle, and end, online documentation has no visible dimensions.

Online documentation requires a computer. This limitation still makes it impractical for some portable applications (although notebook computers and other portable information-access devices are rapidly changing this). You won't use online documentation to help you fix the lawn mower in your driveway; you'll probably use a manual.

Online documentation is restricted by the physical characteristics of the computer—a small screen and letters that are less clear than print. Screens require lots of *white space*—blank areas in which no text or

TABLE 10-1
DIFFERENCES BETWEEN PAPER AND ONLINE DOCUMENTATION

Paper	Online
Fixed and static	Flexible and dynamic
Passive use	Interactive use
Slow, linear information access	Relatively instant, nonlinear information access
Users can find place within whole	Users can get lost
Easier to read	Harder on eyes; requires more white space
Better for long, complex text	Better for short information *chunks*
Time-consuming to update	Easier to keep current
Portable; can be taken anywhere	Portable only for portable-computer owners

graphics appears—to be legible. This limits the amount and type of information that online documentation can effectively present. Small, self-contained "chunks" are best.

Computerized documentation is faster to produce than a book. A CD doesn't need to be printed and bound, and it takes up far less space than a book, making it less expensive to store and ship.

Table 10–1 summarizes the differences between paper and online documentation. The next section shows how you'll use these characteristics to choose the best medium for your communication goal.

ORGANIZING A DOCUMENTATION SET

Most products require more than one document to meet a customer's diverse needs. For example, before buying the product the customer needs to be convinced of its usefulness. Then someone will have to unpack and install or set up the product. The user will need to learn how to use the product, then will need to be guided periodically through product-related tasks, and finally will require quick answers to questions as they arise. When the product malfunctions, the user needs guidance on where to get help or how to correct the problem. Each of these requirements dictates a communication goal that you'll need to address as part of your documentation effort.

For example, documentation for a computer software product might comprise the following:

- sales brochure
- unpacking instructions
- installation or setup instructions
- online tutorial
- online help
- system messages
- error messages
- user's or operator's guide
- reference manual
- trouble-shooting, diagnostics, or error-recovery documentation

By planning a documentation set before planning individual documents, you can provide the optimum medium and organization for each of your communication goals.

Which of these are best suited to paper and which to online documentation?

Documents that lend themselves to online presentation include a tutorial showing how to use the software, online help messages, system messages (as pop-up windows or animated "helpers") that tell users what to do next, and error messages describing what went wrong. These can all be part of the product.

The sales brochure and unpacking instructions are candidates for paper, because both will be read away from the computer. Installation and setup instructions can be on paper, or they can be online provided they don't interfere with computer tasks the user might need to perform while reading them.

User's guides and reference manuals can also be either on paper or online, depending on their complexity—complex on paper; simple online.

These examples illustrate a few of the ways you might decide which medium to use when you plan a documentation set.

William Horton, in his helpful guide *Designing and Writing Online Documentation,* makes the point that you don't need to choose between paper or online. You can choose either, both, or a "hybrid" (which lets users search electronically, then print out what they need). The point is to find what best suits your purpose.[2]

Horton quotes numerous studies proving that online documentation is better or worse than paper, and then concludes:

> The only thing these studies really prove is this: Good online documenta-tion is better than poor paper documentation and good paper documenta-tion is better than poor online documentation. Online documentation does not guarantee success or failure. Only good design guarantees success.[3]

At the same time as you are designing your document set, you should also develop style guidelines and consistent terminology, so the user won't be confused by conflicting usages among documents. Style is discussed later in the chapter "Editing Your Work."

SUMMING IT UP

This chapter began describing the documentation process by introducing the document plan and scheduling. It compared paper and online docu-mentation and suggested some appropriate uses for each. The next chap-ter describes ways to organize technical information in a manual.

---

[1] R. John Brockmann, *Writing Better Computer User Documentation: From Paper to Hypertext,* Version 2.0 (New York: John Wiley & Sons, 1990), p. 89.

[2] William Horton, *Designing and Writing Online Documentation,* Second Edition (New York: John Wiley & Sons, Inc., 1994), p. 12.

[3] Horton, p. 15.

11

Organizing a Technical Document

This chapter provides some ways to organize a technical document. Although it focuses primarily on paper documents, this chapter describes principles that apply equally well to online documents. It reviews basic outline form and then describes the reference aids and other components that make technical books accessible to readers.

ORDERING TECHNICAL INFORMATION

Following the principles of recognizable structure and user orientation, what are some ways to organize a technical document? The following types of organization are familiar to most readers, and therefore fulfill the first principle—recognizable structure. Each will be "user oriented," however, only if it is the best type of organization to meet the user's specific needs:

Chronological	Events are described in the order in which they occur.
Known-to-Unknown (or *Simple-to-Complex*)	Information builds from familiar, simpler to less familiar, more complex concepts.
Question-and-Answer	Information anticipates the user's questions and provides answers.
Alphabetical	Information is tied to terms that can be alphabetized.
Task-Oriented	Information and instructions are organized in the order in which the reader customarily does her job.

Most technical documents don't purely follow any single organizational type. Documents tend to combine an overall order (for example, a chronological order) with different kinds of organization within their sections.

The book you are now reading is chronologically organized to match the steps in a beginning technical writer's career. It's meant to be read through first, then used for reference later. Chronological order works best for books that lead readers through a sequence of steps and for books that will be read from start to finish.

Information organized from known-to-unknown (or simple-to-complex) is common for a tutorial or any teaching text. It begins with what the user knows and proceeds to teach new concepts based on familiar ones.

Troubleshooting material frequently follows question-and-answer order. Online FAQs (Frequently Asked Questions) are another example of this order. This "order," however, does no more than put a question before its answer. You therefore need to organize questions and answers further, either by need (most frequently asked questions first) or by difficulty (simple-to-complex).

Common examples of alphabetical material include glossaries and bibliographies. Reference material that describes computer commands is often ordered alphabetically.

Task-oriented documents provide information about tasks, usually in the form of instructions, in the order in which the reader performs them. Studies have revealed that of all the reading people do on jobs, only 15 percent is reading to learn—that is, to retain information. The rest is reading to do[1]—that is, to complete a task or procedure. Writing for the doer requires task orientation. Rather than focusing on the features of a product, you direct the actions the reader performs. When the reader completes a task, he or she puts the manual away—or exits the online instructions—and can even forget the documented information.

Says R. John Brockmann in *Writing Better Computer User Documentation:*

> Readers only use documentation to get their job completed. . . . Documentation is only a tool and not an end in itself. Thus, the best design for software documentation is one that fits the reader's method of working and requires the least attention and learning. This self-effacing design for documentation is where we need to begin, and this type of design is called task orientation.[2]

How does task orientation dictate document organization? A great example on my shelf is an old manual for consumer accounting software. The product allows users to track and balance their various accounts, including checking, credit cards, mortgage debt, and so on. Unlike professional accounting programs, this software is geared to the layperson, and the manual guides the user through tasks she would normally perform, in the order and language she would use. The first few chapters are listed below:

• Opening your first account
• Using the register

- Writing checks
- Printing checks
- Reconciling your records

Research has shown that while task-oriented documents take 42 percent more time to create than product-oriented documents, they increase user productivity by 41 percent. Also, users are happier with them—79 percent of those who were asked to compare the two preferred the task-oriented documents.[3]

One more way of ordering information—*by need*—requires mentioning here because it can be useful for some documents. Ordering by need means placing frequently required information before information the user needs less frequently. This order can defy the reader's expectations. For example, most experienced readers of technical documents expect installation instructions to appear before reference information, even though reference information is needed more frequently than installation instructions. If you place reference first and installation last, users will find the organization confusing.

However, most sales or marketing-related documents—including most Web sites—benefit from being organized by need because the reader is there by choice. If you don't provide what the reader most needs up front, you will lose him!

No matter how logical a structure seems, it won't work well unless users can find their way in it. In a manual organized by need, you will have to provide excellent reference aids, because the manual structure is less readily recognizable to readers than some other structures. Later in this chapter, you'll learn how to use a "road map" to clarify this type of document organization.

Outline Form

You'll organize your document by writing an outline. Some writers skip this step. Don't. An outline is your document structure made manifest. It is the framework upon which you will build everything else.

An outline can be tedious to write. Like the framework of a building, it is not as beautiful or creative as the final edifice. (The outline for this book sent me to the coffeepot more times than I will admit.) But once in place, an outline allows you to create the headings, transitions, and cross references that will make your text flow.

During whatever happens between high school English and the present, most of us forget how to write an outline, so let's review. Figure 11–1 illustrates basic outline form.

For nontechnical material, your outline can guide your discussion without each level corresponding to a heading. In contrast, for technical material, each move between topics and subtopics is always signaled by a heading.

FIGURE 11-1
OUTLINE FORM

I. First level
II. Another first level
  A. Second level
  B. Another second level
    1. Third level
    2. Another third level
      a. Fourth level
      b. Another fourth level
  C. Back to second level

A few rules accompany this essential tool:

- You can move "in" only one level at a time; you can move "out" as many levels as you want. For example, Figure 11–1 shows a second level (**C**) after a fourth (**b**).
- You must include at least two headings per level before you move back out. In other words, if you have one second-level topic, you must include another one before you move back out to the next main topic.
- Each heading, including the chapter title, must be followed by text. No heading should lie next to another heading like slices of bread in an empty sandwich.

That's all there is to an outline. Now let's fill it in.

HEADINGS

Headings are rhetorical signposts that tell the reader where you're going. As such, they should clearly express the contents of the section.

Readers often scan to find the information they need. Specific, descriptive headings speed your readers' search. They provide topic information in an easy-to-read format or type font, saving readers from the frustrating task of scanning text to determine where they are in the material.

The level of a heading indicates whether what follows is a main topic or a subtopic. You can indicate head levels either by the *milspec* (military specification) numbered format, still common even in some nonmilitary documentation, or by typographical emphasis. Figure 11–2 illustrates the milspec numbering system.

Typographical emphasis uses font size, capitalization, and boldface to visually increase or decrease the importance of a heading. Thus, a chapter heading might appear in 16-point type, followed by a level-one heading in 14-point type, and so on. The headings in this book use typographical emphasis to differentiate heading levels.

FIGURE 11-2
MILSPEC NUMBERING

```
1. First level
    1.1  Second level
    1.2  Another second level
        1.2.1  Third level
        1.2.2  Another third level
            1.2.2.1  Fourth level
            1.2.2.2  Another fourth level
    1.3  Back to second level
```

REFERENCE AIDS

Reference aids help the reader identify the structure of your document. These include the table of contents, the index, dividers with tabs, "icons," and introductory road maps that summarize the contents of a manual.

Nothing prevents user confusion better than a good index. All manuals and online help documentation should have one. You'll learn the principles of indexing in the chapter "The Production Process," later in this book.

Dividers with colored tabs are an inviting way to give the reader access to information quickly. They're particularly helpful in a large reference manual with distinct sections or a binder containing multiple manuals about the same product. Each tab should bear the name of the section or manual.

Icons are small symbols, usually placed in the margin, that alert a reader to a type of information. For example, some hardware setup instructions use an exclamation point inside a triangle to indicate cautionary information about possible damage to equipment. You can use this technique to indicate other kinds of information as well. For example, every time you define a term, you can include a small dictionary symbol in the margin to help your reader find the definition.

As with all graphic elements, icons should be used sparingly and only when they add meaning. Otherwise your page can start to look fussy.

An introductory road map is a fine way to lead a user to needed information. A road map is a table or diagram that summarizes information and indicates where to find it. Web sites sometimes display a road map called a *site map* as either a contents list or a graphic representation of links.

The road map for a manual can be organized in the following ways:

- by audience definition, for a multiple audience document
- by questions
- chronologically
- by need

Figure 11–3 shows a road map I designed for a manual. Because the information in the manual was organized by need rather than chronologically, installation information was at the back and everyday usage information was toward the front. To let the user know where to look to perform specific tasks, I provided a task-oriented chronological road map, which I labeled "QUICKSTART."

FIGURE 11-3
EXAMPLE OF A ROAD MAP

QUICKSTART

To do this:	Refer to this section of the manual:
1. Set up your directories	"Before You Index" in *Chapter 3 Creating an Index*
2. Install the software	*Chapter 4 Installing AutoINDEX*
3. Collect text from drawing files	"*Word Index*" in *Chapter 3 Creating an Index*
4. Create the index	"Build Index" in *Chapter 3 Creating an Index*
5. Find drawing files	*Chapter 2 Using AutoINDEX*

COMPONENTS OF TECHNICAL BOOKS

This section briefly summarizes the most common components of a technical book and tells you about the kinds of information you'll need to include in them.

Front Matter

The front matter includes the title page, copyright notice, trademarks, table of contents, figures and tables lists, and sometimes a preface. Its pages are numbered in small roman numerals.

Check to make sure the copyright notice shows the year the book will be available and is not outdated. Make sure the trademarks for all products named in the book are listed correctly in the trademarks section. Sometimes a legal department will help you with this.

A preface usually includes a brief description of the book's organization. It can include a road map, like the example just given. It might also include a summary of conventions, described next. Be aware that readers hardly ever read the preface, so do not place essential information there.

Summary of Conventions

Often a technical manual includes a table showing how certain typographical conventions are used. For example, a computer manual might include a table, like the one in Figure 11–4, showing how keystrokes will appear.

FIGURE 11-4
KEYSTROKE CONVENTIONS

Esc	Escape
Ctrl	Control
F1-Fx	Function keys F1 through Fx

You might also provide a conventions table for icons and their meanings (such as caution and warning symbols) and for any other visual cues that are not inherently obvious to the reader.

Overview

An overview, or introduction, gives readers a big picture of the product organization. It summarizes the product's uses or features and places them within the whole. Like a preface, an overview often is not read. However, it's valuable to new product users who are not familiar with similar products. It also can compensate for design flaws in the product by pointing out the unexpected. If a reader becomes perplexed about where to find information in the manual, he or she might turn to the overview to get a clearer sense of how the product works before proceeding.

Glossary

A glossary is an alphabetized list of technical terms and their definitions. It is an excellent addition to any manual. It helps new users and old alike. Often even engineers are unaware of certain terms in their field.

A glossary also gives you an excuse to pin down technical experts about their use of terminology.

Appendixes

An appendix is information that is "appended" to the book. It is not an afterthought, although it's occasionally misused as a repository of late-arriving information. Appendixes follow chapters and are assigned letters rather than numbers—Appendix A, Appendix B, and so on.

Any information that would be useful to readers but is not critical to your main communication goal should go into an appendix. Appendixes can include long tables, like conversions between different kinds of measurements, temperatures (e.g., Celsius to Fahrenheit), and the like, as well as long lists.

The appendixes at the end of this book are examples of the kinds of information to include. Two are lists and one is a lengthy example. These appendixes provide information that is useful to some readers but that would interrupt the organizational flow if included in the main text.

Bibliography

A bibliography lists books on the same or related subjects. While many nonfiction books include a bibliography at the back, a technical manual will often list related titles at the front.

Index

This critical reference aid follows all appendixes and the bibliography at the back of the manual. It's discussed in detail in the chapter "The Production Process."

SUMMING IT UP

In this chapter, you looked at some ways to organize technical information, particularly in paper documentation. You reviewed outline form and you learned about common components of technical books. The next chapter will look at how to organize online documentation and will introduce you to some of the concepts and skills you can use to write online.

---

[1] Janice C. Redish, "Reading to Learn to Do," *The Technical Writing Teacher,* Fall 1988, p. 223.

[2] R. John Brockmann, *Writing Better Computer User Documentation: From Paper to Hypertext, Version 2.0* (New York: John Wiley & Sons, 1990), p. 90.

[3] Brockmann, pp. 92–93.

12

Designing Online Documentation

"**A** writer has about 10 seconds on the Web to make her point, from the time the user first clicks the link," says online documentation specialist and technical writing instructor Freda Salatino. Online writing deals with the most impatient user of all: the computer user in search of an answer.

"Look very critically at the bells and whistles," warns Freda. "There are a lot of sexy effects that you can do, but if you're not subservient to the information and you're letting your ego get in the way of what the user is going to see, you're eating up their 10 seconds. Don't dare do that."

Freda is referring mainly to Web-based documentation, which has rapidly become a common medium for technical writers. Nonetheless, her advice applies to all online documentation. Writing for online users requires crisp, concise writing and the ability to place most needed information where the reader can grab it and run.

This chapter guides you through the concepts you will need to begin documenting technical products online. At the end of the chapter, you will find a "Glossary of Online Documentation Terms," which you can refer to if you see an italicized term you don't understand.

Now a simple definition: *Online documentation* is text and graphics displayed on a computer screen. Its purpose is to teach, guide, or inform the computer user about a product. For this discussion, online documentation includes online help, Web pages, *multimedia* tutorials, system messages, manuals *ported* from paper to online, and any other product-related communication that can be made to display online where product users will read it.

As a beginning technical writer you will probably write or update online documents that were designed by a senior writer or an engineer. These documents will most likely be one of the following types:

- Online Manuals
- Online Help

- Web sites
- Tutorials

Online manuals are often versions of paper manuals that are placed online because a product manager or marketing person decided the product needs online documentation to be competitive with everybody else's. Such documents are not well designed for electronic viewing and are often difficult to use. Nonetheless, they serve an important purpose—they provide the user with printable documentation. And the user bears the printing cost!

Online help usually is an integral part of a software product and allows the software users to "click Help" when they have a question about how to proceed. To write online help, you will use a help authoring tool, described in the section "Authoring Tools" later in this chapter.

The term *authoring* is used to describe designing online documents, because the term *writing* is too restrictive. For example, authoring Web pages requires visual design skills as much as, if not more than, writing skills. It also requires some skill in using the underlying *markup language,* such as HTML (Hypertext Markup Language). I know this might sound intimidating, but knowledge of basic HTML is actually quite easy to acquire. You can even find free HTML tutorials on the Web.*

Tutorials teach readers—or in this case, viewers—about a product. The most elaborate tutorials are multimedia, incorporating music, voice, and either video clips or animation. To write such tutorials, you will create a storyboard, showing the sequence of screens the user will see, much as if you were writing a television commercial. You will need to know about audio and video technologies to incorporate them without overloading or conflicting with your user's computer system.

Before discussing the elements of online documentation, let's look at a common example—an online library catalog.

A FAMILIAR EXAMPLE

Once upon a time, library catalogs were cumbersome things. They consisted of cards, stacked several feet thick, inhabiting huge wooden file cabinets. Now, almost all libraries offer some form of online catalog, which lends itself so perfectly to online search capabilities. Because these catalogs were among the first computer applications available to consumers, they have been designed to be simple and user-friendly. They demonstrate many of the basic elements of online documentation.

Whether you are computer sophisticated or not, you know how to use such a catalog to find information about a book. First your eyes scan the screen for directions on how to use the system. Then you choose from among simple commands that let you enter your data. Perhaps you begin

---

* Enter the words *HTML tutorial* in your favorite search engine and you'll get quite a list.

by typing the author's name or some words you remember from the title. To find information about a specific book, you might need to search in other ways. Here are some "online searches" you might perform regarding the book:

- You will probably type or select the exact title to locate the book.
- You will then type a command to display the book's status—is it available or checked out?
- If the book is checked out, you might search to find another library in the area that has the book.

The kinds of information the system displays are answers to the questions you have about the book. Each kind of information is connected to both the author's name and the book title, and each appears on a separate screen.

These screens are examples of displayable *information units* that can be connected to each other in any of a variety of patterns. As a user, however, you are unaware of these patterns. You see only the information in front of you.

The information you seek is layered. It begins with the simplest, most general information about the book and proceeds, with each command you give, to more detailed, specific information.

The way you seek the information is typical of an online-documentation user. You first scan the screen to orient yourself; then navigate through the information in a unique, nonlinear path.

If you were to help a user such as yourself to find what he is looking for, how would you begin? What are the building blocks you would use to get there?

ORGANIZING FOR USERS

The most important thing to know about your online readers is that they read online documentation for one reason only—to find an answer to a question. Knowing this will help you focus on your document purpose— to provide the answer.

In the library catalog example, the question was: "How can I get the book I want?" To find the answer, you navigated through successive screens of information.

Navigation is a term describing the way users move through online information. According to William Horton, "*Navigation* means jumping from topic to topic in a systematic, but free-form, quest for knowledge. . . . The user jumps to a topic and reads it, considers what has been learned, and jumps to another topic to read some more and jump again. Each jump takes the user closer to the answer to his or her question."[1]

Before designing online help systems, Linda Urban considers the following types of questions users might ask:

- How do I do something?
- What is this?
- Where's the command?
- Where do I start?
- What am I doing wrong?

If an online document is well designed, only one or two jumps will be necessary to bring the user to the answer she seeks.

If you have used online documentation in any form, you know the frustration of not finding what you are looking for, then realizing you don't remember where you started in the first place, nor how to return to those almost-answers you found along the way.

One of the difficulties in designing online documentation arises from the fact that the user's navigation path is unpredictable. Understanding how users access information online can help.

How Users Access Information Online

The first thing most users do online is scan the screen in front of them, visually searching for recognizable information. Once they are oriented to their visual environment, they will search for the answer to their question.

Searching can take many forms. Technically, the term *search* refers to the use of a *search engine,* a piece of software that helps the user find information in a database. However, in a more general sense, all online navigation is searching.

Users most commonly search for information in the following ways:

- Visually scanning, while viewing a single screen or paging through an online document
- Clicking *context-sensitive help* while using a piece of software
- Selecting a topic from an alphabetical list, such as an index or table of contents
- Selecting a topic from a document map or *site map* on the Web
- Clicking a *button* or *link*
- Typing a *query* or *keyword* in a search engine

Your user will try one or several of these ways either to move purposively toward an answer or to browse.

Browsing means exploring without a definite goal. Users browse online information when they are unsure of their question or of the type of answer sought.

Whether or not your user is certain of his goal, your goal as an online author is to make information accessible by clearly defining the path ahead.

Making Information Accessible

As stated in the chapter "Planning a Writing Project, on Paper and Online," the main principles for online organization are the same as for books—user orientation and recognizable structure. How do these principles guide the organization of online documentation?

As with paper documentation, user orientation means studying audience characteristics and giving them what they need. In *Standards for Online Communication,* authors JoAnn T. Hackos and Dawn M. Stevens advise: "To provide the right information in an easily accessible manner, you must take the time to understand thoroughly your users and their jobs."[2] This advice parallels the advice in the chapter "Know Your Audience," in which you learned to get acquainted with your audience's characteristics.

Hackos and Stevens suggest creating user *portfolios,* which describe members of your audience, and *scenarios,* "detailed descriptions of goal-directed activities that users perform as part of their job activities. A scenario might describe, for example, how users perform a routine task such as receiving deliveries at the company's loading dock. . . . At each point in the workflow, you learn how information at that point might support the tasks." By placing users from your portfolio into your scenario, you can begin to imagine their reactions and information needs.[3]

For online documentation, even more than for paper, put yourself in your users' places by using the document as they would. Anticipate their questions.

Once you have developed a software version of your online document, you can find representative members of your audience to test it. To ensure user orientation, nothing takes the place of user feedback!

The second organizational principle, recognizable structure, is often an illusion online because, unlike the linear order of a paper document, the structure of an online document is nonlinear and invisible to the user. In the section "Online Structures," later in this chapter, you will learn about this invisible realm.

Because the underlying structure of your online document is hidden, your user can become disoriented. You can help him in two important ways: by providing consistent functional and visual elements, and by offering navigation aids, such as a table of contents, to allow him to move comfortably in the online environment.

PROVIDE CONSISTENCY

Design functional elements, such as commands, to look and act the same way throughout online documentation. Have the user select them from similar-looking menus located in the same area of the screen, type them from the keyboard, or click on a consistently placed graphic or textual unit. For example, if the user is to click a command from a list on one screen, don't have him click a button to issue the same command later in the same documentation. Whatever way you choose, stay with it.

In discussing consistency for Web pages, the *Yale Manual for Web Design* advises: "Users need predictability and structure, with clear functional and graphic continuity between the various components and subsections of your Web site . . ."[4]

Whatever kind of online documentation you design, your consistent use of functional elements will allow the user to recognize the structure and to concentrate on his or her information goal rather than on the means to get there.

Similarly, make visual elements stylistically consistent. If you place boxed text on a blue background on one screen, give it a blue background throughout. Use blinking or moving text sparingly, if at all, and always to indicate the same kind of information. For example, a blinking message is sometimes used to signal the arrival of electronic mail. You would not notice that your mail had arrived, however, if the screen were dotted with blinking elements like a Christmas tree. You will learn more about screen design and the importance of consistency in the chapter "Planning for Visual Impact."

OFFER NAVIGATION AIDS

Navigation aids allow online users to find information efficiently. Just as you would provide a table of contents in a paper manual, you can give online users a contents list or list of links they can click to get to a topic. Similarly, you can provide a more detailed list of topics in the form of an index, commonly used in online manuals and help, or a site map on the Web.

Another way to enable users to navigate your document is to show a set of keys with labels indicating what will happen if you press them. For example, a typical online library catalog, described earlier, shows keys on every screen that allow the user to move **Forward, Back,** or to **Start over.** Well-designed Web sites often give users links that perform similar functions, such as **Next, Back, Top,** and **Home.**

An additional navigational aid, *bookmarking,* lets the user electronically "mark" a place in an online document, so that he or she can leave the document and return later to the same place. The familiar analogy of a bookmark is quite apt.

Context sensitivity is a kind of navigation aid used in online help documentation. In this case, the software navigates for the user: When she clicks a Help button, the software "knows" where the user is in the program and displays information related to the action she is trying to perform. For example, if she clicks a Help button in a dialogue box, a window opens to display detailed information about the options in the dialogue box and may provide cross references (via links) to task-related topics.

As a user, I've frequently been annoyed with context-sensitive help that incorrectly guesses what I'm trying to do or that gives superficial or insufficient information and does not provide a way for me to get the answer to my real question.

Context-sensitive help is tricky to write because you have to antici-pate the user's questions when you don't know what action came before, nor why the user has requested help. The book *Online Help: Design and Evaluation,* by Thomas M. Duffy et al., describes the problem help devel-opers face:

> If we naively assume that users want to know about the current tool when they choose help, we'll often be wrong. Often users are in the mid-dle of a larger task and have just finished adding text. They may want to know about their next goal. . . . If the system guesses incorrectly, it will frustrate users, not help them.[5]

If you write context-sensitive help, first spend as much time as possi-ble using the product. Your intimate knowledge of its problems and fea-tures will allow you to help the user experience success.

ELEMENTS OF ONLINE DOCUMENTATION

Online documentation consists of displayed information units and the links among them. Behind the scenes, these displayable units are software files that the computer opens within an area of the screen. *Hyperlinks* (or *links*— the terms are interchangeable) connect units of information in meaningful relationships, helping users move toward the answers they seek.

Information Units

Information units are simply pieces of information that can be packaged for easy online consumption. They can be text, graphics, audio or video clips, hyperlinks, or *hypermedia.* The online author's palette contains a dizzying array of colors! Fortunately, most technical documentation online comprises text, graphics, and links. So as a beginning tech writer, you will be well armed if you understand how these basic elements are used.

Writing as simply and concisely as possible is critical in any technical documentation, but it is doubly important online. Studies have shown that users read about 25 percent slower online than on paper.[6] Therefore, online writers divide information into *chunks* that are as small and self-contained as possible. Dividing information into such units is called *chunking*—a buzzword that will take you far.

To be self-contained, each chunk should describe only one topic and should provide enough information to be useful to the user.

"If good online documentation is a question-answering machine, then *topics* are the answers to the user's questions," says William Horton, who uses the word *topic* to mean a chunk of text.

> The best way to ensure coherence in a topic is to first write out the sin-gle question the topic is to answer. Then judge every aspect of the design and writing of the topic by whether it helps answer the question.[7]

Says Linda Urban about online help topics:

> One topic might be as small as a definition of a term. But it might also be a task—numbered steps for how to accomplish something. Or, it could be a high-level summary of a large task, with links to additional topics that contain step-by-step instructions. Or, it might be a conceptual topic, that introduces an idea or a process.

Graphic images are another kind of information unit you will incorporate in online documentation. Many of these are similar to the images used in manuals and are described in the chapter "Planning for Visual Impact." In addition, online you will include graphic images that represent commands (for example, buttons) and links.

One of the truly exciting features of online documentation is that any information unit can serve as a link to other information.

Links

A link (also called a hyperlink) appears as a clickable graphic element or section of text. When the user clicks the link, new information displays on the screen. A graphic or animated link is called *hypermedia*. If the clickable element is text, it's called *hypertext*.

Links connect information online just as transitional phrases connect information on paper. Therefore, links need to establish logical relationships between the information units they connect. For example, you might write a general help topic telling your user how to send a document to a printer and include a link labeled "advanced options," which more experienced users can click to find out how to change printer settings.

William Horton suggests the following kinds of topic links:

- Prerequisites
- Background theory
- More detailed procedures
- Exceptions
- Subsequent actions
- Definitions
- Interesting digressions[8]

Links can be very disorienting if online authors place them willy-nilly, without first organizing the online document. Just as an outline provides the structure upon which paper manuals are written, a map of an online document provides the flow of topics, which can then be filled in.

ONLINE STRUCTURES

Organizing an online document helps the writer as much as the reader. Even if the reader won't see the structure of your information, creating it will help clarify your ideas and establish relationships among them. When you begin to write, you will know where each topic fits.

Additionally, your written structure, or map, allows reviewers to give you feedback before you begin. In other words, structuring an online document is just as important as outlining a paper one, and for the same reasons.

Your map can be much more complex than the linear outline of a paper document because links provide an added dimension. Links that connect to increasing levels of detail allow topics to be layered. This layering is similar to the levels in an outline: The top layer contains the main topic, and users can choose to explore in greater depth by clicking links to more detailed or advanced information.

Your map might look like an organizational chart, a flowchart, a table with columns and rows, or a loop that allows users to move through topics and finish where they began. The possible combinations are virtually infinite because links let you connect any information unit to any and all other units in your document.

The important thing to remember about online structures is to design one that will provide the clearest, most direct access to the information your user most needs.

For more details about online structures, refer to the titles listed under "Writing Online" in the bibliography.

AUTHORING TOOLS

"If you're lucky," says Freda Salatino, "you get to use any tool that you master for a couple of years before the next great thing comes out." This is why Freda concentrates on teaching writing skills, rather than software tools, in her online-writing classes. Nonetheless, online writers need to understand their authoring tools, particularly if they are responsible for designing a new document or for creating links from a product to a document.

Linda Urban explains that help authoring tools are still developing. "There are things you may want to do in online help that you have to learn to do [without the tool]. You are more likely to have to get under the hood and look at the code."

An online authoring tool, like a word-processing program, lets you write online documents without having to use the markup language or "code" that actually shapes what appears on the screen. Unfortunately, online authoring tools don't always do what you want them to do, and as stated earlier in this chapter, you will need to understand the underlying markup language as well.

HTML has been the standard markup language used to create Web-based documents, which need to be viewed on different kinds of computer operating systems through different Internet browsers. Newer markup languages, such as XML, offer more flexibility than HTML and may soon become the preferred online authoring language. Such languages and tools are changing as rapidly as other technologies, and as an author of online documents you may need to work overtime to keep up with the changes!

SUMMING IT UP

This chapter gave you the online documentation concepts you will need to begin your journey into *cyberspace, hyperspace,* and beyond. You learned that, despite the glitz of new technologies, good writing is good writing. Online, your purpose and audience still guide your work, and clear organization is as important as it is on paper.

The next chapter describes the visual elements you'll need to control as part of the documentation process.

GLOSSARY OF ONLINE DOCUMENTATION TERMS

authoring tools	Computer programs used to write and format information for online viewing.
bookmark	An electronic place marker.
button	A clickable graphic image containing a command or link.
chunking	Providing information in small, easily absorbed units.
context sensitive help	A help system that displays information about options in the window or dialogue box the user is currently viewing.
cyberspace	All the interconnected information resources available through the Internet, or World Wide Web.
hyperlink	See *link.*
hypermedia	Any graphic element, animated or stationary, that serves as a link to new information.
hyperspace	The connections that form *cyberspace.*
hypertext	Text that functions as a link to new information.
information units	Displayable pieces of information, such as graphic elements or chunks of text.
keyword	Search word associated with online information. When users type a keyword in a *search engine* that is programmed to do keyword searches, the search engine looks for the matching information in its database.
layering	Organizing linked information units so that each link leads to greater detail, more advanced

	concepts, or information that doesn't need to be as accessible as the preceding layer.
link	A graphic image or section of text that, when clicked, displays new information.
markup language	Formatting commands, embedded in text, that tell a Web browser what the text should look like (how to display it) on the user's screen.
multimedia	Online communications expressed in sound, animation, and video images.
navigation path	The sequence of *links* a user chooses to move through *information units* displayed online.
porting	Moving print material from a paper medium to an online medium, including adding markup language and adjusting visual elements for online viewing and printing.
query	Words a user types, in either a help index or a *search engine* field, to describe a question she wants answered.
search engine	A piece of software that can look through sometimes massive amounts of information in a database to find information the user wants.
site map	A map, diagram, or list showing the arrangement of topics on a Web site.

---

[1] William Horton, *Designing and Writing Online Documentation*, 2d. ed. (New York: John Wiley & Sons, 1994), pp. 71–72.

[2] JoAnn T. Hackos and Dawn M. Stevens, "Chapter 2. Learning About Your User's Information Needs," *Standards for Online Communication*, the CD (New York: John Wiley & Sons, 1997).

[3] Hackos and Stevens, "Creating use scenarios."

[4] *Yale Manual for Web Design* at http://info.med.yale.edu/caim/manual-1.html

[5] Thomas M. Duffy et al., *Online Help: Design and Evaluation* (Norwood, N.J.: Ablex Publishing, 1992), p. 119.

[6] Reid Goldsborough, "Words for the Wise: Writing for the Web," *TechWeek*, July 12, 1999, p. 21.

[7] Horton, pp. 99 and 104.

[8] Horton, p. 108.

13
Planning for Visual Impact

"I think there's a problem that writers tend to have," says writing consultant Daunna Minnich. She explains:

> The reason people get into technical writing and stay in it is because they're logical, analytical people who are able to work with logical, analytical programmer types or technical types. And so all these people have a real strong left brain, which is the logical, analytical part. But to be a good communicator—to be a good teacher—you need to appeal to more than just those logical abilities of people. So that's where it becomes important to try to find more than one way to get at an idea. This is where you get into the right brain, which is the part that perceives things spatially and is into music and art.

The visual impact of your document is as important as the text. Yet often writers are not attuned to the elements of good page or screen design and do not know how to visualize concepts very well. This is not surprising, as most writers have not been trained to think visually. Additionally, the visual elements of pages and screens are very complex. Historically, they were handled by a professional designer.

Because design and illustration have their own languages, some of the terms used in this chapter will be unfamiliar. If you see an italicized word you don't understand, refer to the "Glossary of Design Terms" at the end of this chapter.

WRITERS AS DESIGNERS

Today, writers are often responsible for the appearance of their documents, both on paper and online. In fact, one study revealed that writers are responsible for the design of online menus 88 percent of the time and for the display of documentation on the screen 78 percent of the time.[1]

Since the 1980s, desktop publishing software has allowed writers to design the appearance of their own manuals. Most companies have found it convenient to let writers do so. Typesetting can be an expensive and time-consuming process, and some companies believe there's no longer any reason to use it when the technical writer can supply the finished, camera-ready copy. While this is true, it skips an important step.

For typesetting, a manuscript first goes to a book designer who "specs the type"—describes the kinds of type and spacing that will be used for each kind of heading and text. The book designer has an eye for the subtle differences between *typefaces* and is sensitive to the impact a very small shift in spacing can have on readability.

When a professional designer is not involved, document pages—and screens—often look "MacTacky," as a colleague put it. When I asked what he meant, he said, "You know. They look like a ransom note."

What my acquaintance meant is that an inexperienced person can throw in too many different visual elements, just because the tool can provide them. The result looks amateur at best.

Now online authors can also employ color, animation, and even sound in ways that can confuse the user and reflect poorly on the source of the document. Therefore, unless you have a design background, make use of professionally designed document and screen templates and use professional designers and graphic artists whenever you can.

If you must design any aspect of a document, the absolute overriding principles to follow are these: simplicity and consistency!

Using visual elements with controlled consistency helps orient your reader, particularly online, as the authors of *Online Help: Design and Evaluation* advise:

> The reader's eye scans the page first as a purely graphic pattern, then begins to track and decode type and page elements. Settle on as few heading styles and subtitles as are necessary to organize your content, then use your chosen style consistently.[2]

Now I'm going to seem to contradict myself. Within the bounds of good taste (which this chapter attempts to clarify), use as many visual elements as will enliven the page and make it interesting to the reader. You will vary the look of your document with a controlled set of visual elements:

Typographical elements include:
- headings
- text
- labels on art
- typographical emphasis to distinguish certain words

White space includes:
- margins
- indents
- the space between text elements and between art and text
- the space in illustrations

Art is almost anything that's not text and for our purposes includes:

- charts
- graphs
- tables
- pictures of screens
- photographs
- professionally drawn illustrations

Each of these elements is controlled by rules, which I'll call the document's *format*. A document format is sometimes called a template, style sheet, or design specification. They all essentially mean the same thing. Your format ensures consistency by providing a framework upon which to make future design decisions.

Format dictates the kinds of type you'll use; the amount of white space between elements; whether art is boxed or floating, *line art* or *halftone;* and so on.

Now that we are so often responsible for the visual appearance of our documents, we writers have got to hunker down and learn as much as we can about the visual elements. In fact, the visual part is a lot of fun.

AUDIENCE AND PURPOSE

In making visual decisions about your document, first consider its audience and purpose. The reading level of the audience and their patience with the material affect the size of type and the number and kind of illustrations you'll use. For example, an engineer is accustomed to poring over long gray blocks of text in relatively small type. While you can make his or her job easier by providing smaller paragraphs and clear, well-designed headings, you will probably provide a much more visually inviting page to the airplane mechanic, described in the chapter "Know Your Audience," who is covered with grease, working in the rain.

Says a graphic artist who illustrates repair guides for field engineers:

> More and more, I'm doing the art first, and some of the writers will take that piece of art and decide how to pare down the text. What they want to do is put as little text in as possible and only where it's appropriate—especially in our manuals for field engineers who really like to get right to the point, to the purpose of the document. In a lot of cases, I've heard they even skip the text where they can and just go right to the illustrations. If they can get their info right away without having to read several lines, they'll do it.

PAGE AND SCREEN DESIGN

The impact of a page or screen depends upon many things. Distinctions between levels of headings can be clarifying or confusing. The kind of type you use can give a clean or fussy look. The length of your paragraphs can invite or repel the reader.

Ultimately, if you know how to control the visual elements, a page or screen will look professional, creating a positive impression of your document, the product, and your company. This is why large companies develop corporate design formats for their books, online documentation, and Web sites. Companies like Xerox Corporation and Apple Computer go to great lengths to make their documents visually consistent. They're not trying to be dictatorial; they're trying to create a polished corporate "look" that readers will recognize and trust.

If you work for a small-to-medium-sized company, management might not have a clue about what goes into a document's design. It's up to you to package your writing as beautifully as your tools will allow or to contribute to your department's formatting decisions. The principles described in the following sections can help you.

White Space

"White space is the space that is used but not printed," says Daunna Minnich.

> It's like when you speak, there's a lot of nonverbal communication. White space is the nonverbal part of communication in writing. It's the part that gives your eye and your mind some breathing space—some space to kind of invite you a little closer.

Leading, indents, and margins make up the bulk of white space on both the page and the screen. The rest is provided by tables, charts, diagrams, and illustrations. Lists use more white space than regular text and thus invite the eye.

Studies have shown that if at least a third of the page is white space, text is easier to read.

Even more white space is required for online documentation, where text appears to fill more space than on the page. Because users read about 25 percent slower online than on paper, more white space helps them take in text more quickly. However, the small display areas on a screen don't allow for wasted space; clearly grouped chunks of text contribute as much to readability as the white space between them.

LEADING

The leading, or space between lines, will vary with the typeface you use. Larger fonts appear to need proportionally less leading than smaller ones. Line length also affects leading. Research has shown that readability decreases as line length increases. You can compensate for this by increasing the leading between longer lines.

Experiment with different amounts of leading between lines of text on paper. For example, put five short paragraphs on the same page, beginning with no leading and progressing to 4 *points* leading. Ask yourself if the lines appear too crammed together or too spacy. There'll be one paragraph for which the leading and type appear most balanced—somewhere between 1 and 4 points of leading for 9- to 12-point type. But this will vary with the style of type, so use your eye.

You can apply this same learning process online, both by experimenting and by observing the spacing on others' online documentation. By becoming sensitive to the readability and visual accessibility of screens, you can design more effective visual elements in your own screen layouts.

Use extra leading before and after headings and paragraphs, to set them apart. Again this will vary with your font and the effect you're trying to achieve. Start by using twice the amount of leading between paragraphs as you've used between lines. Again, print out variations a point or two apart and let your eye be the judge.

Headings should appear to belong to the material they introduce. Use about the same amount of leading before and after headings as between paragraphs, then adjust it so there's a little less space after the heading. That will separate the heading from the preceding material and lead your eye on to the next.

MARGINS AND INDENTS

Margins can add white space to any format. Many technical manuals and commercial books now use an extra-wide left or outer margin to decrease line length and invite the eye. Major headings are placed on a *hanging indent,* which extends into the margin, so they are clearly visible for fast skimming.

Text can be either *right justified* or *ragged right,* giving the page a very different look. Right-justified text lines up evenly at the right margin. Ragged right extends irregularly at the margin, giving the text a profile that helps readers recognize their place on the page. This makes ragged right easier to read than right-justified text.

You will indent the entire left margin of some visual elements, so that additional white space frames them. Lists, notes, cautions, and art are good candidates for additional indenting. But be consistent. Says one technical illustrator:

Writers need to align stuff. If they have a box, they need to align a margin with it. For example, when you're laying out a design for anything, you may decide you'll have only three indents. Then everything will align with one of those three. It just gives a tighter, cleaner look. Then the eye knows where to look. Particularly in a technical manual, you want the reader to turn the page and not be surprised about the location of something. After a few pages, the eye wants to see something in the same spot on the page.

This idea of consistent placement is particularly important online, where users try to navigate efficiently through your document. They depend on functional elements, like buttons and links, appearing in the same place on each screen, so they can use them to quickly find the information they need.

ART SPACING

Art placed within text needs space around it. The density of the art will make a difference in how much; if the art is very dark or detailed, it will require more space. Art itself can add a lot of white space to a page or screen. If the kind of art you're using is light, place a box around it and use less space between the art and the text than you would for darker art. However, do not vary art spacing within a document. Once you decide on how much space to use between art and text, keep the same increments throughout. The density of the art should not vary either, but should have a consistent look, so the same spacing will work throughout.

Figure and table captions should stay closer to the art they describe than to preceding or following text. A very small amount of space is appropriate between art and caption.

LISTS

Lists are a good tool for both visual and cognitive purposes. Short list items add sparkle to the page or screen by providing extra white space and the staccato of bullets or numerals. Lists are usually formatted with a hanging indent, which provides additional white space and breaks the left margin in a regular pattern. They invite reading.

Lists also organize material in bite-sized chunks the reader can rapidly grasp. They're the fast food of formatting. Therefore, when you mention more than two or three related items, try formatting them as a list.

Typefaces and Fonts

Today writers can choose from a vast range of contrasting typefaces. "At first, explore these extremes," advise authors Jonathan Price and Carlene Schnabel in *Desktop Publishing*. "Later, you'll be able to find a quieter combination of typefaces and layout that gives your document a solid look of unity. As the poet [William] Blake pointed out, the road to the Palace of Wisdom leads through excess."[3]

When I wrote the predecessor to this book in 1991, I reported that I could choose from 19 different typefaces on my computer system, most of which came in several sizes, bold face, and italics. Today, I counted 130 typefaces available on my system! To produce the manuscript for this book, however, I used only two typefaces and three font sizes for different headings. Even when I provide camera-ready copy to a client, I use only two or three typefaces. Again, simplicity and consistency are the guiding principles.

Select one typeface for your headings, another for your text, and stick to them. Distinguish between heading levels through alignment and typographical emphasis, such as font size or capitalization. For example, you can align your level-one headings on a hanging indent and your level-two headings flush left on the text margin. Then you can differentiate, say, between level-two and level-three headings either by varying font size (for example, 12-point, then 10-point type) or capitalization (ALL CAPS, then cap/lowercase style). Do not be tempted to use too many of these forms of emphasis or you will wind up with a page that looks like a ransom note. Select either regular type or **bold** type for your headings, not both. These are general guidelines you're welcome to break, because there will always be exceptions to rules that govern aesthetic decisions.

Type comes in two basic styles: *serif* and *sans serif*. Serif type has small extensions at the ends of letters, whereas sans serif letters have straight, simple lines. Studies have shown that serif type is slightly more readable, and I tend to favor it. But you can compensate for slower readability by using more leading with sans serif type, which some think has a more modern look and which readers tend to prefer online.

Within these type styles, readability and effect vary. Some serif styles can be very ornate and are inappropriate in technical manuals where nothing should distract from the communication goal of the document. Other serif fonts, like Times Roman and Garamond, are highly legible, reproduce well, and do not distract from the document's message.

Sans serif type provides a good contrast in headings, setting them apart from the body text, as this book demonstrates. Sans serif is also more legible than serif type in very small font sizes for which serifs tend to blur. Use sans serif *callouts* in illustrations, where tight spacing limits the size and amount of type.

Typographical Emphasis

Within text, you'll use typographical emphasis to distinguish certain words from regular text. Typographical emphasis includes italics, boldface, uppercase letters, and any combination of them. Below are some reasons you might use typographical emphasis:

- to emphasize a point ("Do *not* touch the wire leading from the battery . . .")
- to indicate a book title
- to distinguish a term you are about to define
- to indicate an example
- to indicate a computer command the reader will type

- to set apart error and system messages a computer might display
- to indicate a hyperlink online

Use typographical emphasis sparingly. Rarely use it to emphasize a point. If your point is important to the reader, set it apart as a note:

NOTE

Only tapes recorded in Hi-Fi stereo will play back with true stereo sound. Standard stereo tapes will play back in monaural sound.

If your point could avoid damage to the product, set it apart as a caution:

CAUTION

When using "nut type" RF coaxial cables, tighten with fingers only. Overtightening may damage terminals.

If your point could prevent physical harm to the reader, set it apart as a warning:

WARNING

Do not touch the wire leading from the battery to the main board. You can receive a severe electrical shock.

Be consistent. For example, use italics for all new terms; do not switch to bold in a different chapter. Avoid using all capital letters, particularly online. They grab attention and should be saved for the times you want to grab attention—such as a warning. Online, capital letters are interpreted as "shouting."

If you have the budget, discreet use of a second color in a manual can be very appealing to readers. For example, text to be typed into or displayed by a computer is central to your reader's task and justifies special treatment. If you use a second color, be particularly conservative with other visual elements. For example, use color instead of, not in addition to, a third typeface.

TABLES, CHARTS, AND GRAPHS

Tables, charts, and graphs are art that lie well within the writer's domain. Lists of related data can be formatted into tables. The progression of milestones in a schedule can be expressed in a flowchart. Percentages of a whole can be presented in a pie chart. Most relationships between two variables can and should be expressed in a graph.

As you write, repeatedly question whether your material can be better expressed in a table, chart, or graph. When a visual representation can convey meaning more economically than words, use it.

ILLUSTRATIONS

Illustrations can consist of only lines or a full range of shading or color, and online, they can include animation. They can be used to realistically describe a tangible product or abstractly represent relationships—for example, between biochemical agents or computer software products.

An artist creates illustrations by using pen and ink, or more commonly, a computer graphics program. You or an artist also can take existing ink drawings or photographs and use a *scanner* to convert them into digitized art.

Illustrations can be used simply to entertain the reader by offering a pleasant visual change from text. Technical illustrations, however, serve a more practical purpose: They communicate technical information. In this role, they supplement text or replace it completely.

If you think about how much time it would take you to verbally describe the location of every screw on a complex piece of machinery, you'll run to your nearest technical illustrator.

Communicating with Artists

Artists can help you generate visual ideas. Approach them at the beginning of your project with a description of the document, the product, and the kinds of illustrations you think might help. A staff artist keeps a library of published illustrations. Often you'll be able to select some drawings from past documents, which can be modified or used "as is" to illustrate your document. You'll provide the artist with a product specification and access to the actual product, so that he or she can modify old drawings or create new ones to show the most current version of the product.

Hardware products are easier to illustrate than less tangible products. For example, the behavior of products like biochemicals or computer software require more imagination for you to conceptualize visually.

Says one artist:

I know so little about software that usually I get a sketch from the writer. They'll try to explain the principle of a sketch, and I'll come up with some ideas, as primitive as they may be, and then we start building from there. And the writer might say, no we can't do that, and then I'll come up with something else. It's like stepping stones—you go back and forth exchanging ideas. With the writer's greater understanding of the product and my understanding of how to present things visually, we usually work something out.

When you are documenting a less tangible product, try to sketch the relationships among parts of the product. For example, a computer network comprises different kinds of computers that communicate across different kinds of communication connections called links. An illustration of a typical network might show microcomputers, mainframe computers, and terminals interconnected with lines representing cables and a cloud representing a conglomerate of all long-distance links. To communicate these complex relationships to an artist, you'll supply a sketch, however crude.

In addition to understanding the art you'll need, the artist might have to schedule your project along with many other writers' projects. Some of these will be higher priority than yours for marketing reasons. A "hot" product goes to the top of the pile. So while you're nervously waiting for the art to get into your document by your deadline, another writer may be breathing down the artist's neck. (Poor artist!)

The best solution is to present the artist with a list of what you need early in the document schedule—as soon as you understand the product well enough to talk about it—then to meet with the artist to jointly plan what needs to be done. At that point, the artist might ask to see certain equipment or blueprints you may not have provided or ask you to sketch something.

Planning Art

The following tips will help you plan the art for a paper document.

TIPS ON PLANNING ART

---

1. Read through your document outline and generate as many art ideas as you can.
2. Make up figure titles for the ideas and number them consecutively by chapter (for example, Figure 2–7 is the seventh figure in chapter 2).
3. Write your figure numbers and titles in two places: on a copy of your outline at the place where the figure will appear and on a separate figures list.
4. Look through related documents for illustrations you may be able to use, either as is or with modifications.
5. On your figures list, write the source document's title and the page or figure number, so the artist will know where to look for the existing illustration. If the staff artist is really on top of things, the illustration might have a serial number you can use.

6. Obtain blueprints or specifications for any piece of equipment the artist will need to draw.

7. Arrange for you and the artist to look at the piece of equipment as soon as a prototype is available.

8. If you want to illustrate an abstract concept, sketch first and go over your sketch with the engineer. Make sure your sketch is technically accurate before presenting it to the artist.

9. Give a copy of the figures list, specifications, your sketch, and any other information you've collected to the artist. Keep copies for yourself.

10. Make an appointment to discuss your document's visual and scheduling needs with the artist.

11. When you meet with the artist:
    - Ask any questions you may have about how best to illustrate concepts.
    - Discuss style issues: if the pictures will be boxed or left open, line drawn or shaded. These style issues can affect your page design.
    - List any information or material you'll need to get for the artist.
    - Find out how the artist will supply the art. Will he or she give you computer art you'll insert in the document, or will the artist paste the art into your document? If the artist pastes the art in, how? By hand or computer? If the artist will insert art into your computer file from a graphics program, he or she will need both an online and a *hard* (paper) copy of the finished document.
    - Discuss how much space to leave for each piece of art.
    - Discuss scheduling considerations: Agree upon the deadline when you'll give the finished document to the artist for pasteup and the deadline when the document is returned to you with the art pasted in.

12. Follow up on obtaining materials and information and on meeting your end of scheduling agreements.

Working with experienced graphic artists can be one of the most rewarding parts of your job, as their contributions will greatly enhance your work.

SUMMING IT UP

In this chapter, you learned about the visual aspects of page and screen design and learned ways to work with a technical illustrator. In the next chapter, you'll explore the golden rules of expository writing and discover clear, concise ways to lead your reader through technical information.

GLOSSARY OF DESIGN TERMS

alignment	Lining up visual objects, like a paragraph and a piece of art, so that they both share the same margin.
bold	Type that is darkened for emphasis.
callouts	Labels describing parts of an illustration.
flush	Lined up against a margin. For example, a piece of art that is *flush left* butts against the left margin of the column.
font	A *typeface* family member with specific properties. For example, a 12-point Times Roman bold font is a member of the Times Roman typeface family. *Font* is sometimes used synonymously with *typeface*.
format	The page design, specifying type fonts, spacing, figures style, and so on.
gutter	The inside edge of the page, which disappears into the binding.
halftone	Shading produced by overlaying a screen of dots on a drawing or photograph.
hanging indent	A reverse *indent* that extends into a margin. The placement of the first line of a paragraph so that it runs into the margin of the page and the rest of the paragraph is indented. This list is an example.
indent	The amount of space text is set in from a margin.
justified	Text lined up at a margin. Almost all text is left justified, and can be either right justified or ragged right.
leading	The space between lines. The word dates back to the time when typesetters used lead bars to separate lines of type.
line art	An illustration drawn with lines, but without shading.
points	The increment typesetters use to measure type and spacing. There are 72 points in an inch.
ragged right	Text that is not right justified contains differing line lengths, which create a ragged effect at the right margin of the page.
rule	A line, usually drawn across a page or column width.
running feet	A line of text, placed at the bottom of a page, usually consisting of a book, chapter, or section title and a page number.
running heads	A line of text, placed at the top of a page, usually consisting of a book, chapter, or section title and a page number.

sans serif type	A plain-type style, with no small extensions at the top or bottom of letters.
scanned art	Art produced by running an illustration or photograph through a *scanner*. A scanner *digitizes* the art, turning it into a file that can be read by a computer. Scanned art is *machine readable*.
serif type	A style of type in which letters have small extensions at the top and bottom. Newspaper type is a common example.
typeface	A family of type designed to look alike, composed of several-sized fonts, which include punctuation marks, special characters (like parentheses), and numbers, as well as boldface and italics.

---

[1] Duffy, Thomas M. et al., *Online Help: Design and Evaluation* (Norwood, N.J.: Ablex Publishing, 1992), p. 36.

[2] *Yale Manual for Web Design* at http://info.med.yale.edu/caim/manual-1.html

[3] Jonathan Price and Carlene Schnabel, *Desktop Publishing* (New York: Ballantine Books, 1987), pp. 2–15.

14

Writing Is the Heart of Your Craft

They're fancy talkers about themselves, writers. If I had to give young writers advice, I would say don't listen to writers talking about writing or themselves.

—Lillian Hellman, *The New York Times,* February 21, 1960

What is good writing? Good writing accomplishes a purpose. It does so economically and without apparent strain.

This chapter provides practical writing guidelines and explores some of the less tangible aspects of writing—developing style, finding your own rhythm within the writing process, and getting through writer's block.

If your background is more technical than literary, refer to the writing books listed in the bibliography for additional guidance. Writing, after all, is too great a subject to be taught in a single chapter.

WRITING GUIDELINES

The rules of good expository writing prescribe simplicity, directness, and precision. You can apply them to any manual, journal article, training script, or for that matter, any nonfiction book.

This section describes writing guidelines as they apply to technical writing. You can use the checklist at the end of this section to review these guidelines while you write.

Choose Short over Long

Favor short, simple words over long, pretentious ones. Engineers and scientists tend to reverse this rule. A common example in technical writing is overuse of the noun *usage,* where the noun *use* can serve. Another is the verb *utilize* in place of the cleaner, simpler verb *use.*

If you can substitute one word for two, do. An example from business writing also corrupts technical writing: the use of *prior to,* when *before* works just as well. Other evils include *in order to, as of now,* and their ilk. *In order to* can almost always become *to,* and *as of now* is simply *now.*

Weed out unnecessary words by asking whether each word does a job. You'll soon learn to recognize suspicious words, like *very* and *particularly*—adjectives that rarely add to your meaning: The *particularly unusual event* is not much different from the *unusual event.*

In technical writing, short applies to sentences and paragraphs, as well. "Let us not fear lest we be too brief," advised turn-of-the-century tech writer Sir T. Clifford Allbutt. "If the matter be meagre padding will not amend it."[1] Confine your sentences to a single thought. This will keep them short and clear. Below is an example of a long sentence that has been rewritten as two shorter ones:

One long: As in the larger network, there is still a problem of inter-ference by other traffic in the network, which may slow the flow in a particular path, or even stop it momentarily.

Two short: As in the larger network, interference from other network traffic still creates a problem. This interference can slow, or even momentarily stop, the flow through a particular path.

Short paragraphs invite reading. Presenting closely related material in short paragraphs is called *chunking* (a term discussed earlier in this book in relation to online writing). Technical writing research indicates that readers absorb material more readily in chunks, rather than through lengthy, ongoing discourse. As with single-thought sentences, construct paragraphs that center tightly on a single purpose.

Choose Active over Passive

The simplest way to judge whether a sentence is active or passive is to ask the question, "Is the subject of the sentence acting or being acted upon by the verb?" In an active voice sentence, the subject of the sentence is per-forming the action. In a passive voice sentence, the subject is being acted upon by the verb.

Passive: When text is created with word-processing software, problems are caused by formatting commands such that machine translation is adversely affected.

Here's the sentence rewritten in active voice:

Active: When you use word-processing software to create text, the software embeds formatting commands that adversely affect machine translation.

The active sentence provides more specific information and interest than the passive version. Often passive voice sentences omit the active agent, leaving the user confused about who or what is performing the action. In the following passive voice sentence, who defines the break character?

Passive: A break character is defined only if the initiating host cannot generate a break signal.

Active: You define a break character only if the initiating host cannot generate a break signal.

Once you know the identity of the active agent, converting passive to active voice is simple.

Passive voice serves best in sentences that stress the verb or object, like the following:

> Serious damage to the system can result if the wires are not connected in the correct sequence.

In this case, the sentence rightfully directs the reader's attention to *serious damage* and *wires,* not to the system or the person connecting the wires.

Favor active voice; then use passive voice consciously, to emphasize the verb or object.

Choose Specific over General

General words leave readers confused. Specific words tell the reader exactly what's going on. Choose specific, precise words over general, vague ones. Here's an example:

General: If you don't type anything for an interval specified in the software, the system times out.

Specific: If you don't type anything for ten seconds, the terminal emulator program automatically logs off the host, and you must begin a new session.

The first sentence leaves the reader wondering: How long can I stop typing? What software? What does "time out" mean? What do I do if it happens? The second sentence provides concrete information the reader can understand and use immediately.

Avoid Redundancy

Redundancy means unnecessary repetition. If you find yourself repeating instructions, definitions, descriptions, and illustrations, it probably means your document is not well organized. Ask yourself if you can reorder the material so the reader doesn't need to read the same information twice. Are you repeating it to emphasize a point? If so, try to repeat the information in a different form, with a chart or table, instead of repeating text.

The exception to this rule occurs when you must address completely separate audiences in a single document. By completely, I mean each audience stays within one section and never refers to other sections of the document.

I was stuck with seven different audiences when I wrote one reference manual. Each audience had purchased one of seven different terminal emulators, but the manufacturer wanted to ship the same manual with all of them. Because each audience would read only the section of the manual for the product it purchased, I made each chapter into a self-contained submanual and repeated many definitions, descriptions, and procedures seven times. I racked my brain to avoid this redundancy. For example, I tried to organize one big manual with tables that summarized product differences. But the result would have been more difficult for the reader to use.

Just as you would avoid repeating explanations and illustrations, avoid redundancy with individual words. Beware of words that mean the same thing, like the ones in the left column below. Choose one word and trust it to do its job:

Redundant	*Improved*
assembled together	together
unrequired options	options
necessary requirements	requirements

Address the Reader

Historically, technical and scientific documents have been written in the third person, and some companies still insist their documents remain in this style. Third person refers to the reader as "the reader"; second person refers to the reader as "you." Third person sounds more formal and professional to some ears than the friendlier second person. But the drawbacks of third person far exceed its surface dignity.

In instructions, third person is unbearably tedious, as the following example illustrates. The imperative, in which "you" is implied, serves more effectively:

Third person: The user then sets the switch by soldering wires 3 and 4.
Imperative: To set the switch, solder wires 3 and 4.

Addressing the reader directly, in second person or the imperative, enlivens your style. You'll write shorter, more active sentences and involve the reader in the action. Make sure, though, that you're clear about who your reader is. If your audience is programmers and you need to talk to them about the users of a computer program, then address the programmers as "you" and refer to the user as "the user"—third person.

Define Terms and Acronyms

In the chapter "Know Your Subject," you learned to list technical terms and acronyms, so that by the time you begin writing, you've researched their definitions.

Define technical terms and acronyms the first time you use them in your draft. If you use them often, the reader will remember what they mean.

If you define a term and then use it infrequently, you may need to redefine it with each use. This is particularly true if you're introducing the reader to a lot of new terminology.

One way to avoid cluttering your document with definitions is to include them all in a glossary, then tell readers to look there.

Eliminate Jargon

Jargon is the slang of a trade. Some jargon from technology has worked its way into everyday English. For example, how many times have you asked for *feedback* or requested *input* from friends or coworkers? After working in a technical field for a while, writers grow insensitive to its jargon. The more experienced they become, the more writers have to fight against jargon creeping into their work.

In most cases, jargon should not be defined—it should be eliminated. It is language that has developed out of laziness, convenience, or a desire to impress. A more meaningful expression can almost always be found. Play it safe—write English:

Jargon: Power up or reset the workstation.
English: Turn on the workstation or, if it's already on, press the reset button on its back panel.

Use Present Tense

In most technical documentation, use present tense verbs, even where you'd normally vary the tense. This convention seems awkward at first, but it's house style for most companies, and readers have come to expect it. The following example illustrates this guideline:

Varied tense: If you select "yes," the program will display the next screen.
Present tense: If you select "yes," the program displays the next screen.

I'm not fond of this convention, because it transgresses the rules of good English. The justification for it, as it was first explained to me, is that the reader is performing all tasks in the present and would be distracted by references to the past or future.

You will develop an ear for present tense by reading technical manuals, and soon it will seem normal. Or I should say, you develop an ear for present tense by reading technical manuals, and soon it seems normal.

Provide Examples

Examples almost always clarify technical material. Once you understand your subject well enough to write about it, you might conclude that your explanation is sufficient for the reader. However, because the subject is now familiar to you, your explanation might reach above readers' heads. An example will bring it down to earth again.

Create Effective Lists

Lists are critical in technical writing, both to describe step-by-step procedures and to group similar items in an easy-to-grasp, visually pleasing format. The effectiveness of a list depends on its

- consistency
- order
- completeness

In general, favor bullets over numbers. The preceding list is an example of a bulleted list. Use numbers with step-by-step instructions, items that will be referred to by number, and items introduced with a number. For example, the following list is introduced with a number:

> **Beginning programmers should be taught the following three rules:**
>
> 1. Always list the objectives of the program.
> 2. Use a flowchart to diagram the program's operation.
> 3. Always include comments within your code.

CONSISTENCY

Items should be parallel in punctuation, capitalization, form, and content, so the reader can grasp their similarities easily. All items should begin with a capital letter or all with a lowercase letter. All should end with a period or without one. If one item is a complete sentence, try to make all items into complete sentences. Similarly, if one item is a prepositional phrase, all items should be prepositional phrases.

The following examples illustrate lists that are nonparallel and parallel in form. In the first list, three items that are similar in content (all describe a way to begin a data communication session) are expressed in different forms. By presenting them all as prepositional phrases, capitalized and punctuated consistently, the second list is much clearer.

Nonparallel form: A session can be initiated in a number of ways:
- Either node can initiate the session.
- A network manager sends a command to the control software.
- issuing of a command by a third unit.

Parallel form: A session can be initiated in a number of ways:
- By either node.
- By a network manager sending a command to the control software.
- By a third unit issuing a command.

Items in a list also should be parallel in content or meaning; they should be logically consistent. If you have difficulty making a list parallel, ask yourself if all items really belong there. How would you classify them? Your list items should be grouped because they have some meaningful characteristic in common.

The following examples illustrate lists that are nonparallel and parallel in content:

Nonparallel content: Before configuring the software, you will need to:
1. Install the hardware.
2. Plug cable A into the connector on the back panel.
3. Configure the hardware.
4. Check that you have the correct software version.
5. Install the software.

Parallel content: Before configuring the software, you will need to:
1. Install the hardware.
2. Configure the hardware.
3. Install the software.

ORDER

Try to give your lists a logical order. If you cannot arrange items by importance, chronology, or some other logical order, arrange them alphabetically.

Chronological order is particularly important in step-by-step procedures. To ensure that the steps are in the correct order, use your document to perform the procedures. If you do not have access to the product, have someone like a field engineer do it for you.

COMPLETENESS

Completeness means everything is there. Like order, completeness is critical in step-by-step procedures, where a missing step leaves the reader hanging.

Completeness is also critical in lists of required equipment for a project or system. If a piece is missing, the project is held up. This can be expensive and maddening for customers, who will probably blame the documentation. Don't give them this excuse. Ask your technical resource person to check equipment lists for completeness, preferably by looking at the lists during a face-to-face interview.

Avoid Anthropomorphizing

"The problem is not that it is difficult to make people accept a computer as human but that it is all too easy," says William Horton in his column "The Wired Word."[2]

Anthropomorphizing means referring to nonhuman entities, like computers, as if they were human. Programmers are particularly prone to this. Beware of machines that *think, believe, assume,* and *conclude.* These are a few of the words programmers sometimes use to describe computer software. Usually you can replace these words with a simple action. For example,

Anthropomorphic: If you stop typing for ten seconds, the system assumes you're finished and blackens your screen.

"Computermorphic":   If you stop typing for ten seconds, the screen turns black.

Some technologies have adopted anthropomorphic terms to describe, for example, certain software entities. *Users, clients, masters,* and *slaves* are all classes of data communication software, and their meanings are accepted in the field. Therefore, you cannot eliminate these words without depriving your reader. The best you can do is use them as adjectives: *user process, client process, master node,* and so on.

For online documentation, anthropomorphizing is particularly worrisome. William Horton describes a computer program named ELIZA, which was designed to function as a Rogerian psychologist. Its mimicry was so complete that, after a few minutes using it, even someone who knew the "psychologist" was only a computer program asked to be left alone in the room with it, so their privacy would remain undisturbed.[3]

Computer instructions that use the first person are cloyingly cutesy to experienced users. And ultimately, first-person instructions break down, because the human model is inaccurate. The computer is simply not an *I*—it's an *it*!

"Don't pretend it isn't a computer," says Horton. "Help the user understand and anticipate how it operates." For example, in place of the computer message, "My memory is overloaded," Horton suggests the message, "Too many items to process."[4]

CHECKLIST 14–1. WRITING AND REVISING

This checklist summarizes the guidelines presented in this section. Refer to it when you need help writing and revising your document.
- Choose short over long.
- Choose active over passive.
- Choose specific over general.
- Avoid redundancy.
- Address the reader.
- Define terms and acronyms.
- Eliminate jargon.
- Use present tense.

- Provide examples.
- Create effective lists.
- Avoid anthropomorphizing.

WRITING STYLE

We usually use the expression *writing style* to mean the rhythm, tone, and various other intangibles that lend a piece of writing its character or effect. For example, words can sound formal or colloquial. Sentence lengths—short, long, or varying—provide rhythm. Each choice lends a particular quality to a piece of writing.

In technical writing, choices are limited, and style is dictated by the kind of writing you do, rather than by your preferences and personality. In the chapter "Get Ready," you learned about six major kinds of technical writing: marketing communication and support, technical manuals and specifications, training materials, technical journalism, online documentation, and Web sites. In this section, you'll find examples of writing styles from each of these broad categories.

Whatever kind of writing you do, develop an ear for the nuances of language so that you can control your writing style. An inexperienced writer might waver between a scholarly and chatty style, creating an amateur impression and distracting the reader from the document's purpose. Remember that anything that distracts from your communication goal does not belong in technical communication, or in any good writing.

Marketing Communication and Support

The goal of marketing communication and support is to convince potential customers to buy your product. Advertising provides the clearest examples of this communication goal. Here are parts of ads in *PC World* for a variety of high-tech products:

> Berlin? Beijing? Barstow? (You never know where it's going.) But you always know it's working . . . [Ad for a mobile PC card]
>
> A GRAPHICS REVOLUTION IS HERE. [This product] redefines the creative process by liberating you from the burden of multiple applications . . . [Ad for graphics software]
>
> Give Your Computer the Finger! Forget passwords! Replace them with your fingerprint. Gain instant, secure Windows and Internet access with one touch. [Ad for a fingerprint-recognition security system]

Notice the choices that make up the writing styles of the ads: attention-getting questions and exclamations simulate the verbal style of a salesman; most-needed or desired information up front attempts to hook the reader's interest; superlatives like *revolution* and *instant* communicate emotional excitement found in no other kind of technical writing.

Technical Manuals and Specifications

Technical manuals and specifications include as their readers both the technically sophisticated scientist and the uninitiated consumer. The readers are captive—that is, they have to read your document to understand a product or process. The following example is from an installation and operation manual for a hardware device that stores computerized engineering drawings, or *plots,* and sends them to a printer:

> The RemotePlot handles both serial and parallel communication. To select whether output will be serial or parallel, use the serial/parallel switch, located on the RemotePlot front panel. When this switch is in the serial position, the RemotePlot outputs its data through the 9-pin serial port on the back of the unit. In serial mode, the RemotePlot can perform either XON/XOFF or hardware handshaking.

This paragraph's style is terse and direct. The writer doesn't try to draw the reader in. There's no need—the reader is actively installing the equipment while reading the material. The audience is made up of engineers, so the writer doesn't define terms like *serial* and *handshaking.* Sentences are moderately long, but words are short, making the material easy to read. Notice the complete absence of adjectives, emotionally colored words, or personal words. Every word serves a function.

For technical manuals, your personality and ego must be kept out entirely. This is a sore point with ambitious new writers who want to express their individuality in their prose. Never in technical manuals! Well, hardly ever. Exceptions exist, but to master good technical writing, first cultivate invisibility. Then reappear, with caution, in the rare technical manual that would benefit from a more personal style. For example, you might inject humor into a software guide for a young reader.

Training Materials

The goal of training materials is to impart knowledge or skills that can be applied later to some task. Training materials are based on consciously formulated prerequisites and objectives, which are often stated in the beginning. The following example is from a training guide to be used with a textbook teaching System Network Architecture (SNA) fundamentals (SNA is a set of communication protocols developed by IBM):[5]

Audience   This course is designed primarily for programmers and other technical people who will be working with SNA data communication networks.

Prerequisites The recommended prerequisites for this course are:
- Introduction to System 370.
- Introduction to an IBM VS operating system.
- Knowledge of communications systems concepts, which include . . . .

Objectives   At the completion of this course you should be able to:
- Define SNA terms.
- Identify the major components of an SNA network and describe their major functions.
- Describe data formats that are used in an SNA network . . .

After stating objectives, the guide provides exercises and answers that test whether the student has reached the objectives. Like technical manuals, this kind of writing is terse and direct, without adjectives or emotionally colored words. It is strictly formulaic: Each section of the guide is parallel and organizational structures repeat. For example, each section contains an "Overview," "Objectives," "Required Materials," "Estimated Study Time," and so on. Terminology is stringently consistent.

Technical Journalism

Technical journalism can be either scholarly or consumer oriented. Scholarly journals present scientific or technical papers either ghostwritten by a technical writer or written by a scientist and revised by a technical writer to conform to a journal's style. Consumer publications, available through newsstands and direct mail, are closer relatives of other consumer magazines. They provide product reviews and how-to advice written in an informal style. Here's an example from *Light Plane Maintenance Magazine:*

> Replacing these cables is a perfect job for the aircraft owner who likes to work on his or her plane, since the job is more tedious than exacting, involving as it does removing and reinstalling seats, upholstery panels, and many little clamps, ties and knots. You'll have to have the job inspected and signed off by an A&P, but it's the sort of job it would be hard to screw up badly.[6]

The writer, Steven Lindblom, used a conversational style. His adjectives (*tedious, little*) and colloquialisms (*screw up*) lend a deceptively homey feel to the piece, which is professionally written. He doesn't shy away from long sentences, yet his style flows seamlessly from long through short, creating a conversational rhythm. (You can tell I'm fond of this piece.)

This kind of technical writing allows the writer more freedom to develop a personal style than other, more restrictive forms.

Online Documentation

Online documentation authors have the same audience as writers of technical manuals and training materials, and their purposes are also similar. The differences lie in the demands of media with small display areas and in the expectations of readers who want information instantaneously. The following example shows what the Microsoft Windows Help system displayed when I selected **Insert dates and times** from the Help index:

Insert dates and times

What do you want to do?

<u>Insert the current date and time</u>

<u>Automatically insert the current date</u>

<u>Insert the date and time a document was created, last printed, or last saved</u>

<u>Not sure what choice you want?</u>

Additional choices

Unlike a manual, online help is *interactive*: it can dialog with the user to focus more specifically on what the user wants to know.

Web Sites

Web surfers are on the move. As a Web author, you face the challenges of the marketing writer: You must catch and hold your reader's attention. Your medium, however, is interactive, more visually inviting than the magazine ad, and offers multimedia effects to hook readers.

For an example of a well-crafted Web page with lots of tips on Web page authoring, look at the online magazine for Web developers:

www.webmonkey.com

For examples of Web pages with some of the latest multimedia bells and whistles, check out:*

www.liquidaudio.com
www.macromedia.com

THE WRITING PROCESS

The writing process differs greatly among writers. All technical writing, even the kind that tends to be formulaic and impersonal, is nonetheless a creative endeavor. As such, it relies on intuitive as well as mechanical solutions, and the writing process is affected by the writer's personality.

The order of the writing process described in this book should help your writing flow smoothly. You'll research your topic and audience first, then organize your document and plan its visual characteristics, and

---

* Web sites change fast. If you can't find the ones listed here, have fun surfing!

finally begin to write. It's a good order. However, no two writers are alike. You may need to begin writing first, as a way of exploring what you know and don't know about your subject. Some writers can't outline a complete project without writing parts of it first. (I confess I'm such a person.) Other writers outline the whole thing. "It's always the first and most important task," says writing consultant Linda Lininger. "And once I write an outline, I don't deviate from it."

So find your own way. Your first draft can be anything from a mass of scribbles to a finished manuscript. But no matter how carefully you write, edit your work to make sure it holds together and is mechanically perfect.

If the writing guidelines in this chapter are new to you, don't try to apply them all at once. Instead, write the best first draft you can, then use the guidelines to review the draft and rewrite it. Good writers sometimes revise a draft two or three (or more) times to perfect it.

ABOUT WRITER'S BLOCK

Writer's block besets writers for a number of reasons. One definition of writer's block is the failure of the writer's bottom to maintain contact with the chair.

"A writer will do anything to avoid the act of writing," says William Zinsser in *On Writing Well.* "I can testify from my newspaper days that the number of trips made to the water cooler per reporter-hour far exceeds the body's need for fluids."[7]

Causes of writer's block include:

- perfectionism
- inexperience
- fear of being wrong
- lack of information

The following sections describe these causes and suggest ways to break through to productive work.

Perfectionism

Perfectionism can lead to writer's block. If you worry about getting every word perfect on the first pass, you might not get past word number one. A solution to this kind of block is to just write, even if it's garbage. You can delete the garbage later, but don't stop to judge it during the writing process.

Inexperience

Inexperienced writers suffer from a second kind of writer's block: Sometimes they just don't know how to begin. They look at a blank page and think there's some mysterious process that gets the first word on the page.

If you are such a person, consider—you use words every day to communicate, and spoken words are not that different from written words. If you don't know how to begin, try describing the product out loud, as if you were describing it to a friend over coffee. Then write it as you'd say it. Don't worry about the "well, sort of" and "I think it kind of." You can weed those out later. First just write.

Fear of Being Wrong

Writer's block sometimes has an emotional component: You're worried about what others think of you or you're afraid of being wrong. In technical writing, you have to accept that someone is always going to criticize your writing and that you will always get something wrong. Once you can live with those two realities, you'll probably get on with writing and never experience this kind of writer's block.

Lack of Information

A fourth kind of block for technical writers comes from lack of information. If you try to write before you understand your subject well enough, you can experience great difficulty. Yet the lack of information is not always obvious. You may think you know enough to begin, then get stuck and not know why. Try asking yourself basic questions about your communication goal:

> **What do I want to accomplish in this chapter?**
> I want to describe how the product relates to other products the company sells.
> **O.K., which other products?**
> Well, there's a database that keeps track of engineering drawings, and . . .
> **Good. How does your product relate to the database?**
> I think it has something to do with . . . I don't really know.

Using this questioning process, you'll find the holes in your knowledge. Write down your unanswered questions; then look through product specifications, use the product, or question the engineer until you understand the answers. The writing process will proceed more smoothly when you know what you're writing about.

SUMMING IT UP

This chapter described principles of good technical writing, showed some ways writing styles vary, and discussed the writing process. The next chapter tells you how to edit and proofread your work, as well as how to communicate with editors.

[1] Sir T. Clifford Allbutt, *Notes on the Composition of Scientific Papers* (London: Macmillan and Co., Limited, 1904), p. 14.

[2] William Horton, "The Wired Word," *Technical Communication,* Journal of the Society for Technical Communication, Third Quarter 1989, p. 252.

[3] Horton, "The Wired Word," p. 252.

[4] Horton, "The Wired Word," p. 252.

[5] Luther Bonnett, *SNA Fundamentals: Personal Reference Guide* (Chicago: Science Research Associates, Inc.), p. v.

[6] Steven Lindblom, "Replacing Aluminum Battery Cables with Copper," *1991 Pilot's Guide to Maintenance and Operations* (Reprints from *Light Plane Maintenance Magazine.* Greenwich, Conn.: Belvoir Publications, 1991), p. 4.

[7] William Zinsser, *On Writing Well* (New York: Harper Perennial, 1990), p. 22.

15

Editing Your Work

"**E**diting," says one writer, "saves you from making an ass of yourself. A good editor gets rid of your blunders before thousands of eyes can see them."

Editing imparts professional polish to your document. This chapter distinguishes between writing and editing and explains the importance of editing. You'll learn about different kinds of edits and find checklists to help you edit and proofread your work. You'll find guidance on dealing with a staff editor and on how to perform as one, if none is on staff.

WRITING AND EDITING—WHAT'S THE DIFFERENCE?

Technical writing and technical editing share a flexible boundary. Writers are responsible for content; editors for polish. The many responsibilities in between are defined as writing or editing depending on the history of the publications department and its members' skills and backgrounds.

A technical document should receive at least three editing passes:

1. substantive editing
2. mechanical editing
3. proofreading

For our purposes, the following definitions will serve:

writing	selecting, organizing, and writing the content of a document
substantive editing	revising to present material in the most usable, flowing manner
mechanical editing	repairing flaws in grammar, usage, and punctuation and applying house style rules (later in this chapter, you'll learn about this kind of style); sometimes called *copyediting*

proofreading   correcting typos and errors in formatting; fixing disagreements between headings in the table of contents and in text, in the index and in text, and the like

Substantive editing forms the gray area between writing and editing and almost always lies within the technical writer's domain. This chapter concerns itself primarily with mechanical editing and proofreading.

WHY EDIT?

Editing increases readability. One way it does this is by treating similar elements consistently. For example, if a marketing brochure refers to a product as Power Tool, an editor can ensure that the reference manual and online information for the product also refer to it by the same name, spelled and capitalized the same way.

This consistency prevents customer confusion and also gives the product a "corporate look." When terms are used consistently, customers easily recognize them. Product names and terms, like trademarks, gain loyalty through recognition.

Consistency, consistency, consistency: This chapter emphasizes it because consistency is almost synonymous with editing. You might get tired of seeing the word, but it's repeated for good reason.

Consistency is difficult to achieve in large companies, where a product might bear several names until it's announced to the public and may not acquire a public name until the last minute. Engineers usually give a computer product a name as they develop the software or hardware. Meanwhile, the company gives the product a code name. For example, the product called Power Tool might be called "P-tool" by engineers and have the code name "bullet." Thus, it's not uncommon to see, in specifications and online, three product names, each with several capitalization styles.

Consistent terminology is only one reason to honor the editing process, but it's a good one, affecting as it does the total impression the product creates. Other edits, such as eliminating typos, also influence product acceptance. Would you trust a product if you found numerous typos in the manual?

You can see that polished documentation reflects product quality. Now let's explore the three editing passes.

SUBSTANTIVE EDITING

When you perform a substantive edit, you might arrange material more logically to eliminate redundancy and make the document easier to use. You'll substitute specific words for vague ones and redefine terms to inject clarity. A good substantive edit requires some technical knowledge, and rightly rests in the writer's hands, although some writers do not have the skill required.

If a document is written by a subject matter expert, like an engineer, the responsibility for structuring the material might fall to an editor.

The principles of substantive editing are the same as those for good writing. Therefore, to perform this kind of edit, you can follow the writing guideline described in the chapter "Writing Is the Heart of Your Craft."

MECHANICAL EDITING

Mechanical editing lies squarely on the technical editor's turf, provided you have such a person on staff. If you do not, you'll need to do it yourself.

When you perform a mechanical edit, you'll apply the rules of grammar, usage, capitalization, and punctuation. In addition, you'll check that technical terms are defined and are consistent in spelling and in the way they're used. You'll make sure like items are parallel. And you'll enforce *house style,* which dictates the spelling, punctuation, and typographic emphasis of product-related terms. The elements of house style and use of style guides are described in the section "House Style," later in this chapter.

Whether you edit your own document or work with an editor, learn to recognize and use the editing marks shown in Figure 15-1.

A complete treatment of grammar, usage, punctuation, and consistency is beyond the scope of this book. The following sections list a few rules writers frequently abuse.

For more details about punctuation and word treatment, as well as editing marks, see *The Chicago Manual of Style,* published by the University of Chicago Press and frequently revised. If you plan to edit much, buy a copy.

Agreement Between Subject and Verb

When a singular subject is separated from the verb by a plural noun or a series of nouns, the verb should be singular. Writers sometimes use a plural verb, creating subject-verb disagreement. Here's an example:

Disagreement	The graph showing dates, sources, and responses appear on the facing page.
Agreement	The graph showing dates, sources, and responses appears on the facing page.

The ear tends to hear a plural verb after plural nouns. However, the verb *appear* refers to *graph,* and not the series preceding the verb.

Commas in a Series

When you write a series of nouns or phrases within a sentence, you have a choice about whether or not to place a comma before the *and.* That last comma is called a *series comma.* For example:

No series comma   Before opening the case, make sure you have on hand a $1/4$-inch screwdriver, a $3/4$-inch wrench and some wire clippers.

Series comma   Before opening the case, make sure you have on hand a $1/4$-inch screwdriver, a $3/4$-inch wrench, and some wire clippers.

FIGURE 15-1
EDITING MARKS

ℒ	delete
⊂	close up
¶	begin new paragraph
tr	transpose; exchange positions
stet	let it stand (do not implement marked changes)
lc	lowercase
caps	capitalize (letters to be capped are underlined three times)
ital	italicize
bf	boldface
a/	insert letter
=/	insert hyphen
⊙	insert period
word/	insert word
#	insert space
∫	break line

Technical manuals almost always use series commas. The important thing is to be aware of your company's style preference and to be consistent: Either always include a series comma or never include one.

Commas and Periods with Quotation Marks

A comma or period should appear before the final mark in a quotation, rather than after it:

> When you reach the heading "Software Agreement," begin reading carefully to make sure you understand the terms.

However, the computer industry has corrupted this rule. This corruption began when writers placed quotation marks around computer commands. If a comma or period appeared within the quotes, the user was likely to type it as part of the command. If the punctuation mark truly wasn't part of the command, it fouled things up. So, rightly, tech writers moved all extra punctuation outside quotes, leaving within them only those characters the computer could recognize. Since many writers weren't quite sure of the rule anyway, commas and periods started creeping out of quotation marks in all instances.

A comma or period belongs inside quotes unless it will confuse the user. One way around the computer-command problem is to use typographical emphasis, like bold type or a different color, to set commands apart, rather than placing them inside quotations.

If your company uses quotes when describing commands and online messages within a manual, do not use commas or any other characters within the quotes except exactly what the user must type or what appears on the screen. In other text, however, place these punctuation marks within the quotes where they belong. For example:

Computer command	After you type "HELP", a list of topics appears on the screen.
Other text	The resin-curing process is "air-inhibited."

Hyphenation of Compound Adjectives

Hyphenate compound adjectives when the first word modifies the second. For example:

> quick-reference guide

In this example, quick-reference describes the kind of guide it is. The word "quick" modifies "reference" and is rightly joined to it by a hyphen.

Do not hyphenate two-word adjectives when the second word modifies the noun. For example:

programming reference guide

In this example, a reference guide provides programming information. "Programming" does not modify "reference." Instead, "reference"
modifies "guide." Notice that a noun and preceding modifier are not
hyphenated.

See *The Chicago Manual of Style* for a more complete treatment of
compound words.

Consistent Person

Refer to the user consistently as either "the user" or "you." Do not
switch between second and third person in your document. For example:

Inconsistent	The purpose of this manual is to help you operate the XYZ machine. Users can learn all XYZ features easily by following the step-by-step procedures in chapters 2 and 3.
Consistent (third person)	The purpose of this manual is to help users operate the XYZ machine. Users can learn all XYZ features easily by following the step-by-step procedures in chapters 2 and 3.
Consistent (second person)	The purpose of this manual is to help you operate the XYZ machine. You can learn all XYZ features easily by following the step-by-step procedures in chapters 2 and 3.

Consistent Capitalization

First, some editing terms: when editors tell you to *capitalize* a word,
they usually mean only the first letter. *Initial cap* also means the first
letter in a word is a capital. All other letters are lowercase, like so:
Aardvark. *All caps* means all letters in the word are capitalized, like so:
AARDVARK.

In general, use capitals only to distinguish proper nouns, like the
name of a product. Engineers tend not to know this rule and can randomly capitalize words in specifications and online. This practice is particularly troublesome when you're trying to create consistency between
your document and computer screens designed by engineers.

House style sometimes dictates that commands and file names be
capitalized, although other forms of typographical emphasis work just as
well. Boldface, for example, can be used to indicate a command: **exit**.

Educate your engineers and fellow writers to use capitals only for
proper nouns and for their usual roles in titles, captions, headings, and at
the beginning of sentences and some list items.

If you do capitalize an element like command names, make sure to do so consistently throughout the product documentation and online to avoid confusing your audience.

Capitalization of Titles, Captions, and Headings

Capitalize titles, captions, and headings consistently. Titles, captions, and headings generally follow these rules: Always capitalize the first word. Use lowercase letters to begin prepositions (*to, with,* etc.), articles (*the, a, an,* etc.), and conjunctions (*and, or,* etc.). Capitalize all other words. The heading for this section is an example.

Follow house style, which may differ from this rule. Then edit all titles, captions, and headings to ensure that they conform to the same capitalization style.

Capitalization and Punctuation of Lists

Capitalize and punctuate list items consistently. For bulleted lists, capitalize or lowercase the first word in each list item, depending on house style. You'll almost always capitalize the first word and place punctuation at the end of list items that form complete sentences. Here's an example from the "Résumés" checklist earlier in this book:

- Have you listed your technical skills?
- Is the layout attractive?

Often you'll lowercase list items that are nouns or that complete a sentence begun by the introductory phrase. End punctuation is optional. However, house style might specify end punctuation after the items if they complete a sentence.

The following example shows lowercase nouns listed with no end punctuation:

- one external disk drive
- one internal hard disk
- two coaxial cables

Parallel Wording

Phrase list items and headings in parallel form. For example, if one heading contains a gerund (a verb form functioning as a noun and ending in *-ing*), use a gerund for all similar headings of the same level in the same section.

The following examples show nonparallel and parallel headings:

Nonparallel:	Planting for Maximum Air Circulation
	The Use of Insecticides
Parallel:	Planting for Maximum Air Circulation
	Using Insecticides

Similarly, edit list items to be parallel, as described in the chapter, "Writing Is the Heart of Your Craft."

PROOFREADING

Proofread every draft you send for review, as well as the final copy. After you type in corrections, proofread your changes to make sure you haven't introduced new errors.

When you proofread, you'll correct spelling and typos, check headings and page numbers against the table of contents, check index entries against pages to which they refer, and so on. (The principles of indexing are described in the chapter "The Production Process," because the index is the last thing you'll do—and the last thing you'll proofread.)

If you do not have an editing or production staff, you'll proofread formatting elements to ensure that they've been implemented consistently. You'll check things like type fonts and sizes, as well as spacing.

Some of these proofreading tasks belong to the final phase of document production and are described in the chapter "The Production Process."

Use the proofreading checklist later in this chapter to remind yourself of elements that need "proofing."

Spelling and Typos

Most technical writers use a word-processing program that includes a spelling-checking function or they use a separate *spell checker*. Spell checkers are computer programs that refer to a standard dictionary, stored in the computer's memory, to check the spelling of every word in your document. Most of them do this very quickly—faster than you can grab your dictionary. Nonetheless, they don't catch all errors. Here are the common ones spell checkers usually miss:

- incorrect words spelled correctly, like "than" where you meant "then"
- product-related terms and acronyms
- double words, like "the the" (some spell checkers catch these)
- incorrect number of spaces between words and sentences (some spell checkers catch these, too)

Therefore, despite the aid of this high-tech tool, you need to proofread your document for spelling errors and typos.

Cross-references

Check all cross-references (and hyperlinks online). If the text states "see page 9 for a description of binary notation," turn to page 9 and make sure the description is there. If a hyperlink says "How Gizmos Work," click it and make sure the linked page provides the promised explanation.

To reduce the risk of incorrect cross-references in paper documents, you can refer to chapter or section names instead of specific page numbers. References to page numbers are easily rendered inaccurate because as you edit a document, you delete and add material, thereby changing where one page ends and the next begins. Material that fell on one page soon falls on another. Therefore, use names rather than page numbers, unless house style dictates otherwise. Proofread cross-references, the table of contents, and the index at the end, when the pagination or online document is final, to make sure the wording matches between each reference and the heading to which it refers.

Formatting

Proofread headings, captions, running heads, and running feet to ensure their consistency. Make sure margins, indents, and leading look consistent around parallel elements.

Similarly, scan text for font errors. Word processing can introduce stray fonts and paragraph styles, and in your hurry to meet the deadline, you don't notice them. When you proofread, stray fonts will appear somewhat darker or lighter than the text around them, but you have to look closely for them. The following paragraph contains an example of a stray font:

> When you type your password, it does not appear on the screen and you cannot backspace to correct errors. An invisible password ensures that someone watching over your shoulder will not be able to learn your password and use it to illegally gain access to your account.

As you proofread, look for paragraphs that are incorrectly indented and spaced; they may be formatted as list items, headings, or in some other style. Similarly, proofread other text categories, such as list items, to ensure they are formatted correctly.

CHECKLIST 15–1.   PROOFREADING

Use this checklist to remember those elements that require proofreading.

- Look for spelling errors and typos your spell checker missed.
- Check for correct numerical order of numbered lists and procedures.
- Check for correct alphabetical order of alphabetized lists.
- Verify cross-references for content.
- Make sure spacing and type style are consistent for all headings and captions of the same kind, including running heads and running feet.
- Check headings (including chapter heads) against the table of contents to ensure they agree in level, wording, and capitalization.
- Check captions against the figures and tables lists for agreement.
- Check text for stray fonts.

- Check art placement (described in the chapter "The Production Process").
- Look for widows and orphans (described in the chapter "The Production Process").
- Proofread page numbers in cross-references, the table of contents, figures list, and tables list.
- Check index entries for correct alphabetical order.
- If you've used a computer program to create the index, spot check index page numbers to ensure that they refer to correct pages. For a manually created index, proofread the whole thing.

HOUSE STYLE

House style is a set of rules that govern the treatment of product-related terms and of elements, like lists, for which no universal rules exist.

Consistency (that word again) is the heartbeat of house style.

You've already learned about some of the decisions dictated by house style—decisions such as how to emphasize command names and whether or not to capitalize list items. You've also heard about formatting elements, like fonts and margins.

House style also includes rules about the spelling, hyphenation, and capitalization of product-specific terms. For example, a computer manual needs to present commands, keystrokes, and online messages in consistent styles.

At one company with no staff editor, I found a manual that told users to simultaneously type the Control key and the letter "T" in seven different ways. Obviously, the manual needed editorial rescue!

Most technical publication departments use a style guide to ward off the confusion engendered by multiple representations of like elements. The style guide specifies one correct way to present terms that might otherwise appear haphazardly. The following is an example from a style guide for computer manuals.

Capitalization and typographic emphasis for technical terms:
- Show commands lowercase and boldface, unless the command must be typed in capital letters.
- Show product labels capitalized as they appear on equipment.
- Italicize file names.
- Use initial capital for program names.

If the responsibility for style decisions falls in your lap, as it may in a small company, you need to produce at least a style sheet, which you can refer to and pass to other writers working on the same product documentation. You may even need to create a style guide from scratch. The sheet or guide should specify how to handle the elements listed in the following checklist. The list is not complete. You will constantly update your style reference to include new elements as you find them.

CHECKLIST 15–2.   STYLE ELEMENTS

When you create a style guide, you'll decide the following issues:

- Capitalization, font, typographical emphasis, and spacing of chapter titles, headings, and captions
- Number of heading levels to use
- Capitalization, typographical emphasis, and spelling of product-related terms, like commands
- Typographical emphasis and placement of notes, warnings, and cautions
- Capitalization, spelling, and punctuation of measurements, like weights and rates
- Whether to abbreviate or spell out measurements
- Capitalization and punctuation of acronyms and abbreviations, as well as their definitions
- Punctuation and division of terms that can be represented as two words or one, for example, *log-in, log in, login*
- Placement and punctuation of table and figure captions
- Capitalization, punctuation, and indent of list elements and index entries
- Use of series comma

You will also need to choose a dictionary and style guide to use for more general spelling and style decisions—those that plague everyone rather than those that apply only to your company. Dictionaries vary in how they spell and hyphenate certain terms, so choose one source. *The Chicago Manual of Style* is the style guide preferred by most technical publications departments and is an excellent reference to use in preparing your company-specific style guide.

WHO EDITS?

The roles of technical writers and technical editors are not sharply delineated, and in the business world, these two job titles are sometimes used interchangeably. For example, when I was employed as a technical editor, I sometimes rewrote technical material, whereas in one technical writing position, my work was confined primarily to mechanical editing. As a technical writer, I confronted my first blank page, to be filled with original writing. However, I've met people with the title of editor who also do original writing.

Be aware of your preferences. Some technical editors want only to edit. That is, they do not want to have to know about a technical product or to be responsible for the technical content of a document. Similarly, some writers (I, for one) prefer the intellectual challenge that comes with learning technical information and structuring it into some form of communication.

If you have a strong preference for either editing or writing, do not mistake a job title for a job definition. Find out what a title means at the company you're approaching for a job.

Negotiating with an Editor

If you have both writers and editors within your publications department, the editor will edit your draft. If polish is a priority at your company, the editor may go through your draft as many as three times, at different stages. First he or she might recommend organizational changes; a second, thorough mechanical edit might come next; and during a third edit, the editor will check that you've implemented mechanical corrections and will proofread formatting, table of contents, and so on.

Some writers see editors as persecutors, to be argued with at every turn. Others lean too heavily on them, submitting rougher drafts than an editor can be expected to rescue. Striking a balance between these two positions is best. Editors are your colleagues. Particularly in technical writing, their job is not that different from yours. They will make mistakes, but they will also help you enormously to produce a professional publication.

You are responsible for letting editors know when they have inadvertently compromised technical accuracy. You should have the final say about content matters. On the other hand, don't leave all the cleaning up for the editor. The more you edit your own work, the fewer red marks will appear on it during the editing process. Your attention to the mechanical details of a manuscript also shows editors you value what they do. Editors appreciate your efforts, and your work relationships with them will go more smoothly.

Peer Editing

If your department does not define a separate editorial function, you will edit your own work. To provide consistency among a group of writers, members must agree to follow a shared style. This requires a team effort.

When I began as senior writer at one company where no staff editor existed, I found the company's manuals contained a hodgepodge of styles. Product-specific terms varied haphazardly in their spelling, capitalization, and punctuation.

I offered to help clear up the confusion and organized a weekly usage panel, which writers voluntarily attended, to decide style issues. Together we divided up issues, researched style guides and good manuals from other companies, and brought recommendations back to the group.

The writers all felt involved, yet there were drawbacks. When it came time to implement the recommendations, writers who didn't attend the panel or hadn't researched a particular issue continued in their old ways. For whatever reasons—deadline pressures, habit, lack of managerial follow-through—inconsistencies continued to appear.

This experience taught me to respect the role of a staff editor. Someone whose job it is to keep track of the details will do so with greater diligence than a writing team can possibly afford to do. Nonetheless, a team effort is better than no effort at all.

Self-Editing

Without a staff editor, and sometimes even with one, you are ultimately responsible for the consistency and polish of your work. If you have little time, make every effort to edit your draft at least once, even if it means taking it home for the weekend. Prefer at least three passes: substantively edit, mechanically edit, and proofread the draft. Ensure that, at least within itself, the document is consistent and that it is error free.

SUMMING IT UP

This chapter described the editing process and the value of consistency. It guided you in editing your own work, in deciding style issues, and in working with a staff editor. The next chapter tells you how to prepare for the review process, how to submit your work to reviewers, and how to use their comments to improve your work.

16

The Review Process

To be accurate and useful, your work must be reviewed several times by experts from different areas of your company. During this process, you'll learn to take criticism, to incorporate technical changes consistently, and to reconcile differences among reviewers.

THE MYTH OF EGOLESS WRITING

Your technical document will pass under many often unsympathetic eyes during the review process. I've had more than one acquaintance ask, "How can you stand it?" when they hear about this aspect of technical writing. How do you survive the review process? Experienced writers recommend that you get your ego out of the way. However, pure egoless writing is a myth.

If you care about your writing and strive to make the best choices you can in its form and content, you feel bad when a reviewer says your work is garbage. Very few writers get their egos out of the way completely. Often those who do are simply burned out, and their poor-quality work reflects their lack of ego involvement.

TAKING CRITICISM

Learning not to take criticism personally takes time, and is never complete, because it is your ego—your pride and confidence in your work—that guides you in dealing with reviewers' comments.

One way to take criticism less personally is to realize that your document is a company product. Others have vested interest in it, and as a team player, you're responsible for soliciting their contributions. In doing so, you need to cultivate a corporate, rather than personal, perspective on your work.

"When I started in the field, having never been seriously challenged about my writing, it was very difficult," says biomedical writer Dan Liberthson. "I got my back up for a while until I realized that [the review process] was valuable."

You'll find after a while that your problem won't be how to take negative review comments but how to convince reviewers to make more of them. Because you depend on product experts to make your document as useful as possible, you'll look for thorough reviewers—as many as you can get—and you'll grow impatient with those who send your draft back with few comments.

How do you discriminate between useful and hurtful review comments? If you incorporate every criticism, your writing loses its coherence. If you reject every criticism, you lose opportunities to improve your writing and you become known as a difficult person. Worst of all, you risk the technical accuracy of your document. Taking criticism demands that you balance subjectivity and objectivity; respect for your own point of view and that of others. It's an art.

The following checklist will help you sort through changes reviewers request.

CHECKLIST 16–1. THE REVIEW PROCESS

Apply the following criteria to reviewers' comments to determine whether they help or hinder your communication goal.

Make a requested change if it:

- improves the technical accuracy of the document
- improves the organization of the document, making information more accessible
- clarifies an explanation or procedure, making it easier to understand

Do not make the change if it:

- introduces material irrelevant to the stated audience
- compromises the document's mechanical correctness, coherence, or readability
- conflicts with other reviewers' comments or with technical accuracy as you understand it. (Such changes need to be discussed with reviewers, as described in the section "Incorporating Review Comments" later in this chapter.)

WHO ARE YOUR REVIEWERS?

Reviewers are usually selected from each of the following departments:

- marketing
- engineering
- testing
- customer support
- publications
- editing

Your company might have different departments from the ones listed here, and representatives from those departments, or from other branches of the company, will review your work. The following sections describe typical reviewers, so you'll know the kinds of comments to expect and how to use them.

Marketing

If you're writing directly for a marketing department, marketing reviewers will comment on your document as an effective sales tool. If you're writing for a different department, reviewers from marketing will help you coordinate your terminology with theirs. They will probably try to delete any negative references to the product. Be careful about making these deletions, as they can deprive the user of necessary information.

Make sure that in response to a marketing review you do not delete information that warns users about hazards to themselves and their equipment. Also state positively, rather than delete, descriptions of bugs engineers could not fix before the product was released. For example, if a computer command that appears on the screen does not work yet, let the user know it "will be implemented in the next release."

Engineering

If you are writing technical manuals or specifications, you should give review copies to several engineers. If you are writing other kinds of material, an engineering reviewer is still essential. Engineers are closest to the product and most able to ensure the technical accuracy of your work.

Quality Assurance (QA), Product, and Usability Testing

Testing professionals use the product to ensure that it runs smoothly. Try to have them review the manual or online documentation by testing it alongside the product. They can determine if your written procedures really work, and their comments are invaluable.

If you are fortunate enough to have document usability testing professionals at your company, they will test the document during the review process.

Customer Support

Customer support engineers (including field support and sales support) help set up the product and ensure that it runs smoothly at the customer site. Your company might also employ customer support engineers to do telephone troubleshooting and on-site repairs when customers have difficulty operating the product. Reviewers from customer support not only help with technical accuracy, but also help you define the audience for your document. They know the customer. They may inject different terminology, perhaps even jargon, that the customer regularly uses to refer to the product. You might need to include these terms (in addition to company standard definitions) to reach your audience.

Publications

Sometimes a review copy will go to a writer in your publications group, or a lead writer, for a peer review. Usually your supervisor will receive a copy. A writing reviewer can help with organization, writing style, and clarity.

Editing

The editor will review your document for mechanical correctness, house style, and consistency, as described in the chapter "Editing Your Work."

Other Reviewers

A reviewer from the training department can also provide helpful recommendations about a range of concerns, including terminology, technical content, and document organization.

In addition, a review copy should go to the artist, who can use it to anticipate art placement and recommend changes affecting art. Inevitably you'll also send out some "political" review copies to people who never have time to read your work but nonetheless reserve the right to review it. These are usually engineering and marketing managers, and you'll need to deal with them more delicately than reviewers who are actually expected to return comments to you by a deadline.

ASKING FOR TROUBLE—SUBMITTING AND RETRIEVING THOSE REVIEWS

You will send your work out for review after you complete the first draft and again after you have incorporated reviewers' requested changes. Sometimes a third review is necessary, if reviewers have requested extensive changes or if the product has undergone changes.

When you submit your work for review, you'll include a cover memo with your name and phone number, the name of the document, the names of reviewers, and the date reviews are due. Distinguish between critical and "FYI" (for your information) reviewers. All your main reviewers are critical. The most critical is your primary technical resource person, whose comments help ensure your document's accuracy.

Your artist, your manager, and the political reviewers mentioned earlier are less critical. Unless you write training materials, training reviewers should also be FYI, rather than critical, because waiting for their comments might hold you up—trainers are often out of town.

Figure 16–1 shows an example of a review cover memo.

Only one task is more difficult than submitting your work for review, and that is getting it back from late reviewers. It's hard enough to ask for trouble in the first place. Having to beg for it is a disgrace!

FIGURE 16-1
REVIEW COVER MEMO

March 23, 2001

TO: Reviewers

FROM: Janet Van Wicklen, ext. 897

RE: Second review of *The Wild Widget User's Guide*

Please review the attached document for technical accuracy. Comments not related to technical content are welcome but might not be incorporated. I need your comments by **Friday, March 31**. Critical reviews received later than this date will jeopardize the document's schedule. If you will not be able to review the document by this date, please call me immediately.

Please write corrections directly on the draft. Make comments specific: If you mark something as wrong, also write in the corrected information.

Thanks for your help making this an accurate, user-friendly document.

REVIEWERS:
Critical Reviewers	*FYI*
Susan Black, Engineering	Harold Schwartz, Engineering
Grant Smith, Engineering	Jane Townsend, Marketing
Lisa Downing, Marketing	Betsy Long, Technical Publications
George Freeman, QA	John Ferrero, Technical Publications
Pete McMann, Customer Support	Jim Hartford, Training
Pam Brown, Technical Publications	

When writer Lisa Peters (fictional name, but real incident) asked one late reviewer when she would receive his comments, he answered, "When pigs grow wings." That afternoon, Lisa bought colored construction paper and glue and created a mobile for this engineer. When he returned to his office the following morning, he found flying above his desk a winged pig.

Lisa's creativity paid off, but it also cramped her deadline-ridden schedule. Late reviews can cost hours of a writer's time and can delay the manual's publication date. At meetings on the subject, writers brainstorm such ideas as attaching lottery tickets or five-dollar bills to reviews as bribes, or including quasi-humorous threats like "REVIEW THIS OR ELSE." The best solution is to convince reviewers' managers that document reviews are an essential part of the production process and that late reviews can hold up the product.

INCORPORATING REVIEW COMMENTS

You will receive many incomplete, illegible, or confusing review comments, despite your request for specific information. Reviewers either don't read your cover memo or do not know how to write the correction clearly. One common, maddening review comment is "See me"—maddening because you are under deadline pressure, have comments from a half dozen or so reviewers to coordinate, and cannot possibly sit down with all of them to clarify their concerns.

Nonetheless, try to follow up on incomplete review comments. You'll quickly learn who your most helpful reviewers are—those who know the product best and who know how to describe its intricacies. You'll take more time clarifying their comments than those of less-experienced reviewers.

Consistency

Apply requested changes consistently. Changes to names, parameters, commands, filenames, procedures, and product descriptions need to be made throughout the product documentation. If a reviewer marks a change in one part of your document, make the change wherever else it applies. For example, if a procedure appears in both the user's guide and the quick-reference card, and a reviewer marks a change in the user's guide, take responsibility for changing it in the quick-reference card as well. To do this may mean you have to team up with other writers in your department.

Conflict Resolution

Inevitably, two or more reviewers will disagree about how the product works. Try to convince reviewers over the phone to resolve their differences and get back to you. Often you can ask your technical resource person to clear up the confusion. If resolution isn't possible, host a review meeting, inviting the disagreeing parties to bring their comments for discussion. Some publications departments routinely hold review meetings to enable document reviewers to agree on changes face-to-face.

SUMMING IT UP

This chapter described how to approach the sometimes harrowing review process and use it to improve your document. The next chapter describes your document's graduation from a rough draft to camera-ready copy.

17

The Production Process

The production process described in this chapter applies mainly to paper documents and manuals converted to online, but the process of indexing is critical for online help documents as well.

Think of the production process as gift wrapping. You've done everything you can to create a finished document, but you still need to package it to present to your reader. This stage involves polishing your format, proofreading the final draft, and creating that vital part of your document—the index.

When you've completed these steps, you'll admire your work, update your résumé to reflect your new accomplishment, and celebrate a job well done.

Large companies sometimes have a production staff that handles this phase. In most companies, however, you will be responsible for the final copy.

POLISHING YOUR FORMAT

The manuscript you send to the printer or place online should be perfectly formatted, with final placement of art, nicely balanced pages, and no *widows* or *orphans*.

Placing Art

Changes you made during the review process may have affected the placement of tables and figures. Perhaps some of them now precede the text explaining them. This can confuse the reader, who will wonder why the art is there. Now it's time to proofread the text around tables and figures to make sure that the text refers to them before they appear—not after.

Balancing Pages

Next, proofread running heads, running feet, and page numbers to make sure that they align horizontally across facing pages and vertically with margins. Also, check that even and odd pages mirror each other. Page numbers should appear on the outer edge of the page, so the reader can flip through your document to find his or her place. Therefore, the page number should appear on the left side of an even-numbered page and on the right side of an odd-numbered page, although some formats might specify that page numbers be centered. Similarly, running heads or running feet should also mirror each other.

If your format includes a hanging indent for headings, such that the heading protrudes into the margin, these, too, can mirror each other, extending into the left margin on even pages and the right margin on odd pages.

Facing pages should also be balanced in length. If one page is filled with text and graphics and the facing page is only a paragraph long, space is wasted and the reader will pause to consider whether material might be missing. A short page usually occurs when large art or a long list follows it. Because the art or list needs to appear all on one page, the preceding text won't fit and gets left behind. Juggle your text, reduce the art, or break the list so the preceding page is full. Ideally, the bottoms of your pages should line up, although most formats allow a little unevenness. The last page of a chapter can be any length, as long as it does not contain a *widow* (the next subsection explains what a widow is).

Begin chapters on an odd-numbered page. If the preceding chapter does not end on an even-numbered page so that the next page is odd, insert a blank page. The blank should be even-numbered and in sequence.

Eliminating Widows and Orphans

A *widow* is a short line of type that gets moved to the next page, and an *orphan* is one that gets left behind. The segment is so short, it seems stranded on the page, cut off from the rest of its meaning and visually isolated.

You can consider the last and first lines of paragraphs as widows and orphans if the page break strands them. However, the introduction to a list, no matter what its length, is an orphan if it becomes separated from the list items it introduces. Similarly, any phrase followed by a colon or *em-dash* (a long, introductory dash) should appear on the same page as the material it introduces.

Most word-processing programs now have a "widow control" function that makes sure at least two lines of a paragraph appear on a page. Some programs also have a page-viewing feature that reduces the size of your pages on the computer screen. This feature allows you to see their layout and check facing pages for balance, as well as for widows and orphans. At the very least, current word-processing programs show where pages break, so you can proofread page breaks on your computer screen before printing a draft.

If your word processor does not have these functions, you will have to correct widows and orphans by proofreading a draft of your manual.

You will always proofread your final draft to check that introductory elements, like introductions to lists, are not orphaned.

PROOFREADING THE FINAL DRAFT

After you polish your format, you'll perform a number of proofreading checks, some of which have already been described in the chapter, "Editing Your Work." The following production checklist provides guidelines.

CHECKLIST 17–1. PRODUCTION

Proofread the following elements during the production process:

- Be sure that art (including tables, graphs, and so on) appears after the text introducing it.
- Check that page numbers, running heads, margins, and similar format elements mirror each other between odd and even pages.
- Make sure pages are visually balanced and approximately even in length.
- Check that each chapter begins on an odd-numbered page. Insert blanks where necessary.
- Eliminate widows and orphans.
- Proofread spacing before and after paragraphs, art, and captions to ensure consistency for each element.
- Proofread page numbers in cross-references, the table of contents, figures list, and tables list.

INDEXING

For your document to be useful, an index is essential. Don't underestimate its value. Even if your publication department does not usually take the time to index, you can take the time to do it yourself. Think about it this way: Your document going out the door without an index is like the product going out the door without your document.

An index is more than a reference aid. It's the user interface, the guide, the entryway to the information your document contains.

Characteristics of a Good Index

The reader looks in the index for concepts, operations, and actions, and often does not know the technical term associated with them. In fact, that's what an index is for—to help the uninitiated find the unfamiliar by looking up the familiar. A good index works well for the same reason a good document works well—it anticipates the reader's needs. In fact, the two organizational principles described in the chapter, "Planning a Writing Project, on Paper and Online," apply to indexes as well. Remember them? They are *recognizable structure* and *user orientation*.

An index has a recognizable structure to anyone who has been to school. The familiar alphabetical sections need not be explained. However, user orientation for an index means that the index lists terms the reader is most likely to seek. These might be terms that do not even appear in the text.

What an Index Is Not

An index is not an alphabetical list of words. Unfortunately, that is what you'll get from computer programs, called *index generators,* that automatically create an index. Designed by programmers, these tools generally do not allow for the complex decisions that go into creating a useful index.

Some index generators automatically list all pages containing a particular term. Many of these pages might offer no useful information about the term. Perhaps it is just used in a sentence. An index generated in this way is practically useless. After the poor reader looks up three or four pages and finds nothing of value, he or she gives up in disgust.

Most index generators let you highlight words in a computer file. The program subsequently lists the words, alphabetically, with page numbers. This is only slightly better than an indiscriminate list. The highlighted list still does not contain most of the words an uninitiated reader will try to find.

The drawbacks of index generators don't render them useless. They excel at finding page numbers associated with terms. You then need to add topics and to edit the index, as described in this chapter.

Selecting Index Topics

To select an index topic, first imagine how the reader will approach the book. What information does the reader expect to find and where will he or she look? Then phrase the index entry descriptively, to indicate the kind of information it points to.

Include index entries for

- descriptions of important concepts and operations
- explanations of actions the reader needs to perform
- definitions of terms, abbreviations, and acronyms
- restrictions, such as notes and cautions, informing the reader of the product's limitations

Good index entries are descriptive. They give the reader some sense of what he or she will find on the listed (or linked) pages. For example, let's say a student pilot wants information about night landings. She looks up *landings* in the index of a flight training manual. She finds the entry lists 29 pages with information about landings. To find information about night landings, or to find out whether or not the book even contains the information, she might have to look on all 29 pages.

A descriptive index entry contains subentries pointing to specific information. The following example shows an entry that would help the student pilot find information on night landings, as well as many other aspects of landing a plane.

Landings
   180° point, 3–10
   aiming point, 3–14, 3–26
   approach, 3–10
   approach airspeed, 3–10, 3–12
   approach angle, 3–13
   at night, 7–21
   base leg, 3–11
   best angle-of-glide speed, 3–14
   bounced, 3–17
   crosswind, 3–18

This portion of an index entry from *Private Pilot Maneuvers* tells the reader exactly the kind of information to expect. The entire entry contains 25 subentries, referring the reader to 29 different pages.[1] A similar online index would show 25 descriptive hyperlinks.

Form of Entries

Index entries for paper documents have two parts—a subject and a reference. The reference can be one or more page numbers or a pointer to another subject ("*see* topic"). Certain rules govern the form of index entries.

ENTRIES AND SUBENTRIES

Index entries can either stand alone or contain subentries. Subentries describe specific aspects of entries. They can be either *nested* (on the next line and indented a few spaces to the right of the main entry) or continuous. The *landings* entry in the preceding section is a good example of a nested entry. A long, detailed index might have more than one level of subentries, with sub-subentries providing even finer detail.

A short, simple index with only one level of subentries can contain entries formatted in a continuous line rather than nested. The following example shows a continuous entry:

searching: multiple text strings, 2–11 through 2–14; single text string, 2–8 through 2–10

SEE REFERENCES

A *see* reference appears in place of page numbers and directs the reader to a main entry containing page numbers. Use it for synonyms of the main entry. For example:

ending a session (*see* logging off)

This entry tells the reader to look up *logging off* for pointers to information about ending a session.

A *see* reference contains no page numbers and sends the reader to another part of the index. Therefore, use it only to refer to long entries. If a main entry is small, include page references for the synonym, as well as for the main term, and place the main term in parentheses. By including page numbers, rather than using a *see* reference, you save the reader the trouble of looking elsewhere. For example:

ending a session (logging off)   40–41

SEE ALSO REFERENCES

A *see also* reference directs the reader to another index entry for related information. It also expands the reader's search by indicating topics the reader might not have considered looking up. For example, to tell terminal users how to log on to a host computer, you will list *logging on* in the index and include page numbers where logging on is explained. Then, to point the reader to information about how security keeps unauthorized users from logging on, you would include a "*see also* security" reference.

A *see also* reference usually appears as the first subentry, with the words *see also* italicized:

logging on   88–93
  see also security

PAGE NUMBERS

Individual page numbers are listed with commas separating them. The following example shows a topic discussed on two separate pages:

fluid levels
  checking   9, 15

Continuing page numbers indicate an extended discussion of a particular topic and are listed by first and last number, separated by an en dash. The following example indicates such a discussion:

fluid levels   9–17

Index generators often don't provide easy ways to indicate continuing page numbers. Therefore, check long lists of individual page numbers in a computer-generated index to see if they are all part of a continuous discussion; then edit the page reference for proper form by listing the first and last page numbers, separated by an en dash.

If you have used hyphenated page numbers in text, you cannot use a hyphen to indicate continuing page numbers. You will have to edit the index and substitute the word "through" for the hyphen. For example, if fluid levels are described on pages 9 through 17 of Chapter Four and Chapter Four contains hyphenated page numbers, continuing page numbers will be listed as follows in the index:

fluid levels   4–9 through 4–17

Creating an Index

You can create an index either manually or with the help of an index generator. Because most word-processing programs now come with indexing capabilities, you'll probably do the latter. This section assumes you'll use an index generator.

You can use the information in this section to guide you through a manual index as well, but you'll have to list entries and page numbers manually and alphabetize them yourself.

When you index your document, you will

- go through a *hard copy* (computer printout) of your final draft and mark terms you want to index.
- enter the terms in the index generator.
- run the software to generate the index.
- edit the index.

MARKING A HARD COPY

On a hard copy of your finished document, highlight or underline those terms you want to index. Remember to mark only those places where the reader will find significant information about terms; do not mark every occurrence. In the margin next to the highlighted term, write additional entries you'd like to include that refer the reader to the information. For example, if you mark the words *engine maintenance,* you might write in the margin *tune-ups* (see *engine maintenance*).

Also write subentries that describe the kind of information the reader will find on the page. For example, if a page describes how often engine maintenance procedures need to be performed, you might highlight *engine maintenance* and write *frequency* in the margin.

USING AN INDEX GENERATOR

Once you mark a hard copy, you can open your computer file and either highlight the terms online or enter them in whatever way your index generator requires. Because these indexing programs differ quite a bit, details on how to use them are beyond the scope of this discussion.

If you have experience using index generators and the one you're using is particularly flexible, you might be able to highlight terms directly online, without first marking a hard copy. Some index generators allow you to type additional entries and subentries in your document, using *invisible text* (text that does not appear in your printed document but that can be read by the indexing program). These capabilities can save you a lot of time. However, fancy software can provide the illusion that you're creating a good index. Don't skip the step of first learning what makes an index useful. You will always need to edit an index, and one created by computer software needs editing more than one you create without such help.

EDITING THE INDEX

You will edit an index both to increase its usefulness and to correct errors. This subsection describes the editing and proofreading passes that lead to a polished index. You can use the checklist at the end of the section to remember them later.

All indexes, even manually created ones, will contain multiple forms of the same terms. For example, the entries *logging on* and *log on* might appear in separate places.

> logging on   2–5, 8
>
> log on   8, 17

Because they are synonymous, these entries' page references should be combined next to the entry the reader is most likely to look up. You can delete the other entry or turn it into a *see* reference, depending on how frequently readers are likely to look up the entry. In this example, you would delete *log on,* because readers looking it up will easily find *logging on* nearby:

> logging on   2–5, 8, 17

Once you have cleaned up your topic entries, read through the index and ask yourself what additional entries and subentries might help someone who is unfamiliar with the product. Add them now.

Next, edit the mechanical errors in your index.

Correct any misspelled terms. If a page reference appears next to a misspelled term, and the term appears correctly spelled elsewhere in the index, move the page reference to the correct entry and delete the misspelling.

Delete page numbers that repeat within the same entry. For example, in the following entry, the first two page references should be deleted:

> logging on   2, 3, 2–5

Proofread the index for correct alphabetization.

Proofread page references against the text to make sure that the page referred to contains the information listed in the index entry. For a long computer-generated index, you can spot-check page numbers rather than proofreading every one against the text. If you find even one error, however, your index generator has a bug and you'll need to go back and proofread all page references.

Proofread all page numbers in a manually created index.

Finally, polish the format of the index as thoroughly as other parts of the document, checking for proper alignment, spacing, and widows and orphans.

CHECKLIST 17–2.   EDITING THE INDEX

Refer to this checklist when you edit and proofread an index:
- Combine page references from multiple forms of the same entry (e.g., *log on* and *logging on*) into one entry.
- Create new entries and subentries that will increase the usefulness of the index.
- Delete page numbers that repeat within the same entry.
- Proofread the index for correct alphabetization.
- Proofread page references against the text.
- Proofread spacing, alignment, and other formatting elements.

SUMMING IT UP

With this chapter, you've come to the end of the documentation process. You now know how to produce a draft that is ready for the printer, complete with index. The next two chapters discuss aspects of the technical writing profession that affect your performance and your future.

---

[1] Excerpted from the index of *Private Pilot Maneuvers* (Englewood, Colo.: Jeppesen Sanderson, Inc., 1989), pp. 1–2.

PART 4
DOING BUSINESS

18

The Hazards of Being a Tech Writer

The price one pays for pursuing a profession, or calling, is an intimate knowledge of its ugly side.
— James Baldwin (*Nobody Knows My Name,* 1961)

All professions have an ugly part—the part you don't hear about until you're in the middle of it. However, if you know about problems before they happen, you can prepare yourself to deal with them.

Let's look at some of the unpleasant aspects of a high-tech career, such as stress and computer-related injuries, with an eye toward their solutions.

STRESS

Doing business as a technical writer means producing high-quality documentation under often stressful conditions—conditions caused by aggressive deadlines and a variety of irritants inherent in a high-tech environment. Learning to deal with stress can help you avoid burnout and excel at your work.

"Job stress costs American business at least $200 billion a year—in absenteeism, diminished productivity, direct medical expenses, employee turnover, insurance premiums, and workers' compensation awards," says corporate consultant Robert K. Cooper. "Put in perspective, that's already more than the profits of all the Fortune 500 companies combined."[1]

Every job provides stress. A certain amount of stress creates challenge and makes an otherwise boring job more interesting. Too much stress, coupled with lack of appreciation for your efforts, can lead to burnout.

Tech writers do burn out. Feelings of futility lead to caring less about the quality of a document, becoming cynical about their company and its products, gossiping about uncooperative engineers, and slowing down on the job. How can you avoid burnout? By assessing the stresses in your unique situation and taking control of them before they control you.

Stresses Inherent in Tech Writing

You already know the most common stresses tech writers face. They're listed in the first chapter of this book. And they're listed again below because now we'll look at them in relation to stress management. They include:

- difficulty obtaining information
- reticent or uncooperative engineers
- canceled projects (after the work's been done)
- unreasonable or unclear deadlines
- unwieldy tools and equipment
- office politics

Writers' occupational injuries can be added to this list of stresses. These are the physical problems born of spending long hours using a computer.

Strategies for Dealing with Stress

Independent-minded, creative people—the kind of people who become tech writers—tend to blame themselves when they have difficulty coping with a stressful situation. Yet, according to psychologists, burnout is a situational problem, rather than an individual failing. Most of the stresses that lead to burnout are caused by organizational and environmental problems.[2]

Some stresses can be changed, others cannot. And many of the ones that cannot be changed become bearable if sufficient rewards are present. One of the first strategies for coping with stress is to distinguish between those problems you can solve and those you'll have to live with.

For the stresses that can be changed, take action. The more control you have over setting your own limits, the less likely you are to burn out. To cope with those problems that can't be changed, you'll need a support group of sympathetic peers, some stress-reductions techniques, and the ability to extract either pleasure or meaning from some aspects of your job.

COMMUNICATING PROBLEMS AND SOLUTIONS

Most problems that can be changed should be taken up with your manager. It's part of a manager's job to solve problems like unclear or unreasonable deadlines and unwieldy tools. Similarly, problems with office politics can often be "delegated upward" to your manager. If you recall from the first chapter of this book, writers sometimes are forced to play diplomat between engineering and marketing departments that disagree about how the product is to work. Your manager should be able to get you out of the middle of the more stressful interdepartmental feuds.

Phrase the problem to your manager in a non-blaming way and be ready to suggest one or more solutions. Your manager might not even be aware that the problems exist and might welcome your help solving them.

Get involved in the solutions. For example, volunteer to set up a scheduling procedure for your department's publications and to research the amount of time each phase of manual production takes.

Sometimes a manager won't be there as a buffer and you'll need to take charge of unrealistic deadlines directly, by confronting a product team.

Says a writer at Apple Computer:

It's really easy for people to look at the product schedule and say, O.K., your documentation can fit in here, here, and here. That was creating a tremendous amount of pressure for me because, first of all, their schedules probably weren't realistic to begin with, but then I was being pushed to fit their schedule without even looking at what I needed and what the document needed. At that point, I stood up in one of our meetings and said, look, this is the way I think schedules should be done—I should sit down and look at what's needed for my document. And that's what I did.

When I did redo my schedule, based on the way I thought it should be, and I put it out there, nobody objected. But still, with me, people will keep pushing—Can't you get this done sooner? Can't you do this? So a lot of it, for me, is setting limits as far as schedules are concerned; setting limits as far as what I'll do and what I won't do—meetings that people want you to go to that you haven't got time to go to—saying no, I can't do that.

This writer discovered what psychologists have discovered about stress. The more you feel in control of the forces affecting your work, the less likely you are to burn out.

CULTIVATING A SUPPORT GROUP

Stress sometimes creates tension among coworkers, leading to cliquishness, gossip, and mistrust. Avoid judging coworkers. Instead look for opportunities to express your appreciation of them. They're experiencing stress, too. And whether problems are solvable or not, you'll benefit from a support group of coworkers who understand the stresses you're experiencing.

Fortunately, camaraderie of writers is one of the rewards of tech writing. They'll not only understand what you're going through, but can also help with feedback about your work.

Lack of appreciation for your work is a significant factor in burnout. You can compensate for lack of support from an overworked manager by setting up a peer review system. Ask fellow writers for feedback. Offer to give it. Make sure that, in addition to diplomatically phrased, constructive criticism, you include a healthy dose of praise.

PRACTICING STRESS REDUCTION

Stress takes its toll on the body, in the form of hypertension, heart problems, and other stress-related diseases. Two ways to counteract the physical ravages of stress are relaxation and exercise.

Psychologists recommend taking time to relax after work, through meditation or whatever means works for you. One tech writer I know goes for a long walk with his two dogs. Another practices classical guitar.

Tech writing consultant Carolyn Curtis maintains an elaborate garden of vegetables and native California plants. She advises:

> The natural world is a good antidote to all of this rectilinear, techie kind of stuff. Random vegetation, in particular. If you don't have your own yard, go to some wild place, like the city park or whatever. Just something that doesn't grow in straight lines!

Now imagine doing something that not only reduces stress, but also helps keep your weight down, increases your strength, improves your resistance to a long list of diseases, tones and shapes your body, regulates your breathing, helps you sleep better, and increases your sense of well-being. Exercise is one of the few bargains in life.

I used to hate gym class in school and have never been athletic. But my first tech writing job just happened to be across the street from a health club that extended discounts to neighboring businesses. I joined mostly for the Jacuzzi. Once I started exercising there regularly, however, I was hooked and have made exercise a habit ever since. I notice after a workout a significant reduction in physical and emotional tension. I also almost never get the winter colds and flu I took for granted before I started exercising.

Don't think you have to join a health club or become a jock. Short, brisk walks, gradually increasing in length, can provide most exercise benefits at no cost. And if you already enjoy bicycling, swimming, skiing, or dancing, do it more often. Start considering it a necessity rather than an indulgence.

FOCUSING ON REWARDS

"You've got to be interested in what you're doing to do it well," says biomedical writer Dan Liberthson. "It was my interest in medicine—which I rediscovered when I went to work as a technical writer for a medical equipment firm—that really led me to make a career as a technical writer. If I hadn't found that interest, I wouldn't have had a career.

"I think there are very few people who can be happy if they are not interested in the work that they're doing and in the material that they work with."

If you enjoy the rewards inherent in technical writing—the variety, the creative opportunities, and the constant learning—its everyday stresses will recede into the background of your awareness.

SETTING LONG-TERM GOALS

Sometimes a particular work situation is just plain unhealthy. Morale is low, unreasonable pressures are beyond your control, and rewards are few. It's time to decide whether to stay or leave.

One of the greatest stress fighters is a clear long-term goal. A long-term goal can be a deep expression of who you are, encompassing your ideals, whom you wish to become, and what effect you want to have on others. If you know where you're going, problems along the way seem much less significant than if they are your whole world.

Perhaps your current, uncomfortable situation is a necessary step toward your long-term goal, and you need to leave honorably, with all your projects successfully completed and your character references pristine. With your eye on the goal, you're constantly reminded of why you are putting up with all the garbage.

Your long-term goal can also help you leave, when the time is right, by providing a vision of a happier future. (The next chapter, "Career Excellence," describes some of the career possibilities open to tech writers.)

WRITERS' OCCUPATIONAL INJURIES

Writers live protected lives, ensconced in temperature-controlled offices, free of health hazards, right? Wrong. As frequent computer users, writers are prone to a host of ailments, which include musculoskeletal disorders, eye strain, and even miscarriages.

Repetitive Strain Injuries (RSI)

The most common musculoskeletal disorders related to frequent computer use are Repetitive Strain Injuries (RSI). They're also called repeated-trauma disorders (among other things) and includes tendinitis, carpal tunnel syndrome, and a host of more esoteric-sounding afflictions, primarily of the hands, wrists, arms, and shoulders. These injuries are common because computer work necessitates sitting for hours and using our bodies in unnatural ways.

"Computer keyboards are a dreadful device," says hand surgeon Robert Markison in an interview reported in *Wired* magazine. "They're one of the worst mass-produced items of the 20th century. ... They [computer designers] decided to make you devolve into a lizardlike creature splayed out flat on a keyboard."[3]

Repetitively straining the body causes injury. RSI can start as a vague discomfort in the forearms, numbness in part of the hand, weakness, tingling, or other variation in sensation—a feeling that something is not quite right. The signs are easy to ignore, particularly when you have a deadline. Because it creeps up slowly, RSI can do a lot of damage before you acknowledge its presence.

In 1996 repeated-trauma disorders made up close to two-thirds of reported occupational illnesses—proportionally twice as high as in 1986.[4] And carpal tunnel syndrome, a disease of the median nerve in the wrist, caused the lengthiest job absences of any work-related injury or illness. In 1997 carpal tunnel syndrome absences averaged 25 days—five times the average absence from all causes.[5] The cost to industry of this injury alone has been enormous.

The greatest irony, from my point of view, is that I reported similar statistics in the predecessor to this book, yet didn't recognize symptoms in myself.

Not long after *The Tech Writing Game* was published, I started having trouble sleeping because of aching in my hands, wrists, and forearms. Nothing serious, it seemed; I just couldn't get comfortable. My doctor gave me some anti-inflammatory drugs, which settled things down until a year later, when the aches came back. This time, they didn't go away. They got so bad, I had to stop work, and eventually, I had to stop everything. I couldn't even open a door without severe pain.

I lost three years of work and a home I loved, which I had to sell to support myself and to pay for the treatments my HMO wasn't willing to provide. Grim, yes. But I hope you'll suffer through these three paragraphs, in place of the three years I endured, and be frightened enough to avoid what I went through. I'll give you some tips on how in the section "Preventing Computer-Related Injuries," later in this chapter.

VDT-Related Injuries

From eyestrain to miscarriages, a host of ailments have been blamed on computer monitors or *VDTs* (video display terminals). Almost 75 percent of computer users experience some form of eyestrain, which can be as slight as dry, itchy eyes, or as severe as burning pain and deteriorating vision.[6] Eyestrain can also lead to strained posture, stiff neck, and eventually, musculoskeletal difficulties.

Reports of other VDT-related ailments as serious as cancer and miscarriages have often been episodic—that is, seemingly isolated incidents that don't prove anything. However, the number of such reports has prompted many to feel more research is needed.

As early as 1983, the California-based health maintenance organization, Kaiser Permanente, responded to concerns about VDT emissions by studying 1,583 pregnant women. The results sent chills up the spines of computer manufacturers and dealers. Pregnant women using VDTs over 20 hours a week showed an 80 percent greater likelihood of miscarrying than women who did not work with computers. Although the study did eliminate factors such as age, education, occupation, smoking, alcohol, and drugs as causes, it did not prove VDTs guilty.[7]

Since then, improvements in VDTs have greatly reduced the electromagnetic emissions thought to be responsible for miscarriages and other health complaints. Flat-panel display emissions are even lower than VDTs. However, the *LCDs* (liquid crystal displays) used in some portable computers can emit strong fields.

Computers themselves, and the office environment that is wired to serve them, are as much or more a source of electromagnetic radiation than the VDT, and the total exposure of office workers may well lead to damaged cells, particularly as a result of *ELF* (extremely low frequency) magnetic fields. These fields have only recently been studied, and while studies have been small and inconclusive, they suggest that ELF magnetic fields affect the growth of developing tissues, promote cancer cell growth, interfere with cell functioning, alter neurological functioning, and indirectly affect the immune system.[8]

What does this mean for tech writers? While opposing factions are debating the hazards, we had best use caution. Recommendations for safe computer use are being disseminated by a variety of organizations in the public and private sectors. Listen for news of current studies on electromagnetic fields, particularly if you are pregnant.

Preventing Computer-Related Injuries

Recommendations for preventing computer-related ills include changes to the furniture arrangement and lighting of your work space, improved body positioning during work, and frequent breaks.

The following tips can help you create good work habits and a safe work environment. I really hope you'll take these tips to work with you and use them. Computer-related injuries are preventable, but only if you actively take care of yourself in the workplace.

TIPS ON PREVENTING COMPUTER-RELATED INJURIES

- Sit relatively straight, but in a relaxed manner, and change your position often.
- Support your lower back with an adjustable chair back or a firm cushion.
- Rest both feet comfortably on the floor with thighs parallel to the floor; avoid crossing your legs.
- Sit at least arm's length from your computer screen.
- Use a copy holder, which you can move from one side of the desk to the other. This will allow you to keep your neck vertical and to vary your head movements, rather than repeatedly looking down at the same spot on the desk.
- Eliminate light sources behind you, which cause screen glare, and in front of you, which compete with the screen. Light should come from the side or above you.
- Use a low-glare screen. If your screen reflects glare, use an antiglare screen cover.
- Use a detachable keyboard. Keyboards attached to a terminal or portable computer cannot be adjusted for comfort and safety.
- When typing at the keyboard, keep your wrists straight; don't bend the hand to the sides or upward to reach keys. Adjust the keyboard height, if necessary.

- Lower your keyboard to the level where your shoulders can relax and where your forearms angle slightly down, or no less than 90 degrees, while you type. If your arms are particularly long, you may need a lap desk or an adjustable keyboard support that clamps under your desk to keep your arms extended in a relaxed position.
- Take a break every hour, even if you feel no tension. And if you feel tightness, break at least every 15 minutes. Set a timer if you need to.
- Stretch! Stretch your forearms, wrists, shoulders, and neck. Studies have shown that an active break, including stretching and light exercise, is more beneficial in preventing RSI than an inactive one.
- If you feel any discomfort while working at the computer, **stop.** Get an ergonomic evaluation and change whatever may be causing the discomfort immediately.

Office equipment manufacturers have responded to distressed computer users with specially designed furniture and computer equipment, such as ergonomic keyboards, foot-operated mouse devices, and so forth. This new equipment and the heightened awareness of employees and employers have reduced the number of occupational injuries over the last few years. To keep this number down, we need to continue to be assertive in requesting ergonomic evaluations and accommodation.

I hope you won't ever need to know anything about treating computer-related injuries. But if you do have any symptoms, act quickly: Educate yourself about the nature of your possible injury (see the bibliography for some resources) and be aggressive about getting help. Some remedies, such as acupuncture, remain controversial, even though studies have pointed to acupuncture as an alternative to anti-inflammatory drugs or surgery for carpal tunnel syndrome. According to one source, "acupuncture and surgery are both about 80 percent successful in curing CTS [carpal tunnel syndrome]."[9]

You may need to pay out of pocket to get timely help for RSI. Do it. Soft-tissue injuries, in particular, take a very long time to heal, and if you act right away, you can shorten the healing time.

If you follow the tips presented in this section, you should be able to churn out prose efficiently and safely.

SUMMING IT UP

This chapter described some of the gloomier aspects of technical writing, such as stress and occupational injuries. But it also gave you some ammunition against them. The next chapter will guide you toward career excellence and provide glimpses of future possibilities.

---

[1] Robert K. Cooper, *The Performance Edge* (Boston: Houghton Mifflin Company, 1991), p. 7.

[2] Christina Maslach and Michael P. Leiter, *The Truth About Burnout* (San Francisco: Jossey-Bass Publishers, 1997), p. 18.

[3] Susan McCarthy, "Hacking the Hand," *Wired,* December 1995, p. 126.

[4] "Most Reported Occupational Illnesses Are Repeated-Trauma Disorders," *Monthly Labor Review,* U.S. Department of Labor, Bureau of Labor Statistics, August 13, 1999.

[5] Martin E. Personick, "BRIEF: Types of work injuries associated with lengthy absences from work," *Compensation and Working Conditions Online,* Bureau of Labor Statistics, Fall 1997, Vol. 2, No. 3 and Table 9. Percent distribution of nonfatal occupational injuries and illnesses ... 1997," *Safety and Health Statistics,* Bureau of Labor Statistics.

[6] Joan Stigliani, *The Computer User's Survival Guide* (Sebastopol, Calif.: O'Reilly & Associates, Inc., 1995), p. 127.

[7] Elaine Clift, "VDT's Can Bring on Medical Problems," *New Directions for Women,* July/August 1989, p. 4.

[8] Stigliani, pp. 211–212.

[9] Gary Perez, "Acupuncture Provides an Alternative," *Connection,* newsletter of the Silicon Valley Chapter of the STC, July 1991, p. 8.

19

Career Excellence

When men are rightly occupied, their amusement grows out of their work, as the colour-petals out of a fruitful flower.
— John Ruskin (*Sesame and Lilies*, 1865)

This chapter describes career development. You'll find suggestions on how to stand out in your current job and how to advance professionally, as well as a detailed section on how to operate as a consultant. You'll also learn about career possibilities open to you as a result of being a tech writer. You can use this chapter to explore your career goals, as a technical writer and beyond.

In the last chapter, you learned about the importance of long-range goals in relation to coping with stress. Long-range goals have the more pragmatic purpose of guiding you in your job choices.

Because tech writers are so individualistic and come from such diverse backgrounds, no single career path is appropriate for everyone. You may want to advance in your organization, move laterally into a different job category, or strike out on your own. You could also choose to stay a tech writer, changing companies for monetary gain and variety. Or you could choose to get out of the high-tech world entirely. Each choice serves up unique possibilities.

SUCCEEDING AT YOUR CAREER

Writing excellent documentation is usually not enough to promote your career as a technical writer. In the real world, some fairly average writers move ahead because they are punctual, they carry themselves in a professional manner, and mostly because people like them. In the business world, how people see you often weighs more heavily than what you produce.

You can take advantage of this seemingly unfair truth by being punctual, dressing well, and making an effort to get along well with your manager, coworkers, and members of the product team. If you add high-quality documentation to these efforts, you will surely excel.

Your documentation and expertise will go further if you share them with your professional network. You can enter your work in competitions sponsored annually by the Society for Technical Communication (STC). These competitions provide a wide range of categories, from reference material to technical illustrations. (You'll find the address of the STC and other writers' organizations in Appendix B.)

Once your career is well under way, you may choose to speak at meetings of professional groups. They are always looking for experienced writers to speak on topics like creating a style guide, designing online help, and so on.

By entering competitions and giving talks, you'll become known within your network as a knowledgeable professional. Should you want to change jobs to advance your career, you'll be one of the first in line for choice positions.

CLIMBING THE CORPORATE LADDER

If you are a people person who enjoys tackling problems, consider moving into management. As one manager pointed out in the chapter "Why Begin?" being a manager means finding rewards in the elusive stuff of problem solving, human interaction, and performance evaluations. The down side is that you don't experience the tangible results you grew to love as a tech writer: holding that published manual in your hands.

To move into management, begin by taking more responsibility within your department. For example, you can organize a group of interested writers to research and suggest improvements to the organization's documentation.

Ask your manager for more responsibility. After you've gained experience as a writer, you can become a mentor or lead writer, teaching newly hired writers about departmental procedures and style guidelines.

Many companies expect senior writers to manage projects undertaken by outside contractors or consultants (described in the next section). If you prove your project management skills, you will eventually earn a supervisory role within your organization, or you'll move on to an organization where such an opportunity exists.

INDEPENDENT CONSULTING

"We all end up earning a living," says consultant Linda Lininger. "At least with being a freelance technical writer, I feel that I'm in control of what I do. I earn a living my way."

As an independent consultant, you are a "freelancer," a "contractor," a self-employed technical writer, and a sole proprietor of a small business. Although I'll use these labels somewhat interchangeably, some define them more precisely. For example, the Internal Revenue Service (IRS) will call you an independent consultant only if you meet certain conditions, as described later in the section "Licenses, Incorporating, and the IRS." Some clients might ask you to meet a majority of those conditions before granting you consultant status and paying you without withholding taxes.

Regardless of how you are paid, you can work independently as either a "plug-in writer"—essentially, as a temporary employee—or as a true consultant.

When I struck out on my own, I began as what I call a plug-in writer in a company I'd worked for on staff. I then contracted through *job shops,* temporary employment agencies that found me similar assignments: I was expected to come up to speed quickly, but basically to fit in and do the work of a staff writer. Through those experiences I grew from thinking of myself as a plug-in to thinking of myself more as a hired gun—or perhaps more appropriately, as a hired pen. I had learned to come up to speed fast and to excel at shaping, scheduling, and completing projects.

Finally, I decided to represent myself without an intermediary, after I realized I was solving somewhat higher-level issues for clients, like communicating with other departments on behalf of a publications manager.

As an independent consultant, you might sometimes perform as a temporary employee and sometimes as a true consultant, providing advice and services that run the gamut from publisher to political go-between.

The joys of independent consulting include being your own boss and setting your own schedule and conditions. The drawbacks of independent consulting include the constant need to hustle work (which is not a drawback if you like hustling), to keep accurate financial records, to know tax laws, and to assume entrepreneurial risk. In spite of having to deal with these challenges, I and many others have chosen the independent route because of the freedom it affords.

Becoming a Consultant

Getting started as a consultant really means getting started as an independent business person. The following prerequisites will help you succeed:

- business contacts
- a good track record
- knowledge of publications procedures
- ability to budget for lean times
- willingness to assume entrepreneurial risk
- ability to sell yourself
- skill at negotiating agreements
- aptitude for accounting and for keeping on top of changing tax laws

You can see that this is not a small undertaking. But a time may come when you'll have the experience and contacts you need to generate a lucrative consulting business. You can begin without knowing all there is to know about taxes and such. You can learn as you go along, and others who have gone before can help with the details.

Your success hinges a great deal on your contacts—who you know. That's one of several good reasons to work in the field for a while before you go it alone. While you build your career as a staff writer, you establish a reputation with managers, supervisors, and lead writers. This reputation will follow you.

For example, six technical writers I've worked with on staff have since become supervisors or managers. Five of them have provided me with contract offers, either directly or through a recommendation to someone else in their company.

Another good reason to work in the field for a while before becoming a consultant is that you will need excellent writing samples, references, and the ability to "land on your feet." As a consultant, you will be expected to know industry-standard procedures for producing whatever kind of documentation is your specialty. You will need to be familiar with how a technical publications department works. Or if you plan to freelance for technical periodicals, corporate newsletters, or some other publishing environment, you will need to know their production and scheduling processes.

If money burns a hole in your pocket, don't become a freelance writer— that is, unless you're comfortable living "close to the bone." To use yet another cliché consultants use frequently, it's either feast or famine.

"I was really nervous in the beginning of my contract career because it was a lousy year to get started," says consultant Carolyn Curtis. "It was 1985, which was a terrible year in the industry. If I hadn't had a cushion saved up, I would have really been in trouble."

During my first years consulting, I turned down a couple of contracts—one because it seemed tedious, another because I sensed conflicting expectations within the organization. Then, when I couldn't find another contract and the phone didn't ring for several months, I spent long hours questioning my wisdom in turning down those jobs.

Some consultants advise taking whatever opportunity comes along. Others advise selecting only those at which you know you'll excel and be happy. I still ascribe mostly to the latter point of view. You'll have to find the level of income and job satisfaction that meets your particular needs.

Meeting Clients' Expectations

As a consultant, you are often called in to "fight fires"—to handle problem projects encumbered by difficult personalities, an unrealistic deadline, or both. Usually these projects are considered undesirable by staff writers, and you are seen as the magician who'll be able to handle them.

The positive way to look at this is that, yes, you can handle them. You are not embroiled in whatever political battle is raging around a particular project, and you are seen as an outside expert—a possible bearer of solutions and sanity. You can set conditions under which you will perform. For example, you can say you'll meet the (unmeetable) deadline, provided that the product is finished and all information is in your hands by a certain date. You can establish contingencies: If the product isn't finished by that date, the deadline will slip.

As a consultant, you'll be expected to ask informed questions about your client company's procedures. For example, when is the beta test for the product? Has a product freeze date been set? Will I be responsible for camera-ready copy?

You will also be expected to produce at a faster pace than a staff writer would.

Some clients might expect a periodic status report, detailing how you've spent your time. It's a good idea to provide at least a general description of your activities when you submit your invoice. Linda Lininger goes even further:

> I keep status reports weekly. In my daily calendar, I make notes about what I do with my time, so that when I do my status report I can write, "I spent this many hours in my day at the keyboard and I edited these files. I spent this much time formatting and printing, and these are the files, or this is what I did." So that when I write a status report, I can account for how I wish to charge my client.

The most important thing to remember is that each client's needs are unique. Try to ascertain what the client expects from you. What can you provide that will be perceived as meeting their needs? Is it a perfectly formatted document? Will a crude, meticulously accurate one do? It may be more important for you to attend meetings and communicate on behalf of the publications department than to produce anything.

If after talking with a client about their expectations, you are still not clear about how to meet them, ask specifically "What would you like to see as evidence that I am meeting your needs?"

Doing Business as a Consultant

Once you decide to freelance, you can begin to learn about business practices. Should you get a business license or incorporate? Should you engage in "fixed-bid" contracts or charge an hourly rate? What contract terms or agreements will protect you?

The answers to these questions fill books and are constantly changing. For example, the tax implications of incorporating and independent consulting change almost annually. Engage an accountant who is knowledgeable about self-employment to help you with the details.

LICENSES, INCORPORATING, AND THE IRS

You can do business as a technical writing consultant without any special licenses or insurance, although it's getting more difficult. Many larger organizations are concerned the IRS might require proof that you are independent. If the IRS determines that you are functioning as a regular employee, your client might be liable for taxes and penalties.

The definition of a consultant is somewhat vague in the eyes of the IRS, but things they look for are "assumption of risk," a workplace off site, multiple clients (as opposed to one client who supplies all your income), and so on. Having a business license or being incorporated is another sign that you are independent. The best way to keep on top of this issue is to join an organization like the STC or the National Writers Union (see Appendix B for addresses) and to network with fellow consultants.

In general, incorporating is a hassle, forcing you to engage an accountant on a regular basis and in some states, requiring a large minimum tax payment. Some consultants feel it's worth it because it shelters their personal assets from liability and, with the help of a particularly agile accountant, can sometimes save on taxes.

WRITTEN AGREEMENTS

You will need a written agreement of some sort between you and your client. Larger companies provide a set contract. Read it before you sign it. If it contains the words "work for hire," you are signing away the copyright to your work. That's O.K. in consulting, and after all, where else are you going to sell a manual on electronic mouse traps except through the company that makes them? However, most companies are not aware of copyright law and so do not include those specific words in the contract. If "work for hire" does not appear in your contract, you own the copyright, and this little detail can help you—if the client claims they cannot pay you, for whatever reason, you can prevent them from publishing your manual.

Even if you sign a client-provided contract, you should write a letter of agreement and ask your client to sign it. The letter should reiterate any verbal agreements you have made with the client, such as your rate of pay, the name of the product you're documenting, the kind of document you've been asked to produce, the time frame, and so on. While verbal contracts are legally binding, they're awfully hard to prove without a paper trail.

A few tech writing contractors prefer to work on a *fixed-bid* contract. *Fixed-bid* means you will be paid a lump sum when you meet one or more milestones, which usually correlate with document drafts. For example, you'll be paid 50 percent of the sum for a first draft, 25 percent for a second review draft, and the final 25 percent for camera-ready copy. This kind of agreement requires you to produce a fairly elaborate written contract, detailing, among other things, contingencies that might inflate your fee. A fixed-bid forces you to estimate your hours very accurately, so that you don't wind up working for free.

A fixed bid is appropriate when you are writing a document, such as a white paper, that describes an existing technology. (A *white paper* is an informational marketing piece that indirectly sells a technical product or solution.) However, unless you are writing a document for an existing technology that will hold still while you produce the document, a fixed bid may not allow you to bill all the hours you work.

Most consultants who document technical products shy away from fixed-bid contracts, because they are working with a moving target, contingencies are inevitable, and such contracts often devolve into hourly arrangements anyway. You can never allow for all the unforeseen problems that can arise during a product release.

OVERHEAD AND SETTING RATES

As a consultant, you are expected to own your own equipment. A computer, a fast modem, and a good laser printer are the minimum you'll need. A fax machine and miscellaneous items like a paper cutter are also helpful.

Remember that your equipment and office space in your home are overhead and should be taken into account in setting your rates. You also need to know how to set your rates. Says consultant Linda Urban:

> It took a lot of years before I realized that what I charged had to include overhead and what that overhead meant. It had to include my vacation pay, my sick pay, my health insurance, the utilities on my office, the upgrades to my software, the training for myself. I'm going to an online help seminar in March. For someone on staff, the decision is, will my company pay for it? For me, the decision is to spend the money. When you start out on your own, it's hard to realize the expense of that. So it may sound like you're making a lot of money per hour, but it covers a lot.

For help in figuring rates, you can contact the Independent Consultants' Special Interest Group of the STC or refer to the numerous books currently available on starting and running a small business.

Working Through Job Shops

Job shops, job brokers, "jobbers," recruiters, contracting houses—all these are names for the agencies that will represent you as a contractor to clients, cut your check, and skim a hefty percentage off the top. Their cut can range from 30 to 50 percent of cost billed the client. This means they might bill the client $80 an hour, and you will see around $45 an hour in pay.

Despite the excessive amount they skim, job shops can help you get started as a freelancer. They provide the contacts, and you provide the rest—your writing samples, references, skills at being interviewed, and finally your skills on the job will establish your value and build contacts in the freelance market.

Before you apply to a job shop, check its reputation carefully. A startling number of job shops are known for misrepresenting the nature of assignments, for misrepresenting writers' skills, and worst of all, for not paying writers. The reputable job shops are reasonably honest about their clients' expectations and will pay you on time, even if the client is late.

In the 1980s, in response to excessive job-shop fees, the National Writers Union (NWU), an organization that promotes fair conditions for writers, started a tech writers' hotline in the San Francisco Bay area. The hotline now serves all kinds of writers nationally. This service brings together contract writers and clients at a greatly reduced fee. To use the hotline, you would need to join the NWU (see Appendix B for the address).

WHAT'S NEXT?

Even though tech writing is a rewarding, creative endeavor, you may choose to move on at some point. Besides the climb toward management or consulting, other career paths become more accessible as a result of your years of technical writing experience.

When my hand injury prevented me from doing technical writing, I decided to try teaching others how to do it. I began by taking classes in training-program development and presentation skills; then I taught night classes in colleges that had been using my book. Now I provide writing seminars to companies. And I continue to seek other ways to express my writing gifts in the world of work.

Lateral Career Change

Perhaps technical writing has sparked your interest in technology. With your product knowledge, you can aim for a technical support job within your organization, changing careers without having to pound the pavement or even return to school. Many technical writers can handle customer support calls with a minimum of extra training. Providing field support at customer sites is another option for technically knowledgeable writers willing to get their hands dirty.

Technical writing sensitizes you to product design defects, which might lead you to transfer into the growing human factors field. According to Vicki King, senior human factors engineer at Intuit, tech writers are drawn to this career path, which is known by many names but which basically involves helping companies design products human beings will want to use. Says Shaunna Pickett-Gordon, lead writer at Sun Microsystems:

> Another thing that has become so huge in the last ten years is human interface engineering (HIE) or human computer interface (HCI) engineering. Ten years ago I hadn't even heard that there was such a thing. The writer's role is as a junior HIE.

As a human factors engineer, your job might be to design the user interface, to usability test the product and documentation, to recommend product design changes, or some combination of these functions—continuing the role of user advocate tech writers already know so well.

Technical training is another career choice for tech writers, particularly those who are extroverted and who can speak knowledgeably about a product. Instead of writing manuals and training material, you'll verbally communicate material written by others to a classroom full of tech support trainees, new employees, or customers.

For the yet more extroverted, opportunities exist to move into marketing and sales.

Within the biomedical field, you can aim for a clinical research associate position, monitoring the outside agencies that perform drug trials. As a clinical research associate, you might design how the study is to be done and act as a liaison between the pharmaceutical company and the testing firm.

And as in other technical fields, your options as a biomedical writer also include training, education, marketing, and sales. In training and education, you can provide project management, supervising outside agencies and contractors in writing training materials. In marketing, you devise a marketing strategy for a specific drug, plan its advertising campaign, and contract with ad agencies to implement the campaign. Additional opportunities exist in public relations, arranging speakers' tours for noted physicians to address groups of fellow physicians on new developments in biomedical research.

Other Kinds of Writing

Many technical writers have other writing interests. Some write children's books, others science fiction, others poetry. Just yesterday, a fellow freelancer told me she's writing books for disabled children, explaining their disabilities to them. During four years of my tech writing career, my avocation was travel writing for newspapers and magazines.

Technical writing prepares you for many of the demands all writers experience—churning out prose to deadline, accepting editing, and dealing with criticism. While most writing pays less than tech writing, it may be your next career choice.

Says Dirk van Nouhuys, a veteran of 35 years of tech writing and a published fiction writer:

Many people get into technical writing who write fiction or poetry, as do I, and they say, How does it affect your writing? And I have an answer for that, which is at first it's a benefit, because it's a benefit to your writing to learn any disciplined subset of writing.

So you learn how to do technical writing, which characteristically has kind of a short breath. It has short sentences and small organizational units. It's very modular. After a certain point—after a certain number of years—that becomes a problem because that kind of gets into your blood. And that's not the only way to write. And there are a great many things that you don't write about in technical writing, like birth, death, love, hate, terror, anxiety. [Laughs] You don't write about them. And your fingers can lose touch with writing about them and with those kind of words—truth and beauty—and so after a while you have to be able to remove yourself from the technical writing mind-set to write other kinds of writing.

Whatever you choose to do next, be it managing, consulting, fixing modems, or writing the great American novel, technical writing will give you many of the skills you'll need.

SUMMING IT UP

This book described to you the joys and pitfalls of technical writing. It allowed you to see into the lives of working writers and the minds of hiring managers. It guided you through the steps of producing a technical document, from scheduling and research right through to last-minute formatting of a camera-ready copy.

Then, this book went on to describe the worst and best of doing business as a tech writer. This final chapter looked at career development and long-term goals.

In all, you are now more ready to pursue a technical writing career than if you had not read this book. You can always refer to it for guidance as you go along. I wish you the best of luck.

APPENDIXES

APPENDIX A

ACADEMIC PROGRAMS

This appendix[1] lists some of the graduate, undergraduate, and certificate opportunities that have been offered through college and university technical communication programs in the past. Most of these programs are still operating, and more programs begin each year. Write to the schools that interest you for details about their offerings.

Alderson-Broaddus College
Box 2158
Philippi, West Virginia 26416
Department: Humanities
Program Name: Writing Degree with Specialization
in Technical Communications
Contact: Barbara Smith

Alexandria Technical College
1601 Jefferson Street
Alexandria, Minnesota 56308–3799
Department: General Education
Program Name: Technical Communication
Contact: Admissions

Algonquin College
200 Lees Avenue
Ottawa, Canada
Department: Computer Studies
Program Name: Technical Writing
Contact: Dave Matheson

American River College
4700 College Oak Drive
Sacramento, California 95841
Department: English
Program Name: Corporate Writing Program and
Professional Communication Program
Contact: Robert Frew

---

[1] Information is from the Web site of the Society for Technical Communications, March 2000, and is used here with permission. For additional programs, details, and updates, go to www.stc-va.org/facademic.htm

American University of Paris
Avenue de New York
Paris 75116 France
Department: Continuing Education
Program Name: Technical Writing Program
Contact: Roberta Vellve

Auburn University
9020 Haley Center
Auburn, Alabama 36849–5203
Department: English
Program Name: English with Concentration in
   Technical and Professional Writing
Contact: Donald H. Cunningham

Austin Community College
11928 Stonehollow Drive
Austin, Texas 78758
Department: Technical Communications Program
Program Name: Technical Communications
Contact: Katherine Staples

Austin Peay State University
P.O. Box 4487
Clarksville, Tennessee 37044
Department: Languages and Literature
Program Name: English Writing Minor with
   concentration in Technical Communication
Contact: James Clemmer

Belleville Area College
2500 Carlyle Avenue
Belleville, Illinois 62221
Department: English
Program Name: Course in Technical Writing
Contact: Roger Christeck

Black Hawk College
6600 34th Avenue
Moline, Illinois 61265
Department: English
Program Name: Course in Technical Writing
Contact: Professor Anderson

Bob Jones University
Box 34631
Greenville, South Carolina 29614
Department: Professional Writing and Publication
Program Name: BA in Technical Writing
Contact: Blake Spence

Boise State University
1910 University Drive
Boise, Idaho 83725
Department: English
Program Name: Technical Communication
Contact: Mike Markel

Bowling Green State University
224 East Hall Bowling Green State University
Bowling Green, Ohio 43403
Department: English
Program Name: Scientific and Technical
 Communication
Contact: Gary Heba

Brigham Young University
3161 JKHB
Provo, Utah 84602
Department: English
Program Name: Technical Writing
Contact: Beverly Zimmerman

Burlington County College
Division of Liberal Arts
Pemberton, New Jersey 8068
Program Name: Technical Writing
Contact: C. DeWitt Peterson

California Polytechnic State University
Department of English
San Luis Obispo, California 93407
Department: English
Program Name: Technical Communication
 Certificate Program
Contact: Dr. Matthew S. Novak

California State University
7750 College Town Drive Street 100
Sacramento, California 95826–2344
Department: Regional and Continuing Education
Program Name: Technical Information
 Development Certificate
Contact: Elizabeth Hough

California State University
1250 Bellflower Boulevard
Long Beach, California 90840–2403
Department: English
Program Name: Certificate in Technical and
 Professional Writing
Contact: Dave Samuelson

California State University
Chico, California 95929–0830
Department: English
Program Name: Technical Writing Certificate
Contact: Kenneth Price

California State University Hayward
School of Continuing and Extended Education,
CSU Hayward
Hayward, California 94542
Department: English
Program Name: Technical and Professional
    Communication Certificate
Contact: Dr. Peggy Lant and Dr. Jude Lopez

California University of Pennsylvania
250 University Avenue
California, Pennsylvania 15419
Department: English
Program Name: Professional Writing Program,
    Technical Writing Track
Contact: Dr. Pratul Pathak

Carnegie Mellon University
5000 Forbes Avenue
Pittsburgh, Pennsylvania 15213
Department: English
Program Name: Technical Communication
Contact: Karen Rossi Schnakenberg

Cedarville College
P. O. Box 601
Cedarville, Ohio 45314
Department: Language/Literature
Program Name: Professional and Technical
    Communication
Contact: Sandra W. Harner

Christchurch Polytechnic, New Zealand
Coventry Street
Christchurch 8032 New Zealand
Department: Faculty of Humanities
Program Name: Diploma of Professional and
    Technical Communication
Contact: Alison Sanders

Cincinnati State Technical and Community College
3520 Central Parkway
Cincinnati, Ohio 45223–2690
Department: Humanities
Program Name: Associate Degree and Certificate in
    Technical Writing and Editing Program
Contact: Pamela Ecker

Clackamas Community College
19600 South Molalla Avenue
Oregon City, Oregon 97045
Department: English
Program Name: Courses in Technical Writing
Contact: Jeff Knorr

Clark College
East McLoughlin Boulevard
Vancouver, Washington 98663
Department: English
Program Name: Courses in Technical Writing and
    Transfer Program: Technical Communication
Contact: Don Erskine

Clarkson University
Potsdam, New York 13699–5760
Department: Technical Communications
Program Name: BS in Technical Communications
Contact: Bill Karis

College of Lake County
19351 West Washington Street
Grayslake, Illinois 60030
Department: Communication Arts Department
Program Name: Technical Communication
Contact: Judy Rosenberg

College of the Rockies
Box 8500
Cranbrook, British Columbia, Canada
Department: Canadian Institute for New Media,
    Research and Development
Program Name: New Media Communications
    Technical Writing
Contact: Stephan Beckhoff

Colorado State University
Room C-225 Clark Building
Ft. Collins, Colorado 80523–1785
Department: Journalism and Technical
    Communication
Contact: Donald Zimmerman and Marilee Long

Columbus State Community College
550 East Spring Street
Columbus, Ohio 43215
Department: Communication Skills
Program Name: Technical Communication
Contact: Susan Moran, Program Coordinator

Concordia University Centre for Continuing Education
1455 de Maisonneuve Boulevard West
Montreal, Canada
Department: Continuing Education
Program Name: Certificate in Technical Communication
Contact: Julia Denker

Cuyahoga Community College
2415 Woodland Avenue
Cleveland, Ohio 44115–3239
Department: Continuing and Professional Education
Program Name: Technical Communications
Contact: Mike Kobuszewski

Danube-University Krems
Dr. Karl Dorrek Street 30
Krems A-3500 Austria
Department: Telecommunication, Information, and Media
Program Name: Technical Communication
Contact: Hanna Risku

De Anza College
21250 Stevens Creek Boulevard
Cupertino, California 95014
Department: Technical Communications
Program Name: AA and Certificate in Technical Communication
Contact: Donna Dowdney

Drexel University
5044 MacAlister/33rd and Chestnut Streets
Philadelphia, Pennsylvania 19104
Department: Humanities and Communications
Program Name: Technical and Science Communication
Contact: Alexander Friedlander

Durham Technical Community College
1637 Lawson Street
Durham, North Carolina 27703
Department: Continuing Education
Program Name: Courses in Technical Writing
Contact: Jim Hines

East Carolina University
English Dept GCB 2129
Greenville, North Carolina 27858–4353
Department: English
Program Name: BA/Certificate (Certificate in Business, Technical, and Scientific Communication), MA (English, Concentration in Technical and Professional Communication)
Contact: Sherry Southard

Eastern Michigan University
Ypsilanti, Michigan 48197
Department: English
Program Name: Written Communication with
concentration in Technical Writing
Contact: Nancy Allen

Eastern Washington University
526 5th Street
Cheney, Washington 99004–2431
Department: English
Program Name: Technical Communications
Contact: Anthony Flinn

Edison Community College
1973 Edison Drive
Piqua, Ohio 45356
Department: English
Program Name: A.S. in Technical Communication
Contact: Dr. John Stibravy

Fairleigh Dickinson University
1000 River Road
Teaneck, New Jersey 07666
Department: English
Program Name: BA in Technical Writing
Contact: Don Jugenheimer

Ferris State University
Big Rapids, Michigan 49307
Department: Language and Literature
Program Name: BS in Technical and Professional
Communication
Contact: Sandra Balkema

Fitchburg State College
Fitchburg, Massachusetts 01420
Department: Communication/Media
Program Name: Technical Communication
Contact: Charles H. Sides

Front Range Community College
3645 West 112th Avenue
Westminster, Colorado 80030
Department: Communications
Program Name: Technical Communication
Associates Degree (of Arts)
Contact: Clark G. Germann

Gateway Technical College
1001 South Main Street
Racine, Wisconsin 53403
Department: General Education
Program Name: Technical Communication
Contact: Richard Gage

George Brown College
Box 1015, Station B
Toronto, Canada
Department: Continuing Education
Program Name: Technical Communications
Contact: Peggy Needham

Georgia Institute of Technology
Atlanta, Georgia 30332–0615
Department: School of Literature
Program Name: MS in Information Design and
  Technology; Certificate in Technical
  Communication
Contact: Professor A. Balsamo

Golden West College
15744 Golden West Street
Huntington Beach, California 92647
Department: Language Arts Division
Program Name: Certificate in Technical
  Communications
Contact: Dr. David D. Hudson

Grambling State University
Grambling, Louisiana 71245
Department: Mass Communication
Program Name: Mass Communication
  (concentration in Technical Communication)
Contact: Pamela Fridie

Hinds Community College
Box 1266
Raymond, Mississippi 39154–9799
Department: English
Program Name: Technical Communication courses
Contact: Nell Ann Pickett

Humber College of Applied Arts and Technology
205 Humber College Boulevard
Etobicoke M9W 5L7 Canada
Department: Business and Industry Services
Program Name: Technical Writing Certificate
Contact: Susan McNulty

Illinois Institute of Technology
3301 South Dearborn
Chicago, Illinois 60616
Department: Humanities
Program Name: Technical Communication and
  Information Design
Contact: Dr. Susan Feinberg

Illinois State University
Campus Box 4240
Normal, Illinois 61761
Department: English
Program Name: Technical Writing Program
Contact: Lee Ellen Brasseur

Institute for New Media, Research and Development
Box 8500
Cranbrook, BC VIC 5L7 Canada
Program Name: New Media Communication
Contact: Jeffrey D. Hunt

James Madison University
800 South Main Street
Harrisonburg, Virginia 22807
Program Name: Technical and Scientific
   Communication
Contact: Alice I. Philbin, Director

Johnson County Community College
12345 College Boulevard
Overland Park, Kansas 66210
Department: Computer and Information Systems
Program Name: Communication Design
Contact: Judy Brazil

Kirkwood Community College
6301 Kirkwood Boulevard SW,
P.O. Box 2068
Cedar Rapids, Iowa 52406
Department: English
Program Name: Technical Communications
Contact: Steve Gates

Lawrence Technological University
21000 West 10 Mile Road
Southfield, Michigan 48075
Department: Humanities
Program Name: BS in Technical Communication
Contact: Dr. Patricia Cornett

Louisiana State University
Baton Rouge, Louisiana 70803
Department: English
Program Name: Business and Technical Writing
Contact: Malcolm Richardson

Louisiana Tech University
Ruston, Louisiana 71272
Department: English
Program Name: Concentration in Technical Writing
Contact: Karen M. Kuralt

Madonna University
36600 Schoolcraft Road
Livonia, Michigan 48150–1173
Department: English
Program Name: Professional and Technical Writing
Contact: Dr. Cecilia S. Donohue

Mankato State
Technical Communication Program
Mankato, Minnesota 56002–8400
Department: English
Program Name: Courses in Technical
 Communication
Contact: Nancy MacKenzie

Mercer University
School of Engineering
Macon, Georgia 31207
and Atlanta, Georgia 30341
Department: Technical Communication
Program Name: BS and MS: Technical
 Communication
Contact: Dr. Marjorie T. Davis, Chair

Metropolitan State College of Denver
Campus Box 35
P.O. Box 173362
Denver, Colorado 80217–3362
Department: Technical Communications
Program Name: BA in Technical Communication
Contact: Lori Allen

Metropolitan State University
700 East 7th Street
St. Paul, Minnesota 55082
Department: Writing
Program Name: Technical Communication
Contact: Dr. Craig Hansen

Miami University
Oxford, Ohio 45056
Department: English
Program Name: BA and MTSC: Technical
 Communication Program
Contact: Dr. Robert R. Johnson

Michigan Technological University
1400 Towsend Drive
Houghton, Michigan 49931–1295
Department: Humanities
Program Name: BA and BS: Technical
 Communication
Contact: Craig Waddell

Middlesex Community College
591 Springs Road
Bedford, Massachusetts 01730–0660
Department: Economic and Community
   Development
Program Name: Software Technical Writing Program
Contact: Kim Burns

Milwaukee School of Engineering
1025 North Broadway
Milwaukee, Wisconsin 53202
Department: General Studies
Program Name: BS in Technical Communication
Contact: Ric Shrubb

Minnesota State University, Mankato
Technical Communication Program
Mankato, Minnesota 56002–8400
Department: English
Program Name: Courses in Technical
   Communication
Contact: Nancy R. MacKenzie

Missouri Western State College
4525 Downs Drive
St. Joseph, Missouri 64507
Department: English
Program Name: English Technical Communication
Contact: Dr. Jeanie Crain

Montana Tech of the University of Montana
1300 West Park Street
Butte, Montana 59701–8997
Department: Humanities/Social Sciences
Program Name: Professional and Technical
   Communication
Contact: Joanne G. Cortese

Montgomery College
20200 Observation Drive
Germantown, Maryland 20874
Department: Humanities
Program Name: Technical Writing Certificate
Contact: Bryant K. Davis

Moorehead State University
Moorehead, Minnesota 56560
Department: English
Program Name: Technical Writing Program
Contact: Jim Bense

Morehead State University
Combs Building
Morehead, Kentucky 40531
Department: English
Program Name: Technical Communication Minor
Contact: Jennings Mace

Mount Royal College
4825 Richard Road SW
Calgary T3E 6K6 Canada
Department: Office of the Registrar
Program Name: Bachelor Applied Communication,
    Technical Writing
Contact: Alice MacKichan

Nazareth College of Rochester
4245 East Avenue
Rochester, New York 14610
Department: English
Program Name: Professional Communication and
    Information Design
Contact: Nancy C. DeJoy

New Jersey Institute of Technology
Newark, New Jersey 07102
Department: Humanities and Social Sciences
Program Name: BA and MA: Professional and
    Technical Communication
Contact: Ms. Michele Collins

New Mexico State University
Box 3E
Las Cruces, New Mexico 88003
Department: English
Program Name: MA in Technical Writing
Contact: Bill Bridges

New Mexico Tech
Socorro, New Mexico 87801
Department: Humanities
Program Name: BS in Technical Communication
Contact: Chuck Campbell

New York Institute of Technology
Program in Technical Writing
Old Westbury, New York 11568
Department: English
Program Name: Coursework in Technical Writing
Contact: George Haber

North Carolina State University
Box 8105
Raleigh, North Carolina 27695–8105
Department: English
Program Name: MS in Technical Communication
Contact: Dr. Stan Dicks

Northeastern University
406 Holmes
Boston, Massachusetts 2115
Department: English
Program Name: Technical Communication
Contact: Kristin R. Woolever

Northern Illinois University
Lincoln Highway
Dekalb, Illinois 60115
Department: English
Program Name: English with a Focus in Rhetoric
  and Professional, Technical Communication
Contact: Christine Abbott

Ohio University
217A Ellis Hall
Athens, Ohio 45701–2979
Department: English Language and Literature
Program Name: Technical Communication
Contact: Paul Dombrowski

Oklahoma State University
900 North Portland Street
Oklahoma City, Oklahoma 73107
Department: Division of Business
Program Name: Technical Communication
Contact: Lesia Strong

Oklahoma State University
205 Morrill Hall
Stillwater, Oklahoma 74078–4069
Department: English
Program Name: Technical Writing
Contact: Dr. Thomas L. Warren

Orange Coast College
2701 Fairview Road
Costa Mesa, California 92628
Department: English
Program Name: Technical Writing Certificate
Contact: Don K. Pierstorff

Oregon Institute of Technology
3201 Campus Drive
Klamath Falls, Oregon 97601–8801
Department: Communications
Program Name: Technical Communication
  Concentration
Contact: Valerie J. Vance

Oregon State University
Corvallis, Oregon 97331–5302
Department: College of Liberal Arts
Program Name: Scientific and Technical
  Communication
Contact: Simon Johnson

Penn State University
Department of English
University Park, Wyoming 16802
Department: English
Program Name: Technical Communication
Contact: Stuart Selber

Pennsylvania College of Technology
One College Avenue
Williamsport, Pennsylvania 17701
Department: Composition, Language and Literature
Program Name: Technical and Professional
    Communication
Contact: Charles F. Kemnitz

Polytechnic University
6 Metrotech Center
Brooklyn, New York 11201–9210
Department: Humanities and Social Sciences
Program Name: Technical and Professional
    Communication
Contact: Professor Harold Sjursen

Portland Community College
P.O. Box 1900
Portland, Oregon 97280
Department: English
Program Name: Technical Communication
Contact: Kate Evans

Portland State University
P.O. Box 751
Portland, Oregon 97207
Department: English
Program Name: Technical Communication
Contact: Tracy Dillon

Purdue University
Room 324/Heavilon Hall
West Lafayette, Indiana 47907
Department: English
Program Name: Technical Communication
Contact: Patricia Sullivan

Purdue University Calumet
Hammond, Indiana 46323–2094
Department: English and Philosophy
Program Name: Technical Writing Major
Contact: Michael Dobberstein

Radford University
Box 6935
Radford, Virginia 24142–6935
Department: English
Program Name: Concentration/Minor in Technical
    and Business Writing
Contact: Donald C. Samson

Red River College
2055 Notre Dame
Winnipeg R3H0J9 Canada
Department: Continuing Education
Program Name: Technical Communication
Contact: Kathryn Davis

Rensselaer Polytechnic Institute
Troy, New York 12180–3590
Department: Language, Literature, and
    Communication
Program Name: Technical Communication
Contact: Cheryl Geisler

Rochester Institute of Technology
92 Lomb Memorial Drive
Rochester, New York 14623–5604
Department: College of Liberal Arts
Program Name: Professional and Technical
    Communication
Contact: Dr. Bruce Austin

Rochester Institute of Technology
31 Lomb Memorial Drive
Rochester, New York 14623
Department: Center for Multidisciplinary Studies
Program Name: Technical Information Design
Contact: Tom Moran

Rock Valley College
Rockford, Illinois 61114–5699
Department: Communications
Program Name: Technical Communication
Contact: David Ross

San Diego State University
5500 Campanile Drive
San Diego, California 92182–4452
Department: Rhetoric and Writing Studies
Program Name: Certificate in Technical and
    Scientific Writing; BA and MA in Special Studies
Contact: Cezar Ornatowski

San Francisco State University
1600 Holloway Avenue
San Francisco, California 94132
Department: Technical and Professional Writing
Program Name: BA, Minor, or Certificate in
    Technical and Professional Writing
Contact: Louise Rehling

San Jose State University
1 Washington Square
San Jose, California 95192–0090
Department: English
Program Name: Certificate in Professional and
Technical Communications
Contact: Bonnie Cox

Sheffield Hallam University
34 Collegiate Crescent Campus
Sheffield S10 2BP United Kingdom
Department: School of Communication Studies
Program Name: Master's in Technical Authorship
Contact: Ms. Florence Dujardin

Simon Fraser University, Harbour Centre
515 West Hastings Street
Vancouver, B.C. V6B 5K3 Canada
Department: Continuing Studies
Program Name: Technical Writing Certificate
Contact: Natalie Makortoff

Southeastern Louisiana University
S.L.U. Box 861
Hammond, Louisiana 70402
Department: English
Program Name: Technical Writing minor
Contact: Dr. Sue Parrill

Southern Polytechnic State University
1100 South Marietta Parkway
Marietta, Georgia 30060–2896
Department: Humanities and Technical
Communication
Program Name: BA, BS, and MS in Technical and
Professional Communication
Contact: Herb J. Smith

Southwest College
5601 West Loop South
Houston, Texas 77081
Department: Technical Communication
Program Name: Technical Communication
Contact: Lloyd Schuh

Southwest Missouri State University
Springfield, Missouri 65804
Department: English
Program Name: Coordinator of Technical Writing
Contact: Kris Sutliff

Southwest Texas State University
601 University Drive
San Marcos, Texas 78666
Department: English
Program Name: MA in Technical Communication
Contact: Libby Allison, Ph.D.

St. Louis Community College, Florissant
3400 Pershall Road
Florissant, Missouri 63135
Department: English/Communications Department
Program Name: Technical/Business
   Communications
Contact: Ken Boyer

St. Louis Community College, Meramec
11333 Big Bend Boulevard
Kirkwood, Missouri 63122
Department: English
Program Name: Certificate in Technical
   Communication
Contact: Maureen Murphy

SUNY Institute of Technology
P.O. Box 3050
Utica, New York 13504–3050
Department: School of Arts and Sciences
Program Name: BS in Professional and Technical
   Communication
Contact: Dr. Daniel J. Murphy

Tarrant County Junior College
828 Harwood Road
Hurst, Texas 76054
Department: English
Program Name: Courses in Technical Writing
Contact: Eddye Gallagher

Terra Community College
2830 Napoleon Road
Fremont, Ohio 43420–9670
Department: Technology
Program Name: Science and Communication
Contact: Sharla Shine

Texas A&M University
College Station, Texas 77843–4111
Department: Journalism
Program Name: Science and Technology Journalism
Contact: Barbara Gastel, PhD.

Texas Tech University
Box 43091
Lubbock, Texas 79409–3091
Department: English
Program Name: Ph.D. in Technical Communication
and Rhetoric; MA in Technical Communication;
BA in English/TC specialization
Contact: Carolyn D. Rude

Thomas Nelson Community College
Box 9407
Hampton, Virginia 23670
Department: English/Communications and
Humanities
Program Name: Technical-Professional
Communication
Contact: Dr. Thomas L. Long
and Dr. Pamela Monaco

University of Akron
Akron, Ohio 44325–1906
Department: Department of English
Program Name: Technical Communication
Certificate
Contact: Diana C. Reep

University of Alabama in Huntsville
215 Morton Hall
Huntsville, Alabama 35899
Department: English
Program Name: Business and Technical Writing
Contact: Rose Norman

University of Arkansas
2801 South University
Little Rock, Arkansas 72204
Department: Department of Rhetoric and Writing
Program Name: BA in Professional Technical
Writing; MA in Technical and Expository Writing
Contact: Dr. Barry Maid

University of California, Berkeley Extension
1995 University Avenue, Suite 300
Berkeley, California 94720
Department: Extension (Business and Technology)
Program Name: Professional Sequence and
Certificate in Technical Communication
Contact: Velma Parness

University of California, Riverside
900 University Avenue
Riverside, California 92521
Department: University Extension
Program Name: Certificate in Technical Writing
Contact: University Extension

University of Central Florida
Box 25000
Orlando, Florida 32816
Department: English
Program Name: BA and MA in Technical Writing
   and Communication
Contact: Madelyn Flammia

University of Colorado
Plaza Building, Suite 102
Campus Box 176
Denver, Colorado 80217–3364
Department: Communication
Program Name: Technical Communication
Contact: Dr. James F. Stratman

University of Delaware
Newark, Delaware 19716–2537
Department: English
Program Name: BA in Technical Writing
Contact: Deborah C. Andrews

University of Denver
University College 2000 South Gaylord
Denver, Colorado 80208
Program Name: Applied Communication Program
Contact: Mark R. Guthrie

University of Findlay
1000 North Main Street
Findlay, Ohio 45840
Department: English
Program Name: Technical Communication
Contact: Tom Stuckert

University of Karlstad
Karlstad, International 651 88 Sweden
Department: Humanities
Program Name: Technical Communication
Contact: Jeanne Lewis-Sturmhoefel

University of Maryland
South Campus Surge Building
College Park, Maryland 20742
Department: English
Program Name: Course in Technical Writing
Contact: Dr. Jean Johnson

University of Massachusetts
210 Bartlett Hall UMass
Amherst, Massachusetts 01003–0515
Department: English
Program Name: Professional Writing and Technical
   Communication
Contact: John Nelson

University of Memphis
Memphis, Tennessee 38152
Department: Department of English
Program Name: Masters in English with
    concentration in Technical/Professional Writing
Contact: Emily A. Thrush

University of Michigan
301 Engineering Programs Building
Ann Arbor, Michigan 48109–2140
Department: College of Engineering
Program Name: Technical Communication
Contact: Leslie A. Olsen

University of Minnesota
64 COB, 1994 Buford Avenue
St. Paul, Minnesota 55108
Department: Rhetoric
Program Name: Scientific and Technical
    Communication
Contact: Billie Wahlstrom

University of Minnesota, Crookston
2900 University Avenue
Crookston, Minnesota 56716
Department: Center for Business and Technology
Program Name: Scientific and Technical
    Communication
Contact: Dr. Traci Kelly

University of Missouri-Rolla
223 Humanities and Social Science Building
Rolla, Missouri 65409
Department: English
Program Name: Minor in Technical Writing
Contact: Dr. Janet Zepernick

University of New Mexico
Humanities 217
Albuquerque, New Mexico 87131
Department: English
Program Name: Concentration in Professional
    Writing
Contact: Scott P. Sanders

University of North Carolina
Charlotte, North Carolina 28223
Department: English
Program Name: Minor in Technical and Professional
    Writing; Emphasis at MA level; Certificate
Contact: Deborah Bosley

University of North Carolina
Wilmington, North Carolina 28403
Department: English
Program Name: Classes in Technical Writing
Contact: Chris Gould

University of North Texas
Denton, Texas 76203
Department: English
Program Name: Minor in Technical Writing
Contact: Brenda R. Sims

University of South Florida
4202 East Fowler Avenue
Tampa, Florida 33620–5300
Department: English
Program Name: BA in Technical Writing
Contact: Phillip Sipiora

University of Southwestern Louisiana
P.O. Drawer 44691
Lafayette, Louisiana 70504
Department: English
Program Name: Technical Communication
Contact: Ann Martin Scott

University of Tennessee
615 McCallie Avenue
Chattanooga, Tennessee 37402
Department: English
Program Name: Technical Communication
Contact: Arlie Herron

University of Tennessee
401 McClung Tower
Knoxville, Tennessee 37996–0430
Department: English
Program Name: Technical Communication
Contact: Russel Hirst

University of Washington
14 Loew Hall Box 352195
Seattle, Washington 98195
Department: Technical Communication
Program Name: Technical Communication
Contact: Jan H. Spyridakis

University of Waterloo
Waterloo, Canada
Department: Continuing Education
Program Name: Courses in Technical Writing
Contact: Maureen Jones

University of Wisconsin
1510 Engineering Drive
Madison, Wisconsin 53706–1573
Department: Engineering Professional Development
Program Name: Certificate in Technical
Communication
Contact: Gisela Kutzbach

University of Wisconsin
141 Harvey Hall
Menomonie, Wisconsin 54751
Department: English
Program Name: Technical Communication
Contact: Daniel Riordan

University of Wisconsin
P.O. Box 413 Curtin Hall
Milwaukee, Wisconsin 53201
Department: English
Program Name: Technical and Professional
Writing
Contact: Gerald Alred

University of Wisconsin
Eau Claire, Wisconsin 54702
Department: English
Program Name: BA and MA in Technical Writing
Contact: Marty Wood

Utah State University
3200 Old Main Hill
Logan, Utah 84322–3200
Department: English
Program Name: Technical and Professional Writing
Contact: Christine Hult

Utah State University
UMC 3200
Logan, Utah 84322
Department: English
Program Name: MA in English/Technical
Communication Program
Contact: Ron Shook

Washington State Community College
710 Colgate Drive
Marietta, Ohio 45750
Department: English
Program Name: Technical Writing
Contact: Thomas M. Sharpe

Washtenaw Community College
4800 East Huron River Drive
P.O. Box D-1
Ann Arbor, Michigan 48106–1610
Department: English/Writing
Program Name: Scientific and Technical
  Communication
Contact: Lisa Veasey

Wayne State University
51 West Warren
Detroit, Michigan 48202
Department: English
Program Name: Courses in Technical Writing
Contact: Richard Marback

Weber State University
1201 University Circle
Ogden, Utah 84408
Department: English
Program Name: Professional and Technical Writing
  Minor
Contact: Mali Subbiah

Western Washington University
Old Main 400
Bellingham, Washington 98225–9042
Department: University of Extended Programs
Program Name: Technical Communication
  Certificate
Contact: Lois Longwood

Worcester Polytechnic Institute
100 Institute Road
Worcester, Massachusetts 01609–2280
Department: Interface Disciplines
Program Name: Technical, Scientific, and
  Professional Communication
Contact: John M. Trimbur

Wright State University
3640 Colonel Glenn Highway
Dayton, Ohio 45435
Department: English
Program Name: Certificate in Technical Writing
Contact: Professor Richard Bullock

York University
2275 Bayview Avenue
Toronto M4T 1B1 Canada
Department: School of Translation
Program Name: Certificate Programme in Technical
  and Professional Writing
Contact: Professor Candace Seguinot

APPENDIX B

PROFESSIONAL ASSOCIATIONS

This appendix contains a partial list of associations that promote technical writing as a profession or further some aspect of technical writing. The list is partial because new groups appear often. Some of the street addresses change as officers change, and Web sites can move, but the contact information below should give you a start in finding associations that will meet your networking needs.

American Medical Writers' Association (AMWA)
40 West Gude Drive, Suite 101
Rockville, MD 20850–1192
www.amwa.org

American Society for Information Science (ASIS)
8720 Georgia Avenue, Suite 501
Silver Spring, MD 20910–3602
www.asis.org

American Society of Indexers
11250 Roger Bacon Drive, Suite 8
Reston, VA 20190–5202
www.asindexing.org

Association for Business Communication (ABC)
Box G-1326, Baruch College
17 Lexington Avenue
New York, NY 10010
www.theabc.org

Association for Computing Machinery (ACM)
Special Interest Group for Documentation
    (SIGDOC)
One Astor Plaza
1515 Broadway
New York, NY 10036–5701
www.acm.org/sigdoc/

Association of Earth Science Editors (AESE)
c/o Mary Ann Schmidt
554 Chess Street
Pittsburgh, PA 15205–3212
www.aese.org

Association of Petroleum Writers
c/o Katherine Reese
Oil & Gas Journal
Box 1260
Tulsa, Oklahoma 74101

Aviation/Space Writers Association
17 South High Street, Suite 1200
Columbus, OH 43215

Computer Professionals for Social Responsibility (CPSR)
P.O. Box 717
Palo Alto, CA 94301
www.cpsr.org

Council of Science Editors
c/o Drohan Management Group
11250 Roger Bacon Drive, Suite 8
Reston, VA 20190–5202
www.CouncilScienceEditors.org

Editorial Freelancers Association
71 West 23rd Street, Suite 1910
New York, NY 10010
www.the-efa.org

Freelance Editorial Association
P.O. Box 380835
Cambridge, MA 02238–0835
www.tiac.net/users/freelanc/

Independent Computer Consultants Association (ICCA)
11131 South Towne Square, Suite F
St. Louis, MO 63123
www.icca.org

IEEE Professional Communication Society
Institute of Electrical and Electronic Engineers (IEEE)
3 Park Avenue, 17th Floor
New York, NY 10016–5997
www.ieeepcs.org

International Association of Business
Communicators (IABC)
One Hallidie Plaza, Suite 600
San Francisco, CA 94102
www.iabc.org

National Association of Government
Communicators (NAGC)
10301 Democracy Lane, Suite 203
Fairfax, VA 22030
www.nagc.com

National Association of Science Writers
P.O. Box 294
Greenlawn, NY 11740
www.nasw.org

National Information Standards Organization
(NISO)
4733 Bethesda Avenue, Suite 300
Bethesda, MD 20814
www.niso.org

National Writers Union (NWU)
www.nwu.org

National Office East
113 University Place, 6th Floor
New York, NY 10003

National Office West
337 17th Street, #101
Oakland, CA 94612

Professional and Technical Consultants Association
(PACTA)
849-B Independence Avenue
Mountain View, CA 94043
www.patca.org

Society for Technical Communication (STC)
901 North Stuart Street, Suite 904
Arlington, VA 22203-1822
www.stc-va.org

WinWriters
3415 Soundview Drive West
Seattle, WA 98199
www.WinWriters.com

APPENDIX C

DOCUMENT PLAN

This appendix contains a sample document plan for a computer software manual. You'll use a "doc plan" to help organize your writing project as well as to present your ideas for review and approval by other members of the product team. Once team members "buy off" on the plan, they are less likely to suggest sweeping organizational changes later, in the review process.

You can use this document plan as a starting point for designing your own. As you send out and get back whatever form you create, you'll modify it to better fit your publication procedures.

April 16, 2001

To:

Susan Black, Engineering

Grant Smith, Engineering

Lisa Downing, Marketing

Harold Schwartz,
Engineering

Jane Townsend,
Marketing

Betsy Long, Technical
Publications

FYI:

George Freeman, QA

Pete McMann,
Customer Support

Pam Brown,
Technical Publications

John Ferrero, Technical
Publications

Jim Hartford, Training

FROM: Janet Van Wicklen

RE: SuperINDEX User's Guide Document Plan

Please review the attached document plan for organizational clarity and completeness. You have received this because you are on my list of reviewers for the document. If you will be unable to review the document during the review periods shown in the document schedule, please assign someone else in your department and let me know whom you've assigned.

Your signature below indicates your approval of the document plan. Please return it to me with your comments no later than April 23, 2001.

I approve the document as is. ❑

I approve the document with changes as marked. ❑

Name _____

Department _____

DOCUMENT PLAN FOR SUPERINDEX USER'S GUIDE

SOFTWARE VERSION 1.0
APRIL 16, 2001

Writer:	Janet Van Wicklen
Product purpose:	SuperINDEX allows users to index CAD drawings and to retrieve them by typing a keyword.
Audience:	Readers are engineers and technicians who are thoroughly familiar with their own CAD software or who have access to CAD documentation. Therefore, this manual will not contain guidance on using CAD features.
Content:	The objective of this user's guide is to provide step-by-step instructions for all SuperINDEX operations. For details, please refer to the attached outline.
Physical characteristics:	The manual pages will be 5 1/2" X 81/2", 3-hole punched, and placed in a binder with the software CD. Each chapter will be marked by a color tab.

SUPERINDEX USER'S GUIDE
OUTLINE

Chapter 1. Introduction
      This chapter will begin with a quick-reference table telling users how to find information.
    I. Overview of the product's operations
    II. Overview of SuperINDEX utilities
    III. Software and hardware requirements

Chapter 2. Using SuperINDEX
    I. Starting SuperINDEX
      [Figure 2-1 SuperINDEX Option Buttons]
    II. Selecting Option Buttons
    III. Using the StartINDEX Utility
      [Figure 2-2 SuperINDEX Main Menu Option Buttons]
    IV. Using the Browse Utility
      [Figure 2-3 Browse Menu]
      [Figure 2-4 Text Viewer]
    V. Using the Smart Index Utility
      [Figure 2-5 Example of Smart Index Search]
    VI. Executing a Text Search
      [Figure 2-6 Text Search Menu]
      A. Boolean Search Syntax
      B. Query Results

Chapter 3. Creating an Index
    I. Before You Index
    II. Word Index
      [Figure 3-1 Word Index Menu]
      A. Word Index Function Keys
      [Figure 3-2 Select All Window]
      B. Word Index Options
      [Figure 3-3 Word Index Options Menu]
    III. Build Index

Chapter 4. Installing SuperINDEX
    I. Running Install
    II. Running Setup

DOCUMENT PLAN FOR
SUPERINDEX USER'S GUIDE

Mar 22-Apr 6	Research (2 weeks)
Apr 7-8	Write doc plan (2 days)
Apr 9-14	Doc plan review
Apr 15	Revise doc plan (1 day)
Apr 16-30	Write 1st draft (2 weeks)
May 1-8	First review
Jun 8	Review meeting
Jun 9-16	Incorporate changes (1 week)
Jun 17-23	Second review
Jun 24-Jul 1	Complete final draft; incorporate final art (1 week)
July 1-4	Holiday weekend
Jul 5-7	Final indexing and production (3 days)
Jul 8-15	Printer turn-around (1 week)
Jul 16	Manuals in stock for distribution

ANNOTATED BIBLIOGRAPHY

This bibliography is organized by topic. The following topics appear in alphabetical order:

- Careers and job hunting
- Computer-related injuries
- Desktop publishing
- History of technical writing
- Interview skills
- Technical writing in general
- Writing online

Within each topic, books are listed alphabetically by author.

CAREERS AND JOB HUNTING

Adams Electronic Job Search Almanac 1998. Holbrook, Mass.: Adams Media Corporation, 1998.

This comprehensive guide, written for beginners, covers every aspect of looking for work online, including details on how to create an electronic résumé, where to find jobs online, and how to research companies online.

Boldt, Laurence G. *Zen and the Art of Making a Living.* New York: Penguin, 1993.

This thinking person's career guide takes you on a wild ride through philosophy, psychology, theology, and metaphysics, in search of your life's work. Along the way, Boldt quotes sages, poets, and saints, and provides his own quotable advice and poetic inspiration. I admit I had this book a long time before I read it because it's fat—600 pages long. Now I dip into it for jewels. Definitely worth a browse!

Bolles, Richard Nelson. *Job-Hunting on the Internet.* Berkeley, Calif.: Ten Speed Press, 1998.

Bolles provides down-to-earth insights on how to find a job online. As a veteran career counselor, his point of view is that, behind the flash of new technologies, the principles of finding a job remain unchanged. The creative approaches that set you apart as an individual, which he describes in his classic, *What Color Is Your Parachute?*, still work best. Bolles reviews job-search sites for usefulness and he doesn't mince words.

Bolles, Richard Nelson. *What Color Is Your Parachute? A Practical Manual for Job-Hunters and Career-Changers.* Berkeley, Calif.: Ten Speed Press, 2000.

Updated annually, this classic guide on choosing a career helps you figure out what you do best, and more important, what you best enjoy doing. It guides you toward a successful and satisfying career choice, then gives you tips on getting a job within your chosen field.

Cooper, Robert K. *The Performance Edge.* Boston: Houghton Mifflin Co., 1991.

In this book, consultant Cooper gives strategies for handling stress and increasing effectiveness on the job.

Criscito, Pat. *Résumés in Cyberspace.* Hauppauge, N.Y.: Barron's Educational Series, Inc., 1997.

This clearly written guide for cyberspace beginners leads you through everything you need to know to use the Internet in your job search. Along the way, Criscito, a professional résumé writer, helps you step-by-step to create an effective résumé. She explains Internet job-search concepts, culture, and procedures, including how to create a home page for your résumé.

Dikel, Margaret Riley, et al. *The Guide to Internet Job Searching.* Lincolnwood, Ill.: VGM Career Horizons, 1998.

Another Internet job-search guide, among several, which may be dated by the ever-changing nature of Web pages! This book is worth a look for its massive lists of job-search Web sites, organized by fields. Of particular interest are sections on entry-level positions for new grads; internships, co-ops, and summer opportunities; and local and international job sites.

Hizer, David V., and Arthur D. Rosenberg. *The Résumé Handbook.* Boston: Bob Adams, Inc., 1985.

This handbook provides 25 examples of good résumés and five examples of bad ones, with terse comments on their good and bad qualities. This is an excellent source of organizational and formatting ideas for résumés.

Lathrop, Richard. *Who's Hiring Who,* 12th edition. Berkeley, Calif.: Ten Speed Press, 1989.

This book provides ways to explore your job-related skills, then present them attractively—both on paper and in the interview—to prospective employers.

Medley, H. Anthony. *Sweaty Palms: The Neglected Art of Being Interviewed.* Berkeley, Calif.: Ten Speed Press, 1992.

Medley gives thorough advice on how to win at a job interview, including how to prepare, communicate, reduce stress, dress, and even negotiate salary.

Oakes, Elizabeth H., editor. *Career Exploration on the Internet.* Chicago: Ferguson Publishing Co., 1998.

Geared toward students, this guide describes over 300 career-information and job-hunting Web sites, including professional associations, employment firms, internship sites, résumé banks, and news groups.

Pincus, Marilyn. *Interview Strategies that Lead to Job Offers.* Hauppauge, N.Y.: Barron's Educational Series, Inc., 1999.

This friendly, readable guide describes how to prepare, through rehearsal and forethought, for different types of interviews and interviewers.

Sturman, Gerald M., Ph.D. *The Career Discovery Project.* New York: Doubleday, 1993.

Sturman provides a self-assessment guide to finding satisfying work. The book is full of tests you can take to clarify your people preferences, personality, preferred skills, values, and so forth. The tests are simple, clear, and nicely laid out, with lots of information on how to interpret the results.

Yate, Martin. *Knock 'Em Dead 2000.* Holbrook, Mass.: Bob Adams, Inc., 2000.

Yate provides a masterful treatment of the job search as a sales effort. He concentrates on the communication skills that will help you get the interview, win the offer, and negotiate the terms you want.

COMPUTER-RELATED INJURIES

Crouch, Tammy. *Carpal Tunnel Syndrome and Repetitive Stress Injuries: The Comprehensive Guide to Prevention, Treatment and Recovery,* 2nd ed. Berkeley, Calif.: Frog, Ltd., 1996.

After two unsuccessful carpal-tunnel surgeries, author Tammy Crouch sought alternative therapies. She shares her discoveries in this book. Crouch includes information about worker's compensation and provides a resource list of organizations, Web sites, books, and articles.

Pascarelli, Emil, and Deborah Quilter. *Repetitive Strain Injury: A Computer User's Guide.* New York: John Wiley & Sons, 1994.

Pascarelli is a surgeon and Quilter a writer and RSI sufferer. Together, they cover the medical and emotional aspects of this difficult problem. This book helped me ask knowledgeable questions and eventually find the right treatments for my RSI. I recommend it highly.

Stigliani, Joan. *The Computer User's Survival Guide.* Sebastopol, Calif.: O'Reilly & Associates, Inc., 1995.

Stigliani has written a detailed, thorough treatment of all the ills to which computer users are vulnerable, from stress to RSI. Her information and advice are well researched and readable, providing helpful guidance to anyone with a glimmer of symptoms.

DESKTOP PUBLISHING

Makuta, Daniel J., and William F. Lawrence. *The Complete Desktop Publisher.* Greensboro, N.C.: COMPUTE! Publications, Inc., 1986.

This book provides a somewhat technical look at the history, mechanics, and aesthetics of desktop publishing. It's a good resource for the computer-literate reader.

Price, Jonathan, and Carlene Schnabel. *Desktop Publishing.* New York: Ballantine Books, 1987.

Price and Schnabel provide highly readable explanations of the elements of page design, from font styles to layouts, with many examples.

HISTORY OF TECHNICAL WRITING

Allbutt, Sir T. Clifford. *Notes on the Composition of Scientific Papers,* 3rd ed. London: Macmillan and Co., 1923 (originally published in 1904).

This is probably the first book on technical writing. After trudging through piles of presumably hideous stuff, Sir Clifford felt compelled to offer advice to his Cambridge medical students on how to write. His advice on brevity, and other writerly virtues, is charmingly couched in ornate Victorian English.

Alred, Gerald J. et al. *Business and Technical Writing: An Annotated Bibliography of Books, 1880–1980.* Metuchen, N.J.: Scarecrow Press, Inc., 1981.

An excellent source for tracing the development of technical writing as a recognized profession by tracing the evolution of books about the subject.

Drachmann, A. G. *The Mechanical Technology of Greek and Roman Antiquity: A Study of the Literary Sources.* Madison: University of Wisconsin Press, 1963.

Drachmann describes the work of the world's first-known technical writers—Hero of Alexandria, Strato, and others—who described the first pulleys, screws, cogwheels, and other inventions of the Greeks and Romans.

Rink, Evald. *Technical Americana: A Checklist of Technical Publications Printed Before 1831.* Millwood, N.Y.: Kraus International Publications, 1981.

Rink provides an annotated bibliography of the earliest handbooks, monographs, and other publications in the United States that address technical topics, from how to "colour hats green on one side" to "descriptions of any curious machinery and improvements in arts and sciences." This is a fun bit of Americana! Rink also lists the libraries that hold these historic documents.

INTERVIEW SKILLS

The references in this section are old, but in a recent search, I could find none better than the sources listed here. Ask your library to find them.

Farber, Barry. *Making People Talk.* New York: William Morrow and Company, Inc., 1987.

New York radio talk-show host Barry Farber provides a richly anecdotal, humorous pep talk on the art of bringing out the best in people. His advice can be applied to interviewing, job hunting, or any situation where you need to positively impress someone.

Metzler, Ken. *Creative Interviewing: The Writer's Guide to Gathering Information by Asking Questions.* Englewood Cliffs, N.J.: Prentice-Hall, Inc., 1977.

Full of anecdotes, this is a very readable, entertaining, and informative treatment of journalistic interviewing. Metzler goes into all stages of the interview process—background research, stages of the interview, categories of questions, and more.

Sherwood, Hugh C. *The Journalistic Interview.* New York: Harper & Row, 1969.

This discussion of the journalistic interview applies to tech writers as well as to journalists. Sherwood covers the whole process, from preparing for the interview through bringing it to a close. An excellent resource.

Stano, Michael E., and N. L. Reinsch, Jr. *Communication in Interviews.* Englewood Cliffs, N.J.: Prentice-Hall, Inc., 1982.

This book provides a detailed analysis of the interview as a communication process. It describes the different stages of the interview, classifies interview questions ("vocalizations") and interview structures, and applies these classifications to different kinds of interviews (for example, journalistic). Good food for thought.

TECHNICAL WRITING IN GENERAL

Brockmann, R. John. *Writing Better Computer User Documentation: From Paper to Hypertext,* Version 2.0. New York: John Wiley & Sons, 1990.

Brockmann describes the technical documentation process and convincingly argues for spending significant time during the planning phase. He also discusses the advantages and disadvantages of online versus paper documentation.

Brusaw, Charles T. et al. *Handbook of Technical Writing,* 5th ed. New York: St. Martin's Press, 1997.

This handbook contains a rich assortment of information useful to professional writers, from descriptions of technical writing forms and formatting to rules of grammar, style, and usage. Highly recommended.

Gunning, Robert. *The Technique of Clear Writing.* New York: McGraw-Hill Book Company, 1968.

Gunning describes the sins of complex, pretentious language and how to avoid them. He also describes his Fog Index and other measures of readability. Gunning writes, "The price of good writing, as that of liberty, is eternal vigilance." What more can I say?

Strunk, William Jr., and E. B. White. *The Elements of Style.* New York: Macmillan, 1979.

An irreplaceable classic on the principles of good writing. Every writer must read this book at least once.

Zinsser, William. *On Writing Well.* New York: Harper Perennial, 1990.

Zinsser informally touches on just about every aspect of writing nonfiction—simplicity and clutter, style, usage, audience, nonfiction as literature, what makes good nonfiction in various genres, and so on. He includes chapters on writing about science and technology.

WRITING ONLINE

Barrett, Edward, and Marie Edmond, eds. *Contextual Media: Multimedia and Interpretation.* Cambridge, Mass.: MIT Press, 1995.

This book offers a collection of 13 papers on the cultural and interpretive aspects (in other words, usability) of multimedia. For example, how does the user's way of accessing information ("search mode") affect how he or she remembers that information?

Duffy, Thomas M., et al. *Online Help: Design and Evaluation.* Norwood, N.J.: Ablex Publishing, 1992.

The authors describe how to design usable online help. They discuss usability research, design issues, and evaluation methods for testing the effectiveness of a help system.

Hackos, JoAnn T., and Dawn Stevens. *Standards for Online Communication.* New York: John Wiley & Sons, Inc., 1997.

In the authors' words: "This book reintroduces the design principles overlooked in the rush to be the first." It takes you through the stages of identifying your audience's needs, designing an online document structure, choosing tools, testing usability, and more.

Horton, William K. *Designing and Writing Online Documentation: Help Files to Hypertext.* New York: John Wiley & Sons, 1990.

In great detail, Horton describes how to plan online documentation, from choosing a suitable structure to designing screens.

Morris, Mary E. S., and Randy J. Hinricks. *Web Page Design: A Different Multimedia.* Mountain View, Calif.: SunSoft Press and Prentice Hall, 1996.

This book provides an excellent, comprehensive treatment of all aspects of Web page design, including authoring skills required, content and "cognitive" design issues, navigational design, page layout, and more.

Nielsen, Jakob. *Hypertext and Hypermedia.* Boston: Academic Press, 1993.

Nielsen clearly describes the basic elements of hypermedia and the history of hypertext, as well as the organization, navigation, and usability issues hypertext authors need to address.

INDEX